MW00974034

"To Live and Die in Dixie"

How The South Formed A Nation

Edited
by
Archie P. McDonald

Gen. Robert E. Lee, the personification of the Southern Nation.

"To Live and Die in Dixie"

How The South Formed A Nation

Edited
by
Archie P. McDonald

Southern Heritage Press
4035 Emerald Dr.
Murfreesboro, TN 37130

Journal of Confederate History Book Series
Vol. XX
John McGlone, Series Editor

Copyright © 1999 Southern Heritage Publications. All rights reserved. No part of this material may be reproduced without written permission from the publisher, except for brief quotes in reviews.

First published as articles in the Journal of Confederate History, Vol. X.

Library of Congress Cataloging-in-Publication Data

———————————

McDonald, Archie P., Editor and Compiler
"To Live and Die in Dixie": How The South Formed A Nation
Includes bibliographic references
ISBN 1-889332-23-2

Front Cover: "Furling The Flag" by R.N.Brooks, courtesy of West Point Museum Collections, United States Military Academy

DEDICATION

To Kelly Marie,

Papa's Delight

IN MEMORIUM

Clayton Ramage Barrow, Jr.
1923 to 1997
M/Sgt. U.S. Marine Corp.
WWII and Korea
Editor-In-Chief U.S. Naval Institute *Proceedings*

and

Elizabeth Barrow Bischak
"Betty"
1926 to 1998
Librarian

"Lovingly Remembered and Sorely Missed"

TABLE OF CONTENTS

CONTRIBUTORS

Anne J. Bailey is an associate professor of history at the University of Arkansas, formerly with Georgia Southern University in Statesboro. She is the author of *Between the Enemy and Texas: Parson's Texas Cavalry in the Civil War,* and contributed thirty-eight biographies to the six-volume series, *The Confederate General.* Dr. Bailey currently serves as editor of the *SCWH Newsletter,* a publication of the Society of Civil War Historians.

Brandon H. Beck is Associate Professor of History and Director of the Civil War Institute at Shenandoah University in Winchester, Virginia. He is the author of several books about the Civil war in the Shenandoah Valley. Beck holds degrees from Gettysburg College, the University of Virginia, and the University of Rochester. He is also Camp Commander of the John S. Mosby Camp of the Sons of Confederate Veterans.

Arch Fredric Blakey is Professor of History at the University of Florida. He is a Fellow of the U. S. Military Academy, Department of Defense, and is listed in *Outstanding Professionals in Human Services* (The American Academy of Human Sciences). He is the author of numerous books and articles on the Civil War, including *General John H. Winder, C.S.A.* and the forthcoming *Rose Cottage Chronicle: The Stephens/Bryant Families and the Civil War .*

Frank Allen Dennis is Professor of History and Chair of the History Department at Delta State University, where he has taught since 1968. He is the author/editor of five books and more than forty articles, book reviews, and scholarly compilations. In 1989, he was named the Outstanding Faculty Member at Delta State University. He is writing, with Professor Herman Hattaway, the volume in the Heritage of Mississippi Series entitled *The Civil War in Mississippi: A Military History.*

Alan C. Downs is a visiting assistant professor in the Department of History at Georgia Southern University. Before moving to Georgia in 1992, Downs, a native North Carolinian, taught at North Carolina State University and the University of North Carolina at Chapel Hill where he earned his PhD. Since 1989 he has lectured on North Carolina's Civil War experience at various seminars and conferences. His publications include entries for the *Dictionary of North Carolina Biography* and the forthcoming *Encyclopedia of the Confederacy.*

The Confederate States

James Marten, who received his Ph.D. from the University of Texas at Austin in 1986, is presently an associate professor of history at Marquette University. He teaches courses on the Civil War era, military history, and African-American history, and is the author of *Texas Divided: Loyalty and Dissent in the Lone Star State, 1856-1874* and *Texas* in the World Bibliography Series.

Archie P. McDonald is Regent's Professor of History at Stephen F. Austin State University. He is the Executive Director and Editor of the East Texas Historical Association, and a Fellow of the Texas State Historical Association. He is the editor of *"Make Me a Map Of the Valley:" The Civil War Journal of Stonewall Jackson's Topographer*, and several books and articles on the Civil War and Texas History.

Carl H. Moneyhon is a Professor of History at the University of Arkansas at Little Rock. He is the author of *The Impact of the Civil War and Reconstruction on Arkansas: Persistence in the Midst of Ruin*, forthcoming from Louisiana State University Press, and co-author and editor of a series of photographic studies of the Civil War in the Southern states entitled *Portraits of Conflict*. He is also the author of numerous articles on the Civil War and Reconstruction in the southwest.

R. B. Rosenburg is Assistant Professor of History at Virginia Polytechnic Institute and State University at Blacksburg, Virginia. His publications include *"For The Sake of My Country": The Diary of Col. W. W. Ward, 9th Tennessee Cavalry, Morgan's Brigade*, and *Living Monuments: Confederate Soldiers' Homes in the New South*, published by University of North Carolina Press at Chapel Hill.

Jason H. Silverman is Professor of History at Winthrop University. He was the 1990-1991 South Carolina Governor's Professor of the Year and was named Distinguished Professor at Winthrop in 1991. He is author or editor of numerous works on Southern history and is completing *Beyond The Melting Pot in Dixie: Immigration and Ethnicity in Southern History* for the University of Texas Press.

John McGlone is the Editor of the *Journal of Confederate History* Series and Publisher of Southern Heritage Press. He holds degrees from Georgetown University, Salisbury State University, and Middle Tennessee State University. He is an Adjunct Instructor at the Junior College level, a former Marine, and the seventh generation of his family to, proudly, call Tennessee home.

Charles Edmund Vetter is professor and chair of the Department of Sociology, Centenary College of Louisiana, Shreveport, Louisiana. He is president of the

The Confederate States

North Louisiana Civil War Round Table and author of *Sherman: Merchant of Terror, Advocate of Peace.*

Phillip Thomas Tucker serves as the historian for the Air Force District of Washington. He is the author of *Father John Bannon, The Confederacy's Fighting Chaplain,* which won the Douglass Southall Freeman Award for Best Book in Southern History in 1993, and *The South's Finest: History of The First Missouri Confederate Brigade.*

EDITOR'S FOREWORD

by
Archie P. McDonald

Thousands of books and monographs contain a niagara of information about the Civil War, one of the pivotal and defining events of United States history. These begin with the apologia of participants and continue to the present through several "schools" of interpretation with each generation and each interest group presenting parts of the whole in ways which defame or confirm one side or the other.

This modest collection seeks no grand purpose, such as explaining why the war occurred – accidentally or inevitably – and it does not attempt bold new interpretations of individuals or events. It sprang from a narrative of one of the Confederate States of America presented to the Deep Delta Civil War Symposium that later appeared as an article in the Journal of Confederate History. JCH editor John McGlone and I began to speculate on the similarity and differences in how the other Confederate states became involved in the Confederate experience and how they fared during passage from statehood in the Union, through secession, to membership in a new confederacy. We knew how the story ended; we wanted to review the plot.

Next came the recruiting of historians of the various state experiences, and we found willing workers. They each lived, studied, and/or taught in the states about which they wrote.

Jason Silverman, South Carolina Governor's Professor of 1990-1991, presents the story of the lead state in the secession process. Allen Dennis, Outstanding Faculty Member at Delta State University, writes of the struggles of Mississippians with the great historian and Floridian, tells the story of neglected but crucial Florida during the war. R.B. Rosenburg, research professor at the University of Tennessee and scholar of Alabama, writes about the secession leadership that came from this Deep South stronghold. Charles Edmund Vetter brought the story west of the Big River to Louisiana. Anne Bailey, transplanted Georgian, relates the experience of the Southern empire state, Texas, "the dark corner of the Confederacy," was represented by the work of the editor. Shenandoah University's Brandon Beck tackled the crucial state of Virginia. Carl Moneyhon presented the story of the Trans-Mississippi commanders and the Confederate experience of Arkansas. John McGlone flew Tennessee's flag beside the Stars and Bars. Alan Downs assumed the duty of telling us of North Carolina's experiences. And James Martin and Phillip Thomas Tucker tell us about Kentucky and Missouri, two states which bore the burden of being both Confederate AND Union in the hearts of their citizens.

Each writer wrote of his state with a minimum of instruction and little contact with each other. This general outline went to each: "The chapters should be approximately twenty-pages, no notes but should conclude with a bibliography, and should be a narrative that features your state concerning attitudes on secession; the process of secession; political, economic, and social conditions; and appropriate military events and personalities associated with the state."

The results are before you. Some found the story of secession itself the most important topic, usually but not always when that state witnessed few battles. Some found the military aspect of the war so compelling that it consumed the majority of their attention and space. All wrote with a critical eye on the failures of political and military leaders but many presented an understanding of the common folk who bore the burden of the war with disrupted lives, families, and fortunes. The editor let each tell the story of their state in their own way, save for attempting to impose some consistency in language usage. Appreciation and gratitude is expressed to each for accepting the challenge, returning requested revisions in the face of other pressing matters, and putting up with the foibles of a curmudgeon. This extends to: Catherine Hull and

Mel Johnson, who aided with preparation of the manuscript in various ways; to Judy Daughtry, who inherited the "clean up" and set the type; and to John McGlone, that Confederate's Confederate, who wrote the chapter on Tennessee and served as publisher of this book.

Archie P. McDonald

SOUTH CAROLINA

by
Jason H. Silverman

State Court Judge and secessionist Robert Aldrich was worried. Aldrich and his fellow South Carolinians had just watched with fear and trepidation as Northern Republican Abraham Lincoln won election as the sixteenth president of the United States. "I do not believe the common people understand it," he wrote a friend regarding the gravity of the situation, "We must make the move and force them to follow. That is the way of all revolutions and all great movements." Above all, Aldrich concluded, South Carolina must not wait to act. Indeed, to the firebrands, South Carolina had been waiting for the rest of the South to act against the federal government for almost three decades, ever since the Nullification Crisis of 1832. Lincoln's election, the most recent in a long line of disturbing events, now signaled what many in the Palmetto State had known all along, that the South no longer could be safe in the Union.

Aldrich's colleague, Federal Judge Andrew G. Magrath, was even more dramatic. Following Lincoln's election, Magrath divested himself of his judicial robes and thanked God that "his temple of justice has been closed before its altar has been desecrated with sacrifices to tyranny." Magrath's act electrified many in South Carolina. Ten years earlier Magrath had opposed separate secession on the part of his home state and had, instead, advocated collective action by the South. Now, however, Magrath's resignation was so profound that it was said to have brought the divided Charleston legislative delegation into unity for immediate action. The emotional resignation of a Federal judge brought much distress in the nation's capitol. As the federal court structure in South Carolina crumbled, lame duck President James Buchanan lamented that this was perhaps the beginning of the end. So it was, and so it would be: on December 20, 1860, a little more than a month after the presidential election, a South Carolina convention unanimously passed an ordinance of secession. For South Carolina, the waiting was over; after agitating for decades, the state had left the confines of the United States of America.

South Carolina's secession, while a long time coming, was inevitable. As early as the 1820s, there was an increasing level of Southern opposition to federal powers and policies and a powerful urge on the part of South Carolina to seek shelter for threatened economic interests in a strict interpretation of congressional powers and a liberal translation of the rights of the states. South Carolina regularly opposed protective tariffs as inequitable and blamed them for an economic decline owed more to soil erosion and competition from the Southwest. South Carolina's favorite son, John C. Calhoun, had even built upon the theory of state "interposition" with the doctrine of nullification in an attempt to prevent the operation of a tariff which South Carolinians regarded as unconstitutional.

In nullifying the tariff acts of 1828 and 1832, South Carolina rendered the tariffs uncollectible within its borders, denied the use of federal force against the state, and exacted an oath from its public officials to support the ordinance of nullification. President Andrew Jackson resisted, blocked all of South Carolina's moves with a request from Congress for a Force Bill to enforce the tariffs, and the nation witnessed a prelude to Civil War.

A compromise tariff mitigated the tension temporarily, but the whole episode reinforced the conviction that Northern and Southern interests were at odds with one another, alienated a number of South Carolinians from the federal government, and developed a disposition that looked to secession as an ultimate necessity. "[This] has prepared the minds of men for a separation of the States," wrote James L. Petigru, "and when the question is mooted again it will be distinctly union or disunion."

The chronic need to defend the institution of slavery only further served to irritate tender sectional feelings on the part of South Carolina. From the Louisiana Purchase onward, South Carolinians were quick to resent anything which remotely resembled a threat to slavery and, hence, to their safety. So tenuous was South Carolina's relationship to theFederal government that as early as 1827, Dr. Thomas Cooper believed that it was "time to calculate the value of the Union."

The desire to secede intensified in South Carolina in the twenty years following Nullification. The increase in abolitionist literature, anti-slavery petitions before Congress, the controversy over the annexation of Texas, and more sectional acrimony over tariffs and the Second National Bank fanned flames of dissolution in South Carolina. Though Calhoun remained more conservative toward secession than most of his fellow South Carolinians, there did emerge leaders such as Robert Barnwell Rhett, the "father of secession," who took every opportunity to call for nullification and disunion. For instance, in opposition to the Tariff of 1842, Rhett launched a movement at Blufton on July 31, 1844, calling for a convention to nullify the tariff and, if necessary, to secede from the Union. Then secretary of state, Calhoun, still harboring presidential aspirations, counseled caution and used his influence to derail the so-called "Blufton Movement." "I had to act with great delicacy," Calhoun wrote, "but at the same time [with] firmness." However much Calhoun may have wished to eschew disunion, he had schooled his state and his region in the necessity of defending their interests through the limiting of Federal authority. By the mid-1840s a growing number of South Carolinians had come to the conclusion that that could only be achieved by withdrawing from the Union.

The Mexican-American War made a bad situation worse. The Wilmot Proviso, which would have prohibited slavery in any territory acquired as a result of victory over Mexico, convinced many South Carolinians that their destiny lay outside the bonds of Union. Instead of serving as a moderating influence as he had in the past, Calhoun reacted to the proposed Wilmot Proviso with great acrimony. Denying that Congress had authority to prevent the extension of slavery into the territories, Calhoun sought to unite the entire South in a program of resistance and he spoke more directly about secession than he had ever done before. "Though the Union is dear to us," he asserted, "our honor and our liberty are dearer." With Calhoun's inspiration, the South Carolina legislature unanimously resolved in 1848 that the time for discussion with the Federal government had passed and that they stood ready to join with their sister states in opposing the Wilmot Proviso "at any and every hazard." Once again, South Carolina poised itself on the precipice of civil war.

For a brief period it appeared that South Carolina would have the cooperation of her fellow Southern states. At Calhoun's urging, Mississippi called for a convention of Southern states to meet in Nashville in June 1850. South Carolina's legislature promptly elected delegates to this convention and resolved that passage of the Wilmot Proviso or the abolition of slavery in the District of Columbia would be, in the words of prominent Greenville unionist Benjamin F. Perry, "tantamount to a dissolution of the Union."

Henry Clay's compromise measures offered in Congress in January 1850 and Daniel Webster's conciliatory speech of March 7 undermined much of the initial enthusiasm for the Nashville Convention. When the meeting convened in June, only nine of the fifteen slave states sent delegates and the moderates dominated all of the action. Twenty-eight resolutions were approved, the most significant of which demanded the opening of all territories to slavery but "as an extreme concession" also consented to accept the Missouri Compromise line of 36 30' north latitude to the Pacific Ocean. The convention then resolved to await final action by Congress and agreed to meet again in November. Ardent secessionist Robert Barnwell Rhett returned to South Carolina extremely disappointed by the Nashville Convention's inaction and at once began a drive for independent action by his home state if other Southern states failed to act. "We will not be governed by the African," Rhett stated upon his arrival home, "neither will we be by the Yankee! We must secede." His colleague E. B. Bryan was even less subtle: *"Give us SLAVERY or give us death!,"* Bryan wrote after the convention.

Other southerners may have been placated by what ultimately became the Compromise of 1850, but South Carolina quickly and angrily repudiated the measures. And at least one measure of the "compromise" further intensified South Carolina's sectionalism. Northern refusal to comply with the Fugitive Slave Law of 1850 and its outright nullification of it in some states by Personal Liberty Laws, enraged the "fire-eaters" in the Palmetto State. Shortly before his death in 1850, Calhoun despaired of the possibility of saving both slavery and the Union. Witnessing the debates in Congress, Calhoun wrote James Henry Hammond, his South Carolina colleague in the Senate, "I trust, it will be of character to satisfy the South, that it cannot with safety remain in the Union, as things now stand and there is little or no prospect of any change for the better. . . . The impression is now very general, and is on the increase, that disunion is the only alternative that is left us."

Hammond's reply was equally revealing. "We must act *now*, and *decisively*," he told Calhoun, "long before the North gets this vast accession of strength she will ride over us rough shod, proclaim freedom or something equivalent to it to our slaves and reduce us to the condition of Hayti. . . . If we do not act now, we deliberately consign, not our posterity, but our *children*, to the flames." Nevertheless, at a Convention of the People of South Carolina called in Charleston in April 1852 to determine South Carolina's course of action, the co-operationists defeated the secessionists by a vote of 25,045 to 17,710. Old political divisions in South Carolina once again reemerged with the plantation districts calling for secession and the upstate and Charleston cautioning moderation. So incensed was Robert Barnwell Rhett with the outcome of this meeting that he resigned his U.S. Senate seat, claiming now to be an inadequate representative of a state adopting submission and merely waiting for cooperation.

Perhaps it was the election of sympathetic Franklin Pierce to the presidency in 1852 that calmed the flames of anger in South Carolina for the moment. But by then political giants Calhoun, Clay, and Webster were dead—succeeded by a generation of statesmen less skillful in the art of compromise and conciliation. Rhett and his fellow "fire-eaters" in South Carolina watched and waited, again, for their opportunity to lead their state out of the Union.

The "fire-eaters" did not have to wait long for sectional antagonisms to flare anew. The Kansas-Nebraska Act of 1854 repealed the Missouri Compromise and introduced the doctrine of popular sovereignty into the national debate over slavery's expansion into the territories. Allowing the people of each territory to decide for themselves whether or not they wanted slavery was a proposal that initially appealed to Northern and Southern Democrats alike. But the proposal also spawned the birth of the Republican Party, dedicated to the exclusion of slavery in all territories, thereby promoting the growth of abolitionist sentiment in the North and an aggressive pro-slavery dogma in the South. The result was that extremists on both sides of the Mason-Dixon Line rushed into Kansas Territory determined to influence the decision on slavery there by either ballots or bullets. Headlines soon sounded the clarion call to "Bleeding Kansas."

It was events in the Hall of Congress and not on the plains of Kansas that pushed South Carolina further down the road to secession. Abolitionist Senator Charles Sumner of Massachusetts, in a speech entitled "The Crime Against Kansas," excoriated his venerable senatorial colleague from South Carolina, Andrew Butler. Three days after Sumner's speech, and determined to avenge the insult of his kinsmen, Butler's nephew, U.S. Representative Preston Brooks used his "gutta percha" to attack the Massachusetts senator while he sat at his desk, hitting him over the head some thirty times. Brooks resigned his seat in the House after failure of a motion to expel him; and missed by only about fifteen votes unanimous re-election to Congress from his home district.

Once returning to Congress, Brooks received canes, cups, walking sticks, and the like, replete with nametags of prominent abolitionist congressmen worthy of his caning, from all over the South. Indeed, South Carolinians even paid Brooks' $300 fine! In the North, headlines blared "Bleeding Sumner" as sectional hatreds further crystallized. Henceforth, the two regions of the country would think of one another only in terms of stereotypes: "Bleeding Sumner" or "Bully Brooks," sadistic slave owners or wild-eyed abolitionists.

In the face of such unrelenting sectional tensions, it seems amazing that Representative James L. Orr, of Anderson, S. C., emerged to provide leadership for the conservatives in the Palmetto State. Believing that South Carolina could, or should, not act alone, Orr contended that his state must work within the parameters of the Democratic Party, a party with which most South Carolinians at least had been affiliated nominally since 1832. Staving off secessionists such as Rhett and L. M. Keitt from Orangeburg, Orr led a South Carolina delegation to the National Democratic Convention in Cincinnati in 1856. Orr's plan was a simple one: have South Carolina assume so major a role in the national Democratic Party organization that it would be able to shape its direction, thwart abolitionist tendencies, and prevent federal policies that were patently anti-Southern. Supported by prominent conservatives Benjamin F. Perry and Francis W. Pickens, Orr convinced many South Carolinians that only through cooperation with Northern Democrats could the South in general and South Carolina in particular prevail. Rhett accused such a program as being treasonous and claimed it would undo the work of an entire generation. The "fire-eater" prophesied, correctly, that the anti-slavery forces ultimately would capture the North anyhow so disunion was inevitable. Northerners, Rhett maintained, would never ally with their Southern counterparts, even within the same political party, to defend an institution and way of life which so many believed to be immoral. Still, when Orr obtained a promise that the National Democratic Party convention would be held in Charleston in 1860, and later when he was elected speaker of the House of Representatives, the plan seemed to be working.

When the Supreme Court endorsed the Calhounian principle of Southern rights in the territories in the Dred Scott Decision (1857), the conservative position in South Carolina and elsewhere in the South was strengthened all the more. The attempt of "fire-eater" Rhett, in concert with fellow radicals Edmund Ruffin in Virginia and William L. Yancey in Alabama to carry the South out of the Union by creating a bold minority analogous to the men who precipitated the American Revolution a century earlier, simply collapsed.

By 1858 the lines in South Carolina were clearly drawn between a small group of secessionists seeking any means by which to leave the Union, and the dominant conservatives, determined to secede if Southern rights were disregarded, but hoping and believing that through cooperation with the national Democratic Party the Union might be preserved. Indeed, South Carolina planter and assistant Secretary of State William H. Trescott later reflected that Orr and his fellow moderates were truly leading the Palmetto State down a new path; one which, given ample time, would have so altered the state that there would have been sufficient patience to prevent disunion in 1860.

But time was something the moderates did not have. In 1859, one man unified the entire South and managed to do in one swift motion what Calhoun, Rhett, Hammond, Ruffin, and Yancey had not been able to do in three decades. Radical abolitionist John Brown's attack on the federal arsenal at Harpers Ferry convinced Southerners to expect the worst while adding much currency to the arguments of the "fire-eaters." Although by no means was John Brown a typical Northerner or abolitionist, Southerners believed that he was and that was all that mattered. To many Northerners, John Brown acted accordingly, and after his execution they made him a martyr, thereby exacerbating an already lethal sectional crisis. Regional stereotypes in existence for most of the *antebellum* era now took firm root in the minds of Americans, North and South alike. In South Carolina the legislature immediately allocated $100,000 for military preparations and men throughout the state began drilling and preparing for war.

In Congress, the bonds of Union and civility were rapidly loosening. "So far as I *know*, and as I believe," wrote South Carolina senator James H. Hammond, "every man in both Houses is armed with a revolver—some with two—and a bowie knife. It is, I fear, in the power of any Red or Black Republican to precipitate at any moment a collision in which the slaughter would be such as to shock the world and dissolve this government. . . . I keep a pistol now in my drawer in the Senate as a matter of *duty* to my section."

Under this shroud of sectional anxiety and paranoia the nation braced itself for the presidential election of 1860. The Democrats, as promised, convened in Charleston. But given recent events, the voices of moderation led by James L. Orr in behalf of presidential aspirant Stephen A. Douglas of Illinois were not heard. When the Alabama delegation determined to obtain a congressional slave code for the territories, all hopes of compromise dissipated. The radicals lost the platform fight, however, and bolted the convention. With the convention now paralyzed, the Democrats decided to reconvene in Richmond, hoping that cooler heads would prevail. But South Carolina's delegation to the new convention was headed by Rhett, a secessionist whose star finally seemed to be rising. Any likelihood of Northern and Southern Democrats compromising on a candidate, was, as Rhett had predicted four years earlier, forever gone.

The splintering of the Democratic Party virtually ensured the election of Republican Abraham Lincoln in the fall. Throughout the summer South Carolina became more resolute about secession should Lincoln become president. Voices on both sides of the Mason-Dixon Line became more shrill. Even the usually restrained *Charleston Courier* wrote that "unless our foes are brought to a sense of their responsibility, unless fanaticism is driven in disgrace, and with the lash, from the pulpits and halls of legislation it has so long desecrated with its foul presence, we may and should apprehend the direst evils."

It was not surprising, then, when the South Carolina legislature acted so quickly after Lincoln's election and called for a state convention to act on secession. On December 20, 1860, this specially assembled convention unanimously passed the ordinance of secession. This time South Carolina did not wait for her Southern brethren to join her; she dared to act alone confident that the other Southern states would follow. And follow they did, as in short order six more Southern states left to form the Confederate States of America. Unionism in South Carolina was now dead. "I have been trying to prevent this sad issue for the last thirty years," wrote one of South Carolina's most prominent unionists, Benjamin F. Perry. But to underscore how much unionism in South Carolina had now acquiesced, Perry continued, "You are all now going to the devil, and I will go with you. Honor and patriotism require me to stand by my State, right or wrong." William H. Trescott was more philosophical. "History will vindicate our purpose," he wrote, "while she explains our errors."

Amidst the excitement, South Carolina prepared for war. Enthusiastic as they proceeded, if not actually jubilant, South Carolinians were convinced the war would be short and sweet. But no amount of preparation could have foretold the story of the next four years. In the coming war, 71,000 South Carolinians would serve; 12,922 (almost twenty percent of the state's white male population) would be killed in action or die of battlefield deaths. As one scholar has noted with pathos, if Americans in World War II had died in similar proportions, the casualty toll would have been almost 2.8 million instead of the actual figure of 332,000. The cost of secession would be a tragically expensive one.

The story of Fort Sumter is, of course, a well-told one. The attempt by lame-duck President James Buchanan to reinforce and supply Fort Sumter, the last visible sign of federal power in the state, failed when cadets from the Citadel fired on the *Star of the West* on January 9, 1861. In the aftermath of the attack, Buchanan hesitated, fearing a second attempt might mean war. Although the Confederate government had been founded in Montgomery without awarding either of the two highest offices to a South Carolinian, all eyes turned to Charleston harbor where the Federals still held Fort Sumter. When shots fired out toward Fort Sumter in the early hours of April 12, 1861, the Civil War began. Two days later, Major Robert Anderson surrendered the fort to the Confederate command.

Chosen as War Governor of South Carolina in the interest of state harmony was Francis W. Pickens of Edgefield, long identified as a moderate in the national Democratic Party. An aristocratic planter from a famous family, Pickens was an extremely intelligent and experienced, if not prickly, individual who possessed the capacity to alienate those around him quickly. Such would considerably work against him as South Carolina labored during the war.

Shortly after the loss of Fort Sumter, the Union made a massive amphibious assault on coastal South Carolina and established a firm foothold on the Port Royal/ Hilton Head area. For the next four years the Federals camped there, providing a constant threat of either westward penetration into the state or a northward assault toward Charleston. The federal presence so close by surely did not go unnoticed in Charleston where fear and paranoia caused many residents to flee inland. A massive fire in Charleston in December 1861 only confounded the anxiety and confusion there.

Under these conditions the nettlesome Governor Pickens came under a torrent of criticism. "Pickens is such an ass," wrote William Gilmore Simms, "that he will drive away from him every decent counsellor. . . . All who will flatter, can rule him. . . . He is at times too inflexible to say no, at other times too mulish to say yes even though every argument called for it." To offset the lack of confidence in Pickens, an Executive Council was created not by the legislature but rather by the Secession Convention still sitting in operation. This Council would have all the usual powers associated with the executive branch of government but "also [with] unlimited wartime powers." Although the governor was a member of the five-man Council, at no time would it function as the governor's cabinet.

Quickly the Council sought to muster the full force of the state behind the war effort. They impressed slaves into work wherever they were needed and attempted to provide all necessary supplies. Foremost among these were powder and lead for the cause and to assure that they were plentiful, John and Joseph LeConte, science professors at South Carolina College, were recruited to be leaders in the manufacture of munitions. But every action of the Council inspired fear and jealousy among one state group or another. Planters resented their slaves being impressed into action while the state legislature's envy of the Council's emergency powers remained unbridled. And even though the Council never abused its powers, when the Secession Convention's mandate expired in 1862, the state legislature quickly moved to destroy its creation—declaring invalid all of the Council's previous actions save for contracts.

Thus did South Carolina go through the war quibbling. Manpower, a perennial problem for all states in the Confederacy, fostered a state-wide debate over who would be exempt from the Confederate draft laws. In the end, South Carolina granted far fewer exemptions from service than did other states, and the number of draftees who hired substitutes was relatively small. Of the 104,428 reported Confederate deserters, only 3,615 were listed from South Carolina.

As the war dragged on, South Carolinians experienced much of the same hardships as other Confederate states. The Union blockade brought growing shortages, spiraling inflation, and disrupted transportation to cities such as Charleston. And the tightening noose of Federal control off the coast progressively diminished profitable privateering. Still, without enemy occupation, Charlestonians functioned as normally as could be expected under these conditions. In Beaufort, which federal troops had occupied virtually since the outset of war, the situation was considerably different. A visiting journalist remarked that the town was "greatly demolished by the rude hand of the invader with the marks of vandalism everywhere." Since most of the community's leaders had fled in the

"Grand Skedaddle" before the Union forces arrived, wrote this journalist, "the days of ancient grandeur are forever gone when field hands and wandering contrabands people the halls of the ancien noblesse of Beaufort."

In the occupied sea islands area many of the plantations were confiscated for nonpayment of Federal taxes. Others were bought by speculators. Some were divided by the government and sold or rented in small plots to former slaves seeking yeoman farmer status, thereby providing the backdrop for what historian Willie Lee Rose called the "Rehearsal for Reconstruction."

But the "real" war arrived for many South Carolinians early in 1865 when General William T. Sherman's army marched into the state. By the time he had entered South Carolina Sherman already had severed the South. Determined on "utter destruction for the hellhole of secession," Sherman announced that he "was fighting not to prolong the conflict but to hasten its end, and total war was the most effective means at hand for securing this object."

Feigning an attack on Charleston, Sherman sent the brunt of this army inland toward Columbia, a city long believed to be safe and whose population had swelled from 8,000 to 20,000 during the war. Even as late as February 1865 the residents of Columbia, confident and content, were anticipating full protection despite ignoring the appeals of Governor Andrew G. Magrath that they rally to the colors. As one officer complained, he had "two brigades and five proclamations with which to oppose Sherman."

Sherman's march through the Carolinas is legendary. The wide swath of destruction through South Carolina by his troops, coupled with explosions at the railroad depot in Charleston and the burning of Columbia, lay waste to much of the state. Sherman accepted the consequences in characteristic fashion. "Though I never ordered it, and never wished it," he wrote after the war, "I have never shed any tears over the event, because I believe that it hastened what we all fought for, the end of the war."

Devastation and destruction reigned supreme in South Carolina. "The very air," Emma LeConte wrote in her diary, "was fraught with sadness and silence." All money invested in slaves evaporated with their emancipation. The value of land drastically tumbled. Surplus invested in Confederate bonds was worthless. And the white citizenry of the state found itself momentarily stunned. Indeed, most would agree with Emma LeConte's entry in her diary equating "Yankee" with all that was "*mean*, despicable, and abhorrent." Among the state's black population was very little animosity or vindictiveness but rather great hopes and expectations for the future—all of which would soon be dashed and then long thwarted. Amid these conditions and moods, rebuilding and building anew would be a difficult road to travel.

SUGGESTED READING

Steven A. Channing, *Crisis of Fear: Secession in South Carolina* (Norton: New York, 1970).

Lacy K. Ford, Jr., *Origins of South Carolina Radicalism: The South Carolina Upcountry, 1800-1860* (Oxford University Press: New York, 1988).

Philip M. Hamer, *The Secession Movement in South Carolina, 1847-1852* (H. Roy Haas: Allentown, 1918).

Harold S. Schultz, *Nationalism and Sectionalism in South Carolina, 1852-1860: A Study of the Movement for Southern Independence* (Duke University Press: Durham, 1950) .

John Barrett, *Sherman's March Through the Carolinas* (University of North Carolina Press: Chapel Hill, 1956).

William W. Freehling, *Prelude to Civil War: The Nullification Controversy in South Carolina, 1816-1836* (Harper & Row: New York, 1965).

John Barnwell, *Love of Order: South Carolina's First Secession Crisis* (University of North Carolina Press: Chapel Hill, 1982).

William W. Freehling, *The Road to Disunion: Secessionists at Bay, 1776-1854* (Oxford University Press: New York, 1990).

MISSISSIPPI

by
Allen Dennis

When South Carolina bit the bullet of secession on December 20, 1860, she found it a far tastier morsel than the bitter pill of nullification in 1832. Knowing that many citizens of her sister states were fairly frothing at the mouth in their zeal for separation from the union, the Palmetto secessionists basked but briefly in their solitary condition. While the ghost of John C. Calhoun breathed a sigh of vindication, the "bonnie blue flag" of rebellion was raised a second time in Mississippi.

Less than two weeks after the Charleston celebration, the Mississippi state capital of Jackson feverishly began to prepare for its own secession convention. Like South Carolina, Mississippi had considered secession before. Early in the 1850s, John Quitman and his legions had flirted openly with the idea before Jefferson Davis and other cooler heads managed to pull Mississippi back from the abyss. As time passed, events seemed to confirm the wisdom of the more conservative Southern position. Davis was rewarded with the portfolio of secretary of war under Franklin Pierce, adding substantially to his already excellent national reputation. When Roger Taney's court rebuffed Dred Scott in 1857, Mississippi took heart; when Stephen Douglas turned back Abraham Lincoln's strong senatorial challenge in 1858, her newspapers rejoiced. The horrid tide of what Mississippians considered abolitionism seemed to have been dammed.

But John Brown's mischief at Harpers Ferry in 1859 sent a shock wave along the Ohio River that surged down the Mississippi to the Gulf. As Mississippi and the South watched in disbelief, Northern newspapers turned a man Southerners thought was plainly mad into a saint. Daily, it seemed abolitionism gained respectability, even making inroads into the Democratic Party. Of all the nation's major institutions, only the Democratic Party could still pitch a tent large enough to contain both Northerners and Southerners. But should one of its stakes become shaky, the Deep South certainly was poised to bolt both the party and the Union. Then, when Abraham Lincoln was elected president, Southern paranoia increased geometrically. Their worst nightmares had come true; their domestic institutions seemed in grave jeopardy.

When the Mississippi secession convention met on January 7, 1861, its decision was a foregone conclusion. The vast majority of delegates chosen were avowed secessionists, and they moved swiftly to take the state out of the Union. The only significant opposition to secession came from the delegates from the hill counties of northeastern Mississippi. By a vote of eighty-four to fifteen, Mississippi joined South Carolina as an "independent nation" pending what most Southerners believed would be the inevitable creation of a Southern republic. When the Montgomery Convention met in February, Mississippi became one of the original seven members of the Confederate States of America. Late in March, Mississippi ratified the Confederate constitution. Certainly, Mississippians were gratified that one of their own sons, Jefferson Davis, was chosen provisional president of the Confederate States of America.

In the warmth of this patriotic afterglow, few Mississippians could have foreseen the frightful cost of what lay before them. By 1865, a once-prosperous agricultural economy was shattered beyond repair. State indebtedness amounted to almost $9 million, all of which was repudiated by the Reconstruction Constitutional Convention of 1868. Once a national economic and political leader, Mississippi's influence would never approach its *antebellum* zenith.

The war also brought considerable political change to Mississippi. Before the conflict, Mississippi had a thriving two-party system, as Democrats and Whigs regularly competed for most state and local offices. Whiggery was strong in the counties along the Mississippi River which were dominated by the planter class, and also in the finger-like Prairie region in the east-central part of the state. Jacksonian Democrats flourished in the hilly northeastern section, the Piney Woods, and in most of the poorer rural areas. At least initially, there were substantial pockets of unionism scattered throughout the state. Wealthier Whigs—almost always political conservatives—were often unionists, as were many hill county residents where slavery was not widespread. Yet, most reluctant secessionists and other skeptics eventually fell in line with Confederate Mississippi. But the war and reconstruction changed Mississippi politics. In the gubernatorial election of 1863, the moderate Democrat (and former Whig) Charles Clark was elected, receiving more than seventy percent of the vote in a three-man race which included a conservative Whig and a full-blown Fire-Eater. A wounded Confederate veteran, Clark presided over Mississippi's decline with dignity and uncommon aplomb. Absent the Civil War and the racial issue, the Republican Party might well have expected to inherit the support of former Whigs in Mississippi who shared many of the party's economic positions. But the polarization caused by the war's emotions and the hatred engendered for Republicans eventually destroyed the two-party system in post-Reconstruction Mississippi. Not until the 1960s and 1970s would the Republican Party even field candidates in most state political races, and not until 1991 did Mississippi elect its first Republican governor since Reconstruction.

But none of this concerned Mississippians early in 1861. As armed conflict approached, Mississippians flocked to their own colors and to those of the Confederacy. By late July, more than 170 companies had been formed, representing nearly all sections of the state. Governor John J. Pettus strove mightily to bring order out of the chaos plaguing Mississippi and its relationship to the Confederate government. Lying in its cradle, the Confederacy greatly resembled a human infant impatiently desiring instant gratification.

Geographically, Mississippi possessed both advantages and disadvantages should revolution become actual war. When Tennessee completed secession's Confederacy in June 1861, the northern border of Mississippi was protected by Confederate Tennessee and by the essentially friendly slave state of Kentucky, located farther north. If invasion came to Mississippi, it would almost certainly not be by land; even if land invasion came, it would not come quickly. Nor was a coastal invasion likely. Mississippi's tiny gulf coastal area contained few points of strategic or economic importance to the Federal high command, and was situated too far away from Washington to be of much concern.

The Achilles heel of Mississippi's defense was the configuration of its river system. Unlike Virginia, whose Potomac-Rappahannock-York-James ladder of east-west rivers afforded natural lines of defense, Mississippi's rivers were essentially north-south streams which virtually invited Federal invasion. The giant Mississippi River flowed past several of Mississippi's richest and most important cities, including Vicksburg and Natchez. Farther to the east, the Yazoo River and its major tributaries, the Tallahatchie, the Yalobusha, and the Coldwater, penetrated deeply into the heart of northern and central Mississippi, potentially opening an inviting back door to Vicksburg. Along the eastern edge of the state flowed the Tombigbee, near such important towns as Aberdeen, Amory, Tupelo, and Columbus.

In addition to the strategic importance of Mississippi's rivers, the state's railroad system was also crucial to its defense. Many of the Confederacy's most vital rail lines lay within the state, and several Mississippi towns and cities astride them became crucial as the war progressed. At Corinth, located in the northeastern corner of the state about five miles south of the Tennessee border and twenty-five miles west of the Alabama line, the Mobile & Ohio Railroad and the Memphis & Charleston Railroad intersected. This little town would later be the Confederate staging area for Shiloh, one of the Western Theatre's most important battles. At Grenada, in central Mississippi, the Mississippi Central Railroad leading from Jackson forked, with one branch continuing north to Memphis as the Memphis and Jackson Railroad and the other meandering through Oxford and Holly Springs to

LaGrange, Tennessee. Jackson, the state capital, was the railroad hub of the state, where the Vicksburg & Jackson, the New Orleans & Jackson, the Great Northern, and the Southern railroads converged. At Meridian, located about eighty miles east of Jackson, the Mobile & Ohio intersected the Southern railroad.

Little military action occurred in Mississippi during 1861, as both Confederate and Federal forces jockeyed for position in Virginia. Ship Island, off the Mississippi coast, was evacuated by Confederate forces on September 17 and occupied by Federals on December 3. Ship Island would become the base from which the Federal navy eventually would launch its successful raid against New Orleans, which surrendered on April 25, 1862. On December 31, 1861, a desultory naval raid on Biloxi from Ship Island destroyed a Confederate shore battery, but the town was not attacked. Apprehension reigned as the year closed, and 1862 would see Mississippi become—next to Tennessee—the western Confederacy's most important battle-ground.

In February 1862, Federal forces under Ulysses S. Grant capturedFort Henry and Fort Donelson, located in north-central Tennessee on the Tennessee and Cumberland rivers, respectively. The loss of Fort Henry imperiled northeastern Mississippi since its demise meant that the Tennessee River was open to Federal invasion as far south and east as Muscle Shoals, Alabama. As Grant's forces moved slowly up the Tennessee (the Tennessee flows north at this point, hence going "up" it is going south), the outflanked Confederate high command elected to concentrate its scattered forces at Corinth. For the next several months, Corinth laid claim to being the most important town in the entire Confederacy.

General Albert Sidney Johnston, with General Pierre Gustave Toutant Beauregard vying for a leadership role from his second-in-command position, summoned troops from throughout the western Confederacy to Corinth. Johnston himself commanded about 20,000 troops, who arrived in Corinth between March 18 and March 24. Greeting him there were 10,000 Confederates under Braxton Bragg, recently arrived from Mobile and Pensacola. Daniel Ruggles brought an additional 5,000 from Louisiana, and Leonidas Polk rounded out the Confederate force when he arrived from Columbus, Kentucky, with his units. By March 25, more than 40,000 anxious Confederates occupied Corinth.

Grant, in the meantime, also had been active. He and his forces evacuated the Fort Henry-Fort Donelson area on March 5, and by March 11 had taken up a position at Pittsburg Landing on the Tennessee River, some eighteen miles northeast of Corinth on the Tennessee side of the border. To the east, Don Carlos Buell's Federal forces sought to link with Grant, leaving Nashville on March 16. Their march was hampered by bad weather and destroyed bridges.

As April 1862 opened, Mississippi was threatened from three sides. Operations were already in progress against New Orleans, which threatened to open the Mississippi River as far north as the strongholds of Port Gibson and Vicksburg. Farther up the Mississippi, Federal assaults against New Madrid and Island No. 10 were about to endanger Memphis. A Federal victory in the Corinth-Pittsburg Landing area would complete the classic triangulation. In Washington, the more optimistic members of the Federal high command surely exulted over the possibility of eventually approaching Vicksburg and Jackson from three directions.

Since the major battle in the Corinth-Pittsburg Landing area occurred in Tennessee (at Shiloh), it will not be considered in detail here. The aftermath of the battle, however, significantly involved Mississippi and laid the foundation for two major actions late in the summer and early in the fall of 1862.

As the defeated Confederates trooped back into Mississippi from Shiloh, they escorted the body of the fallen Albert Sidney Johnston, which lay in state for a time in the parlor of a home in Corinth. The Confederates, now under the command of Beauregard, were reinforced at Corinth by additional troops commanded by Sterling Price and Mississippian Earl Van Dorn. To the north, Henry Halleck had assumed command of the huge Federal army. On April 30, it laboriously began the short journey toward Corinth, where a monumental struggle apparently would result. Halleck had about 120,000 men in his command, of whom 100,000 were combat-ready. Beauregard's force had swelled to nearly 70,000, with 50,000 available for immediate duty.

By May 28, Halleck's army had invested Corinth, ready to lay siege or do battle. But Beauregard was not prepared to endure either. Using an elaborate series of ruses, including massive use of "Quaker guns" (logs arranged and stained to look like artillery pieces), Beauregard evacuated Corinth on the night of May 29-30. Halleck occupied the town, gaining control of the vital rail junction there, while Beauregard moved the Confederate army some fifty miles south to Tupelo on the Mobile and Ohio Railroad.

Command difficulty, which bedeviled the western Confederacy at every hand, reared its head at Tupelo. Beauregard had reported to Richmond that the conflict at Shiloh was a victory, and consequently President Jefferson Davis was bewildered. If Shiloh was a victory, what were Beauregard and the Confederate army doing at Tupelo, and why was Halleck occupying and controlling Corinth? But conflict between Davis and Beauregard was nothing new. The Confederate president still resented Beauregard's overcautious behavior at the conclusion of the Manassas battle in July 1861, and, in fact, had relegated him to the Western Theatre to keep the Virginia wolves from both their doors.

When Beauregard took an unauthorized leave of absence in June to soak in the mineral waters at Bladen Springs, Alabama, Davis exploded. He relieved Beauregard of command, replacing him with an old favorite, Braxton Bragg. At this point, Confederate strategy depended to a large degree on what the Federal high command decided, and vice-versa. Had Bragg remained at Tupelo, Halleck's force may well have moved out of Corinth to bring the Confederates to battle somewhere between Corinth and Tupelo. But Federal supply lines reaching from Memphis might be too long and too vulnerable to make such a campaign feasible. By the same token, the Confederate high command searched for ways to relieve Mississippi and western Tennessee from the Federal threat.

The Confederates elected to undertake an offensive campaign designed to draw Federal forces out of Mississippi and perhaps to entice Kentucky into the Confederacy. Bragg took the Army of Tennessee on a circuitous route from Tupelo to Mobile to Atlanta to Chattanooga, where he conferred with Edmund Kirby Smith, commander of the Confederate Department of East Tennessee. They agreed on a joint invasion of Kentucky, though their armies never served together at any time during the campaign.

This Confederate move left Halleck with two choices. He could continue overland deeper into Mississippi, confronted by few Confederate troops. Or he could send at least a portion of his force to parallel and shadow Bragg's movement into Tennessee and Kentucky, possibly bringing him to battle somewhere in Middle Tennessee. To choose the first option would require tremendous extension of the Federal supply lines, which Halleck did not wish to risk. Too, if Bragg were allowed to move unopposed into Middle Tennessee and Kentucky, dearly-bought occupied territory might fall into Confederate hands.

Consequently, Halleck chose the latter option. He divided his force at Corinth into three parts, two large and one small. He sent one of the larger portions, commanded by Don Carlos Buell, eastward along the Memphis and Charleston Railroad to keep an eye on Bragg's movement. He dispersed the second of the larger forces, overseen by Ulysses S. Grant (who remained temporarily at Corinth), throughout West Tennessee to protect important railroads and rail junctions. These troops eventually would comprise the majority of the Federal force that waged the Vicksburg campaign. Not wishing to leave the vital rail junction at Corinth undefended, Halleck left William S. Rosecrans and about 17,000 Federal troops in and around Corinth.

As he and the majority of the army departed from Tupelo, Bragg left a Confederate force of about 15,000 men under Sterling Price at that city. These units were to keep an eye on any Federal moves from Corinth, and also served briefly to deceive the Federal command at Corinth about Bragg's eventual intentions. Thus the stage was set for potential conflict between Rosecrans and Price.

Bragg considered it essential that Rosecrans be prevented from linking with Buell's forces. Therefore, he ordered Price and his small army north from Tupelo in a sliding motion eastward to prevent any movement by Rosecrans toward Buell. On September 14, 1862, Price's force occupied Iuka, a tiny town located in extreme northeastern Mississippi some twenty miles south-southeast of Corinth and no more than five miles from the Alabama border. Just as Bragg feared that Rosecrans would move to join Buell, Grant feared that Price would try to link with Bragg. Price's occupation of Iuka seemed to indicate a possible move toward Bragg's army, and Grant was determined to stop it.

Grant divided the small Federal force at Corinth into two parts. General Edward O.C. Ord and 8,000 Federals were to move toward Iuka from northwest of the town, while Rosecrans and 9,000 troops were to approach Iuka from the west. According to a rather elaborate battle plan, Ord's forces were to attack first, driving Price and his Confederates southeastward into the waiting arms of Rosecrans. Rosecrans would then roll up the Confederate left (the Confederates were facing west), cutting them off from the Mobile and Ohio Railroad and other sources of supply to the South. If all went according to schedule, the entire Confederate force might be captured. Should this occur, nearly all Confederate resistance in eastern Mississippi would be crushed, freeing Grant and all his forces to focus on Vicksburg.

Seldom in the Civil War did well-laid plans go so far astray, for Price would be no easy mark. Even though a planned juncture with other Confederate forces under Earl Van Dorn did not materialize, Price proved to be a formidable opponent. Command confusion within the Federal ranks led to Rosecrans' force, not Ord's, opening the attack on the afternoon of September 19. As the fighting raged throughout the hot late summer afternoon, Rosecrans wondered where Ord's forces were and when they would join the battle. Meanwhile, Ord's troops were positioned just northwest of Iuka, within seemingly easy earshot of so large an engagement. Ord later claimed that he and his forces did not hear the fighting, apparently caught in what is known as an "acoustic shadow." Supposedly, atmospheric conditions combined with terrain characteristics can create a situation in which a military force cannot hear a nearby battle. Ironically, at least three other similar situations occurred during the summer and fall of 1862, including one at the Battle of Perryville during Bragg's Kentucky campaign.

Without Ord's participation, capture of Price's force became impossible. Receiving information that a large, unengaged Federal force (Ord's) lay just northwest of him, on September 20 Price elected to withdraw from the field toward Fulton, some forty miles south of Iuka. Casualties numbered slightly more than 1,500 for the Confederates and just under 800 for the Federals. While the casualty ratio indicates a significant Federal victory, the chance to capture an entire Confederate force was lost. Rosecrans and Ord verbally sniped at each other as long as both lived, and Price and Van Dorn survived to fight again two weeks later at Corinth.

Earl Van Dorn, who ranked Price, was becoming exceedingly ambitious. He dreamed of clearing northeast Mississippi of the Federal threat, moving on to do the same in West Tennessee, and then possibly driving on St. Louis or Paducah. According to the plan adopted, Van Dorn was to move his force from its position at Holly Springs to Ripley, where he would await Price's arrival from just south of Iuka. By September 28, both forces had rendezvoused at Ripley. That afternoon, they swung into action. The plan was to march north from Ripley to a point just across the Tennessee line near Pocahontas, about twenty miles north-northwest of Corinth. This move was designed as a feint to entice the Federals in the Corinth-Iuka sector to think the Confederates intended to drive deeper into West Tennessee.

But Rosecrans was not surprised. Using some of the entrenchments that Beauregard's men had dug nearly six months before, the Federals fought ferociously when Van Dorn attacked on October 3. Unseasonably hot weather plagued both armies, and the Confederates called off the attack at dusk. Before daylight on October 4, Confederate and Federal artillery set the darkness ablaze prior to the resumption of infantry fighting at dawn. By noon, the disappointed Confederates had had enough and began to withdraw toward Ripley. Rosecrans' forces gave little pursuit, and none farther than the outskirts of Ripley. With Federal intentions regarding Vicksburg unclear, Van Dorn's forces eventually withdrew as far south as Grenada in central Mississippi. From this point, they would be in a position to move either north toward Tennessee or south toward Vicksburg as circumstances warranted.

Meanwhile, Grant considered several possibilities as he developed strategy to move against fortress Vicksburg. From his headquarters at Memphis, he considered a direct push down the Mississippi in conjunction with naval support. But the overland route through Mississippi into Vicksburg's back door beckoned enticingly. Only Earl Van Dorn's force of about 20,000 at Grenada and the cavalry of Nathan Bedford Forrest stood in his way.

In November 1862, Grant's force pushed out of West Tennessee into Mississippi along the Mississippi Central Railroad, reaching Oxford by December 2. John C. Pemberton, commander of the Confederate forces at Vicksburg, clamored for reinforcements from Bragg's army in Tennessee. Bragg had his own troubles trying to deal with Rosecrans in his front, but did detach Nathan Bedford Forrest's cavalry to raid Grant's supply lines in West Tennessee that stretched to Columbus, Kentucky. Forrest so threatened the crucial railroads and rail junctions in West Tennessee that Grant made Memphis his chief supply base so that supplies could come directly down the Mississippi to Memphis, rather than risk the overland routes through West Tennessee into Mississippi.

By December 15, the Federal army was fifteen miles south of Oxford, headed in the direction of Grenada. But his extended supply line gave Grant considerable pause, and a moderate change in strategy ensued. Grant ordered William T. Sherman and four divisions to return to Memphis and embark on a move against Vicksburg by going downriver. In the meantime, Grant intended to bring Van Dorn to battle. If Van Dorn could be defeated, Sherman could move down the Mississippi against Vicksburg while Grant and his forces closed the other side of the vise by approaching the river city from the east.

On December 20, Sherman's forces left Memphis full of hope. Almost simultaneously the erratic Van Dorn, whose grandiose ego would not long abide inactivity, played his best card. On December 18, two days before Sherman left Memphis, Van Dorn took 3,500 of his best cavalry from Grenada, skirting Grant's army to make a lightning strike on Holly Springs, Grant's chief supply base for the overland Vicksburg expedition. The assault came on December 20, and it was Van Dorn's finest hour. More than $1.5 million in Federal ordnance and supplies were destroyed in the raid, and so complete was the desolation and so unlikely its quick repair that Grant abandoned the overland push. By January 1, Grant's army was back in Tennessee, humbled but still ambitious.

Meanwhile, Sherman and his forces had arrived opposite Vicksburg on December 26. Anticipating eventual assistance from Grant, Sherman moved his forces via transport up the Yazoo River, which flowed into the Mississippi just north of Vicksburg. On December 29, Sherman's troops assaulted the Confederate positions at Chickasaw Bluffs, sustaining more than 1,200 casualties. Confederate losses were slightly more than 200. Realizing that Vicksburg was a tough nut to crack, Sherman withdrew to Milliken's Bend, located north of Vicksburg on the Louisiana side of the river, to await further coordination with Grant.

While Sherman and Grant experimented unsuccessfully with canal-building to bypass some of the Vicksburg defenses, another intriguing plan took shape. Far north of Vicksburg, near the present-day Coahoma-Tunica county line, was a prehistoric bayou called Yazoo Pass. In ancient times, the pass was a branch of the Mississippi River that led from the main channel of the Mississippi into the Yazoo River via the Coldwater River and the Tallahatchie River. In 1856, however, planters along the riverside built a levee across the Yazoo Pass to dry the fertile soil for planting, thus cutting off the Mississippi from the Yazoo River system.

Under Grant's direction, this levee was breached on February 2-3, 1863, and the Mississippi's waters once more gradually filled the old channel. By the first of March, it was deep enough to permit Federal vessels to enter the Coldwater River. But the waterway was clogged with brush, undergrowth, and dead trees, many of which were placed there by Confederates to impede the Federal advance. Because of the almost constant dredging that was necessary, the flotilla's progress was slow. This gave Confederates under W. W. Loring time to construct crude river defenses near the point where the Tallahatchie met the Yalobusha, creating the Yazoo. Called Fort Pemberton, this fortified area faced upstream (north), dominating at least a thousand yards of straight river.

In March and April, several Federal naval assaults attempted to break the Confederate defenses and move past Fort Pemberton toward Vicksburg. The land around Fort Pemberton was too marshy to allow a ground assault against the position, and the campaign was abandoned shortly after the Confederates sank the *Star of the West* in the main channel of the Tallahatchie, blocking any additional Federal advance.

At the same time the Confederates were turning back the Federal advance at Fort Pemberton, another amphibious assault unfolded just north of Vicksburg in the Steele's Bayou region. On March 14, 1863, David D. Porter took a flotilla of thirteen ships, including five ironclads, into Steele's Bayou. This move was designed to complement the Yazoo Pass expedition by moving up Steele's Bayou through Black Bayou to Deer Creek, and then on to the upper Yazoo. If successful, this move would outflank major Confederate river batteries ten to twelve miles up the Yazoo from Vicksburg. Then, the forces involved in this effort could either move north to aid in the assault against Fort Pemberton or turn south for an attack on the Yazoo River batteries above Vicksburg.

It was a star-crossed effort. Colonel Samuel F. Ferguson's Confederates rushed to Rolling Fork, where they defeated Porter on March 19. When Winfield S. Featherston arrived with reinforcements, the Confederates nearly captured most of Porter's force. Only a daring night march by units of Sherman's infantry, lighting their way with candles and small torches stuck in gunbarrels, rescued the beleaguered Porter. Grant, perhaps tiring of these esoteric jousts at Vicksburg, doggedly began to pursue more conventional efforts.

The new strategy was quite simple: cross the Mississippi River from the Federal position on the Louisiana side, swing east to position the Federal force between Vicksburg and possible reinforcements from Jackson, and drive on the river stronghold, pinning its garrison against the Mississippi. The land north of Vicksburg in the "V" created by the Mississippi and the Yazoo rivers was too marshy and soft to permit much movement. Hence, the Federal goal was to cross the Mississippi south of Vicksburg on drier soil.

Since Confederate batteries at Port Hudson, Louisiana, prevented supplies or naval support from arriving upstream from New Orleans, it became necessary to rely on David Porter's fleet for these purposes. But Porter's flotilla would first have to run past the batteries at Vicksburg in order to pick up the Federal ground forces south of Vicksburg for the journey to the eastern bank. Porter's task, long dreaded by the Federal high command, proved to be surprisingly easy. On the night of April 16, thirteen Federal vessels challenged Vicksburg's river guns, and twelve made it past Vicksburg. Emboldened by this success, another large flotilla ran the batteries on the night of April 22. At long last, Grant had the means to cross to the east bank for the decisive assault on Vicksburg.

Deciding where to cross the river was another matter. After some confusion, including an abortive attempt to cross at Grand Gulf, Grant elected to ferry the troops across at Bruinsburg, located approximately thirty-five miles downriver from Vicksburg. By the end of the first week in May, most of the Federal troops were safely on the east bank of the river.

John Pemberton, in command at Vicksburg, had far too many irons in his fire. Not only did he have to be concerned about Grant, but he also was worried about what Benjamin Grierson was up to. The Federal cavalryman began his storied raid from LaGrange, Tennessee, on April 17, and it proved to be the consummate diversionary tactic. It confused Pemberton and caused him to disperse his already outnumbered force. With fewer than 40,000 troops scattered between Jackson and Vicksburg and beyond, Pemberton eventually would face a Federal force numbering almost twice that.

Joseph E. Johnston faced a daunting task. As Confederate theatre commander in the West, his charge was to coordinate Pemberton's army with that of Braxton Bragg in Tennessee. Ideally, he was to shift forces from one army to another as the need arose, since the Confederacy had the advantage of interior lines. But if both armies were under pressure from vastly superior numbers, this strategy was rendered moot. While William S. Rosecrans steadily flanked Bragg farther toward Chattanooga, Grant and Sherman menaced the Jackson-Vicksburg area. Johnston could do little more than watch helplessly as the Confederate tide ebbed on two fronts.

On May 12, Confederates under John Gregg fought Federals commanded by James B. McPherson at the Battle of Raymond, some fifteen miles southwest of Jackson. Thick undergrowth stymied both forces in what essentially was an indecisive battle, although the Confederates left the field. Each side suffered about 500 casualties. Gregg withdrew his forces to Jackson, where he conferred with Joseph E. Johnston. Earlier, on May 9, Johnston had left Tullahoma, Tennessee, on orders from Secretary of War James A. Seddon to assume command in Mississippi. Tired from his long journey, Johnston arrived in Jackson late on May 13. Finding that only Gregg's small force was available to protect Jackson, Johnston ordered its evacuation. As the Johnston/Gregg forces moved north toward Canton, units of the Federal army under William T. Sherman occupied the capital city on May 14. Johnston began to collect reinforcements near Canton, but the large Federal army between him and Vicksburg prevented any real coordination with Pemberton in time to save Vicksburg.

On May 16, the final pitched battle of the Vicksburg campaign occurred at Champion's Hill, after which Pemberton withdrew toward the Vicksburg defenses. Further demoralizing action took place on May 17 at the Battle of the Big Black River, and the Confederate return to Vicksburg was more a rout than a retreat. As the Federal forces encircled the city, Grant could not resist making two frontal assaults against the Confederate trenches, both of which were repulsed. Consequently, Grant contented himself with laying siege to Vicksburg on May 22.

As weeks passed, dwindling food supplies and the onset of summer heat ravaged the Vicksburg garrison. Pemberton, perhaps expecting generosity on Federal Independence Day, elected to surrender on July 4. Grant, who always offered only unconditional surrender but was usually more lenient in practice, immediately authorized paroles for most of the Confederate forces. Many would see additional action later in the war.

In the full glow of victory, Grant decided to send Sherman after Joseph E. Johnston, who had made it as far as the Big Black River in a futile attempt to assist Pemberton at Vicksburg. Reinforcements had swelled Johnston's army to more than 30,000, and he could have been a formidable foe. But Johnston, already honing a skill that would make him notorious in the Atlanta campaign, retreated into Jackson. By July 10, Sherman's forces had invested the city, and a sort of semi-siege began. Johnston's escape route to the east was always open, and he took it on the night of July 16-17. Sherman's forces took Jackson on July 17 and did the usual mischief of occupation troops until summoned back to Vicksburg a week later.

Although significant military action would occur again in Mississippi, never would it be on so large a scale. Vicksburg was the one remaining jewel in the crown of Confederate Mississippi, and its capture presaged a decline in the importance of Mississippi to the Confederate cause. Events in Tennessee, Georgia, and Virginia would dominate the war. By the fall of 1863, Grant and Sherman were both involved in the action in the Chattanooga area, winning laurels that would eventually result in Grant's appointment to command all Federal forces and Sherman's promotion to Grant's former command.

But there was still a little unfinished business in Mississippi. At Meridian, eighty miles east of Jackson, lay the junction of the Mobile and Ohio Railroad and the Southern Railroad. Some supplies still reached Bragg's army in Tennessee via this source through Mobile and Atlanta. Sherman returned to Vicksburg late in January 1864, determined to eliminate this irritant. Jackson was reoccupied on February 5, and Sherman's forces continued east the following day.

Opposing this Federal advance were Confederates under Leonidas Polk, who recently had assumed command of the Department of Alabama, Mississippi, and East Louisiana. Still smarting from a near court-martial at the hands of Bragg for alleged dereliction of duty at Chickamauga, Polk was no match for Sherman. Failing to make a stand when approached by Sherman's forces at Morton, Polk fell back to Meridian. Sherman, undaunted, drove his army mercilessly toward the city.

Knowing that he was outnumbered heavily, Polk evacuated Meridian on February 14, and Sherman easily occupied the city that afternoon. After a few days of massive destruction, Sherman and his army returned to Vicksburg early in March. In the meantime, 7,000 Federal cavalry under William Sooy Smith attempted to move overland from Memphis to join Sherman in his assault on Meridian. Bad weather and worse roads slowed their movement, and they were unable to rendez-vous with Sherman. In fact, Sherman gave up on Smith and began his return to Vicksburg at about the time Smith's horsemen reached Okolona, more than 100 miles north of Meridian.

It was a trip Smith probably wished he had never made, for he encountered Nathan Bedford Forrest and his cavalry near Okolona. The Confederate cavalry genius had been given license to operate independently against Federal supply lines in northeast Mississippi and northwest Alabama, and he made the best of it. Smith's forces were routed near Okolona on February 22, and were only too happy to return to Memphis and away from Forrest's little fiefdom. Thus, when Sherman was called to replace Grant in March 1864, he was already too familiar with the threat Forrest posed to his supply line. Unfortunately for him and several thousand hapless Federal cavalrymen, he would become even more familiar.

Late in the spring of 1864, Sherman's Atlanta campaign was in full swing. As the giant blue horde bore down on Joseph E. Johnston's retreating Confederates in northern Georgia, Sherman continued to worry about his supply lines and about the gray wizard Forrest. He had cause to worry. On June 1, Forrest left Tupelo, aiming to strike the rail lines in northern Alabama or southern Middle Tennessee that fed and armed Sherman's force. Almost simultaneously, Sherman ordered Samuel D. Sturgis and his forces from Memphis to locate Forrest and deal with him. When Forrest's superior, Stephen D. Lee, learned of Sturgis' advance, he summoned Forrest back into Mississippi to confront the new Federal threat.

The engagement that followed ranks as one of the finest examples of the cavalryman's art. On June 10, Forrest struck Sturgis at Brice's Cross Roads, located about eighteen miles north of Tupelo. With Sturgis was the hated Grierson, whose famous raid had helped stymie Confederate defensive efforts during the Vicksburg campaign. Whether Forrest knew of Grierson's presence is debatable, but revenge was sweet under any circumstance. He battered Grierson's force early in the battle, and swept violently through demoralized Federal units in the afternoon. The Federal retreat became a complete rout. Wagons and supplies were abandoned wholesale, and few victories in any theatre during the Civil War were more complete. Forrest inflicted more than 2,200 casualties while absorbing fewer than 400. Sherman gnashed his teeth and vowed revenge.

To a degree, he got it. Early in July, Sherman ordered another force from Tennessee into Mississippi in pursuit of Forrest. Commanded by Andrew Jackson Smith, this force of slightly more than 14,000 warily tacked southeastward toward Pontotoc and Tupelo. Evading Forrest near Okolona, Smith formed his battle line slightly west of Tupelo on the night of July 13. At daylight on July 14, the Confederates under Forrest and S. D. Lee attacked. By mid-morning, Lee and Forrest withdrew, vulnerable to a counterattack had not Smith had such respect for Forrest's reputation. After desultory action on July 15, Smith withdrew into Tennessee, leaving Forrest alive, well (except for his raging boils), and angrier than ever. Although the battle was a rather decisive tactical Federal victory, Smith left the field to return to Tennessee, and Forrest resumed his usual role as chief harasser of Federal supply lines. Sherman resumed gnashing his teeth, both at Forrest and at Smith's failure to crush him.

Forrest was not happy, either. Deterred from being able to snipe at Sherman's supply line by the pesky Federal cavalry, he was in no mood to tolerate much more. When A. J. Smith made a second foray into Mississippi early in August, Forrest took the initiative. Two weeks of maneuvering and skirmishing found both armies near Oxford, and Forrest decided to strike. On August 18, Forrest took 2,000 of his best cavalry, skirted Smith's force, and headed for Memphis. On the morning of August 21, the gray cavalry stormed into the city, surprised the garrison there, and generally scared the wits out of anyone wearing blue. After taking a few prisoners and destroying or confiscating some supplies, Forrest fell back into Mississippi. When Smith heard of Forrest's Memphis raid, he also withdrew toward Tennessee, hoping to bring Forrest to battle. But the wily Forrest evaded Smith, and continued to wreak havoc almost at will until he and his command finally surrendered at Selma, Alabama, in April 1865.

Although dozens of skirmishes and minor engagements occurred in Mississippi from September 1864 through April 1865, most of the Civil War's significant military action during this period occurred in Virginia, Tennessee, and Georgia. As Grant closed in on Robert E. Lee in Virginia and Sherman pushed northward from Savannah toward Joseph E. Johnston's force in North Carolina, the war drew to its now inevitable conclusion. Yet, Confederate forces in Mississippi were among the last ground forces to surrender. On May 4, 1865, almost a month after Lee's surrender and more than week after Johnston's, Richard Taylor surrendered his force near Citronelle, Alabama, just across the border from Meridian. For Mississippi and the Confederacy, the war was over.

One issue, however, still hangs fire. And, after decades of historiographical focus on the Virginia theatre, only recently have historians begun to discuss it fully. Why did Jefferson Davis, loyal son of Mississippi, give emphasis and preferential treatment to Robert E. Lee and the Army of Northern Virginia, while furnishing only dribs and drabs to his home state's defense and that of his home region?

SUGGESTED READING

Michael B. Ballard, *Pemberton: A Biography* (Jackson: University Press of Mississippi, 1991).

Edwin C. Bearss, "The Armed Conflict, 1861-1865," in R. A. McLemore, ed., *A History of Mississippi* (2 vols., Hattiesburg, MS: University and College Press of Mississippi, 1973), I, 447-91.

Edwin C. Bearss, "Calendar of Events in Mississippi, 1861-1865," *The Journal of Mississippi History*, XXI (April, 1959), 85-112.

Edwin C. Bearss, *Decision in Mississippi* (Little Rock: Mississippi Commission on the War Between the States and Pioneer Press, 1962).

John K. Bettersworth, *Confederate Mississippi: The People and Policies of a Cotton State in Wartime* (Baton Rouge: Louisiana State University Press, 1943).

John K. Bettersworth, "The Home Front, 1861-1865," in R. A. McLemore, ed., *A History of Mississippi* (2 vols., Hattiesburg, MS: University and College Press of Mississippi, 1972), I, 492-541.

Mark M. Boatner, III, *The Civil War Dictionary* (New York: David McKay Company, 1959).

Thomas L. Connelly, *Army of the Heartland: the Army of Tennessee, 1861-1862* (Baton Rouge: Louisiana State University Press, 1967).

Vincent J. Esposito, ed., *The West Point Atlas of American Wars* (2 vols., New York: Praeger Publishers, 1959).

Patricia L. Faust, ed., *Historical Times Illustrated Encyclopedia of the Civil War* (New York: Harper & Row, 1986).

Herman Hattaway and Archer Jones, *How the North Won: A Military History of the Civil War* (Urbana, Ill.: University of Illinois Press, 1983).

E. B. Long with Barbara Long, *The Civil War Day by Day: An Almanac, 1861-1865* Garden City, NY: Doubleday & Company, 1971).

FLORIDA

by
Arch Fredric Blakey

When South Carolina seceded from the Union in December 1860, it was only a matter of time before the rest of the Lower South followed. There was little if any opposition to secession in the Palmetto State and the same was almost true of Florida. In politics, Florida was a miniature replica of South Carolina; no other Southern state was more eager to depart the Union than those kindred souls in power in Florida. But, there were a few areas of the state where unionism was strong, especially in Jacksonville and the northeastern area of the state. Still, the great majority in that region were as firmly committed to the creation of a new Southern nation as could be found anywhere.

It had been obvious since June 1860 when the Florida Democratic Party opted for secession if Abraham Lincoln won the presidency what the state's future would be; the only question remaining in December was whether to join South Carolina immediately or wait to see what Georgia and Alabama would do. If either of those states did not sever their association with the Union and Florida did, the state would be in an impossible situation.

The sixty-nine delegates who convened in Tallahassee in January 1861 accurately reflected the views of their constituents. The great majority were for secession; most favored an immediate break with the Union, others urged a waiting period until Georgia and Alabama acted, and a few remained loyal to the old flag. The vote came on January 10, sixty-two to seven, for a declaration that Florida was now "a sovereign and independent nation."

Floridians never intended to become a "sovereign nation." They recognized that their future was tied to a new confederation of states because they had none of the resources necessary to exist as a separate entity. To cite the most obvious difficulty, the population numbered but 140,427, of whom 77,747 were white, 932 were free Negroes, and 61,748 were slaves. Eight *cities* in the United States were larger.

In addition, Florida hosted no industrial or manufacturing facilities except for one cotton mill and one shoe factory. The agricultural system was not self-sufficient. Almost everything consumed except corn, pork, vegetables, and forage, was imported. Florida's 400 miles of railroad track did not connect with adjoining states, and the state could not begin to defend its long and vulnerable coastline. Small wonder that a Florida delegation hastened to Montgomery, Alabama, and gladly joined the nascent nation called the Confederate States of America in February 1861.

Despite their liabilities, most Floridians could not wait to sever the ties of Union and the convention actually lagged behind the actions of the citizens. By the time secession was adopted, local "Minute Men" organizations already had seized all Federal property in Florida except for Fort Taylor at Key West, Fort Jefferson in the Dry Tortugas, and Fort Pickens on Santa Rosa Island which guarded the entrance to Pensacola Bay.

Confederate Florida could do nothing about the southern-most city or Fort Jefferson, but Fort Pickens was another matter. Pensacola Bay, the largest deep water port on the Gulf of Mexico, was quite a prize, and in addition to Pickens there were two other forts and a navy yard worth over $1 million at stake. Clearly, these valuable assets would be of enormous benefit to the Confederacy, and there was only one under-strength company of Federal artillery to defend them. By March 1861, there were at least 5,000 Confederate troops from Georgia and Alabama at Pensacola; Fort Pickens could have been taken at any time but a truce was arranged in an attempt to work out a peaceful solution.

The situation in Florida mirrored that at Fort Sumter, South Carolina. These two forts were the only Union possessions under Federal control in the Confederacy, and if war came it would begin at one or the other of these places. In April, the Confederates bombarded Fort Sumter into submission and the war began.

Federal reinforcements poured into Fort Pickens and the Confederates found to their dismay that now they lacked the firepower to force a surrender. Even worse, a daring Federal raid from the fort in September destroyed the dry-dock. Confederate forces were repelled the next month when they tried to take the fort by a night attack on Santa Rosa Island. For the next several months, occasional artillery duels took place and again, Confederate guns failed to silence the fort.

The Confederate line in the West collapsed in the Spring of 1862 and Confederate forces left Pensacola to the Federals and moved to the endangered Tennessee-Kentucky front. Fort Pickens and Pensacola remained in Union hands for the duration of the war, depriving the Confederacy of a valuable port of entry for blockade-runners and the largest naval base on the Gulf.

Many Floridians were dismayed that their own Confederate troops, numbering about 15,000 men, had been sent to Virginia or Kentucky. The loss of Pensacola was a blow, but they feared the worse was yet to come because Florida was virtually defenseless by early 1862. Citizens bitterly concluded that the Confederate and state governments had left them to their own fate, and that fate was soon to prove cruel indeed.

At the outbreak of hostilities, Governor John Milton and high Confederate authorities had agreed that Fort Pickens must be taken and that Pensacola had to be retained. In addition, the entrance to the Apalachicola River, which guarded the cotton kingdom of Florida and southern Georgia and Alabama, must be held. In the eastern part of the state, Fernandina, Jacksonville, and St. Augustine must be protected by activating forts or building new structures to block the St. Marys and St. Johns rivers. All recognized that these points could be seized by Federal forces protected by gunboats unless Confederate or state troops occupied them in strength. Unfortunately, the Confederacy faced collapse in the West in 1862 and had to strip forces from all over Dixie in order to stop U.S. Grant's offensive; this resulted in Florida being at the mercy of Federal invasions after March 1862.

After Union forces captured Port Royal and Hilton Head, South Carolina, in November 1861, they looked for favorable opportunities to establish additional coaling stations and ports to increase the efficiency of the naval blockade declared by Lincoln after the fall of Fort Sumter. Northeast Florida looked to be an attractive target, and the blow fell in March 1862. Federals added Fernandina, the eastern terminus of the Florida Railroad, and St. Augustine to the list of occupied areas in Florida. Jacksonville also was invaded, for the first of four times, but was evacuated in April, much to the dismay of the Unionists who lived there.

Most Floridians strongly supported secession from the beginning of the war until the end, but this was not true of northeastern Florida in general or of Jacksonville in particular. This port, located on the St. Johns River, was the most important city in northern Florida; it was the commercial hub of the entire region before the war and shortages of every thing from boots to brooms and coffee to clothing resulted when this commerce was halted. Although it was not occupied permanently until 1864, the city suffered considerable damage in 1862 when Confederates burned all facilities of possible use to the invading Federals. Some of the holdings of known Unionists also were torched.

Some of Jacksonville's leading citizens planned to create a loyal government and return East Florida to the Union. They called for elections to do so in April and understandably were upset when informed that the Federals would be leaving in a matter of days. These Loyalists had no choice but to depart with the Federal forces; when they returned two years later they found that their homes and most of the city had been destroyed.

The people of Florida and the authorities at state and Confederate levels must have wondered what more Florida could contribute to the cause beyond the troops already in the field. The Federal occupation of Fernandina restricted Confederate use of the Florida Railroad in the east and a naval raid against Cedar Key in January 1862 ruined that railroad's Gulf terminal. The line continued to serve the interior of the state but could no longer distribute goods that had run the Federal blockade successfully. In fact, all of Florida's ports were either nullified or in Federal hands by 1862. On the Gulf, Pensacola, Apalachicola, and Key West were occupied by Federals, and Tampa and Cedar Key were subjected to naval raids that prevented either from attaining any importance to the Confederacy. The fate of Fernandina, St. Augustine, and Jacksonville has been mentioned previously.

Floridians found it almost impossible to transport goods delivered by blockade-runners to other parts of the Confederacy and nothing of major importance was accomplished in this area. The experience of Florida troops in dealing with a contraband cargo early in 1862 serves as an example of the difficulties they faced because of insufficient transport facilities.

Mosquito Inlet (located south of present day Daytona Beach) offered a good landing for blockade-runners, but moving the cargo from there involved a twenty-five mile, overland trip to the St. Johns River. Loaded aboard inland steamers, the journey continued down (north) the St. Johns some forty miles to the Ocklawaha River and westward on that stream for another twenty miles to Orange Springs. Another overland trek of about thirty miles from there to Waldo followed when at last the cargo could be entrained on the Florida Railroad. The cars took the goods northeast some forty miles to Baldwin (about eighteen miles west of Jacksonville), to connect with the Florida Atlantic and Gulf Coast Railroad. The cargo was transferred to the new line and shipped westward about forty miles to Lake City, where it was loaded onto wagons for the final run into Georgia. Once the Georgia railroad east of Valdosta was reached—another forty mile-run from Lake City—the cargo was shipped to Savannah and to any and all parts of the Confederacy. It took about three months for the cargo to go from Mosquito Inlet to Savannah in 1862.

Florida made a much more important contribution to the war effort by producing salt and foodstuffs than by shipping blockaded cargoes to the Confederacy. With the fall of the Confederate West, salt was in short supply but so necessary that all who engaged in the business were exempted from military service.

About 5,000 salt workers, mostly from Georgia, engaged in boiling sea water along the Florida coast from Tampa to Apalachicola after 1862. Federal ships repeatedly destroyed the salt works and Confederates immediately rebuilt them for the duration of the war. Neither the Union or Confederate governments assigned a high priority to the business despite its importance, probably because neither gave Florida as a whole a high priority.

Not being of major importance irritated Floridians, but they realized that this also meant that their state would not host terrible battles such as occurred in the eastern and western theatres. Although not a scene of major conflict, residents of the state did experience difficulties and heartbreaks of all descriptions.

Nothing was worse than news from the front that a loved one had been killed, wounded, or captured, but the *not knowing* for weeks and months at a time was almost as bad for the folks at home. The mail was slow and irregular during the best of times, and weeks passed before letters even written in-state were delivered. Since almost all of Florida's soldiers were out of state, the delay for their relatives and friends usually entailed a wait of at least a month.

The breakage of anything made of metal presented almost insuperable problems. It could, and usually did, take several months to have a wagon wheel repaired, even in northeastern Florida where blacksmiths were more numerous than in much of the rest of the state. Any object that required the attention of a highly skilled repairman went unrepaired, and the cost of mending virtually anything was beyond the means of many citizens. Scarcities of all sorts abounded; everything from whale oil to coffee usually could not be had at any price, and substitutes made of amazing substances had to suffice.

Floridians soon felt the economic impact of government in a manner unheard of in *antebellum* times. Before the war, about the only contact average Floridians had with the national government was with the employees of the post office. The war brought a powerful centralized government into play, and taxes, in money and in kind, increased dramatically. The Confederate government passed three revenue measures that directly affected everyone: the Direct Tax of 1861; the Impressment Act of 1863; and the General Tax Act of 1863. The second measure was not technically a tax law, but it proved to be a heavy burden because Confederate agents impressed food and labor at rates much lower than market prices. Taken together with state, county, and municipal taxes, the average citizen felt put upon indeed.

Increased taxation was a problem, but so too was inflation. Shortages caused by the blockade constantly drove prices up, as did the lack of confidence in the currency. State treasury notes backed up by the public lands fared better than Confederate treasury notes or bonds, and corporation notes and fractional paper notes issued by municipalities virtually had disappeared by 1864. Neither the Confederate or state government had any success in managing the economy and catastrophic conditions were the norm after 1862.

White Floridians were spared in one vital area; many feared that with almost all adult white men absent a slave rebellion might occur, but this did not materialize. Most of the slaves remained on the plantations and farms and continued at their labors. After northeastern Florida was occupied by Federal troops in 1864, slaves in that area did cross the lines, but most waited patiently for the freedom they were certain would come.

While Florida did not become an important battleground it certainly did not escape a good number of raids, skirmishes, and two battles, one of which was fairly significant. The port cities were neutralized by the Union navy but the interior of the state became more important as a food source for the South as the war continued, especially after the Confederacy was cut in half by the fall of Vicksburg in July 1863. Large herds of cattle and hogs were driven from southern and central Florida to rail junctions in northern Florida and Georgia and from there to the rest of the Confederacy. Some estimates assert that Florida beef permitted Robert E. Lee's army to stay in the field for the last year of the war. That may be an exaggeration, but early in 1864 the Union command felt that the salt and foodstuffs were important enough to justify an offensive designed to sever Florida from the rest of the Confederacy.

After the seizure of Fernandina and St. Augustine in 1862, Federal forces had been content to bombard Florida's salt works and raid Tampa and Apalachicola until October of that year when Jacksonville was once again occupied. The region along the St. Johns River was harassed by gunboats and several Confederate steamers were taken, but once again the Federal force withdrew. This time about 300 slaves, called "contrabands" by the Union, departed Jacksonville for an uncertain future in the North.

The enactment of the Emancipation Proclamation in January 1863 changed the war from one to restore the Union as it had been to a revolutionary crusade to abolish slavery in the Confederacy. It also meant that African Americans were soon in Union uniforms, ready and eager to join in the fray. Before the war ended, about 1,000 black Floridians served in the Union armies, many of them entering the ranks in 1863 and 1864.

In March 1863, Jacksonville was invaded again and this time two regiments of black soldiers were in the force. The First and Second South Carolina Volunteers (Colored), under the command of Colonels T. W. Higginson and James Montgomery, engaged in several hot skirmishes with Confederates under the command of General Joseph Finegan. Confederate strength soon convinced the Federal commander to give up the city and what was left of Jacksonville was evacuated on March 29. The use of black troops enraged Confederates, military and civilian alike, and threats were made that no quarter would be asked or given if they were encountered again.

The fourth and final Federal invasion of northeastern Florida came late in the winter and early in the spring of 1864. This was an election year and Lincoln knew he was not likely to win unless the war news changed dramatically. The Union had made progress in 1863 with the capture of Vicksburg and the Confederate defeat at Gettysburg, but what remained of the Confederacy was as indomitable as ever. Lincoln brought Grant to the East and assigned him the paramount task of destroying Lee's army while Union forces under William T. Sherman tried to cut the Confederacy in half once again by marching from Tennessee through Georgia. These offensives began in May 1864, but an attempt to sever the "breadbasket" of the Confederacy was undertaken three months earlier.

Both political and military reasons justified the invasion of Florida in 1864. As mentioned, Lincoln faced a tough re-election bid, and if part of Florida could be conquered and a loyal government enacted, Lincoln likely would receive the electoral college support from the state. In addition, the salt, beef, and pork supplies from Florida were becoming increasingly important to Confederate armies and this was justification in itself for another attack. Finally, a Federal invasion would result in the addition of Florida's blacks to the Union cause and hurt the Confederacy simultaneously. It might also force Confederate General P. G. T. Beauregard to reduce his forces at Charleston and Savannah to such an extent that one or both places might fall to Union offensives. At the least, raiding parties could burn and plunder in the untouched interior of the state if the offensive was of sufficient strength.

In January 1864, Lincoln wrote Major General Quincy A. Gillmore, commander of the Department of the South, that a move "to reconstruct a loyal State Government in Florida" soon would be attempted. Gillmore perceived correctly that his commander-in-chief wanted a military expedition immediately and began to gather a sufficient force to provide one. He assembled approximately 5,500 men and placed Brigadier General Truman Seymour in command.

There were several liabilities about this invasion that were not obvious at the time. Over one-third of the Federals were recently recruited and inadequately trained black troops; in many cases they had never fired their guns. Their courage, coupled with the lack of training, meant that many likely would be slaughtered in battle. Also, Gillmore and Seymour did not have the same plan in mind, and this led to a disastrous defeat. On the other hand, the Federals had an enormous advantage in numbers when the campaign began. Properly led, they should have been able to go deeply into the middle of the state and accomplish their objectives with little effort. They were initially opposed by approximately 1,500 Confederate cavalry, most of whom had never been in anything more serious than a small skirmish. The key to Federal success was speed; if they followed the railroad from Jacksonville westward through Lake City to the railroad bridge over the Suwannee River (approximately 100 miles west of Jacksonville) and destroyed it, the interior of Florida no longer would be a sanctuary for Confederate beef and other provisions. If they then retreated, burning and raiding the surrounding countryside, the military objectives would be accomplished.

As far as establishing a loyal civilian government, that could be done only if the troops stayed in and around Jacksonville and northeastern Florida. The Federal occupation of Fernandina and St. Augustine had convinced the military that a loyal Union government was not possible even with Jacksonville as its capital unless the area was garrisoned by the military. So Lincoln's claim to Florida's electoral votes would be attained only at the point of the bayonet.

The offensive began with promise on February 7. Seymour's cavalry swiftly raided as far west as Lake City, then swung some sixty miles south to raid Gainesville, inflicting about $1 million in damage on Confederate supplies and storehouses and private property. The infantry followed in good fashion but Seymour halted his force just west of Baldwin at Barber's Plantation (present day Macclenny). Gillmore returned to South Carolina, expecting Seymour to withdraw to Jacksonville as soon as his strike was completed. Gillmore was stunned on February 17 when he received a message from Seymour that he intended to launch an all-out offensive into the interior with the objective of destroying the Suwannee railroad bridge. This advance *en masse* with the entire army was not what Gillmore wanted, so he ordered his subordinate to call off the campaign and return to the vicinity of Jacksonville. The telegram came too late; Seymour already had begun his advance.

Despite the presence of Federal cavalry, Seymour did not know the strength or location of the enemy. They were, in fact, directly in his path and now equaled his numbers. Seymour's long delay at Macclenny permitted Beauregard to send veteran troops to Lake City under the command of Brigadier General Alfred H. Colquitt to assist Finegan in the defense of Florida. The Confederates dug in east of Lake City not far from Olustee railroad station and planned to await an attack, but this soon changed and the battle was fought in impromptu fashion.

A small force of Confederates probed eastward to discover the location of the Union troops and ran into Federal cavalry. They quickly formed into the Napoleonic Square, one of the few times it was used during the war, which was the perfect defense against mounted troops. It was, however, virtual suicide against artillery, and this the Confederates found out in a matter of minutes. They retreated with the information that the Federal army—infantry, artillery, and cavalry—was directly east of Olustee and on the march.

Colquitt hurried to the front and began to establish a line about three miles east of the prepared fortifications; they could fall back to that position if necessary, but he determined to confront them where they were. As more Federals came up, Colquitt summoned reinforcements from Finegan, who remained in the rear near Lake City. Colquitt positioned his men in better fashion than did his opponent, and although each side had approximately 5,000 men engaged, the Confederates had superior firepower from the beginning.

The Federal artillery was positioned too close to the front and Confederate infantry cut them down in droves. Federal infantry, particularly the black units, stood and fired in the open while their more skilled enemy used trees and terrain for cover. The result was a foregone conclusion. It took about four hours, but the Federals were thoroughly defeated and driven back toward Jacksonville as darkness fell. Confederate cavalry was slow in pursuit and the defeat did not become the rout that it might have, but this was one of the worst beatings any Federal army suffered during the entire war. Union casualties totaled 1,861 out of 5,000 engaged, a full thirty-seven percent, with 203 killed, 1,152 wounded, and 506 missing. The Confederates suffered ninety-three killed, 847 wounded, and six missing, for a total of 946.

The Union dead and most of the wounded were left on the battlefield and many of the wounded blacks were executed summarily despite their pleas of surrender. The captives, black and white alike, were sent to the newly opened prisoner-of-war camp officially named Camp Sumter but already known as Andersonville, and few survived the summer.

The defeat did not result in the Union troops' evacuation of Florida, but it did confine them for the rest of the war to the northeastern part of the state. From

Jacksonville, Union gunboats ventured up the St. Johns as far as Enterprize, 130 miles to the south, raining destruction upon the plantations, farms, and towns in the area. Increasing numbers of blacks were freed and some immediately joined the Union army and more and more whites gave up the fight and took the pledge of allegiance to the Union. Olustee was a major Confederate victory but it did not bring improvement in the lives of Floridians; conditions actually got worse for the population living near the St. Johns River for the rest of the war.

Federal raids along the river and as far west as Gainesville, some fifty miles inland, intensified in 1864 and 1865. The plantations, farms, and other property of Confederates were destroyed, livestock was killed, and the slaves were freed. Although outnumbered and outgunned, Confederates fought back with skill and tenacity, and sank several Union ships with torpedoes (mines) in the St. Johns. They also launched raids of their own against Federal encampments, but nothing of any real consequence happened in that part of Florida after the battle of Olustee.

As the war drew to a close, Union gunboats continued to raid port cities on the Gulf as well as the salt works, but in March 1865 the decision was made to attempt another thrust at the interior of the state. This time the object was Tallahassee, the capital, and the rich plantations in and around the city.

A Federal fleet brought approximately 1,000 troops from Fort Myers and Key West to Cedar Key late in February, and that force landed at St. Marks, about twenty-five miles south of Tallahassee, on February 28. News of the landing reached the capital on March 4 and a frantic attempt to round up enough troops to resist the invasion proved remarkably successful. Several companies of regulars were rushed by train from as far away as Baldwin, and enough old men, convalescents, and cadets from the West Florida Seminary (later Florida State University) appeared to swell the defender's ranks to approximately 1,500.

The Federal advance from St. Marks was slowed by the difficult terrain and Confederate skirmishers setting fire to everything from bridges to farms as they retreated to a point called Natural Bridge, a land mass above the St. Marks River approximately fifteen miles southeast of Tallahassee. At daybreak on March 6, the Federals made a determined attempt to take the bridge but ran into an extremely effective crossfire and retreated in short order. The battle was a miniature Olustee; Federal casualties were twenty-one killed, eighty-nine wounded, and thirty-eight captured, and the Confederates suffered three killed and twenty-two wounded, none of them boys from the seminary.

The Battle of Natural Bridge marked the end of the conflict in Florida. It was the last successful effort to protect their ravaged homeland and save their capital from capture. Tallahassee was the only state capital in the Confederacy east of the Mississippi River that was not taken by Union troops during the war. It was surrendered on May 20 after both Lee and Joseph E. Johnston had given up, and the survivors began the attempt to cope with what was a strange new world to them.

The small state made about as large a contribution to the war as could be expected. Almost every able man and boy entered the service; about 15,000 served the Confederacy in every theatre of the war and 5,000 of them did not come back. An additional 1,200 white and 1,000 black Florida men served the Union. There were few exemptions granted in Florida and the loss of one-third of the best men was severe.

Stephen R. Mallory from Key West was the Confederate secretary of the navy and performed admirably in an impossible position. Florida also sent two professional soldiers, William W. Loring and Edmund Kirby Smith, who distinguished themselves as general officers. There were no truly outstanding members from Florida in political circles, either at the state or Confederate levels.

Floridians suffered keenly in trying to create an "independent nation." They experienced hardships of every imaginable kind, endured undreamed of economic, political, and administrative problems, and weathered scarcity, inflation, and invasion. In addition to the loss of manpower in the field, the freeing of the slaves was an immense psychological shock. So, too, was the shock of defeat to these proud, even arrogant, people who never imagined that such an end was possible.

SUGGESTED READING

William Watson Davis, *The Civil War and Reconstruction in Florida* (Columbia University Press: New York, 1913).

Joseph T. Durkin, *Stephen R. Mallory: Confederate Navy Chief* (University of North Carolina Press: Chapel Hill, 1954).

Alfred J. Hanna, *Flight into Oblivion* (Johnson Publishing Co.: Richmond, 1938).

John E. Johns, *Florida During the Civil War* (University of Florida Press: Gainesville, 1963).

Ella Lonn, *Salt as a Factor in the Confederacy* (Walter Neale: New York, 1933).

William H. Nulty, *Confederate Florida: The Road to Olustee* (University of Alabama Press: Tuscaloosa, 1990).

Joseph H. Parks, *General Edmund Kirby Smith. C.S.A.* (Louisiana State University Press: Baton Rouge, 1944).

Lewis G. Schmidt, *The Civil War in Florida. A Military History* (4 vols.; privately printed: Allentown, PA, 1992).

ALABAMA

by
R. B. Rosenburg

Alabama had been in the Union for only forty-two years before it seceded in 1861. At that time it was not far removed from what it had always been—a frontier, thinly settled and undeveloped. Mobile, founded by the French in 1702, with a population of 29,258, about one-fourth less than Richmond, Virginia, was the state's leading emporium on the eve of the war. Montgomery, the state capital since 1846, was the next town in size, with nearly 9,000 (of whom half were black), followed by Huntsville and then Selma, with about 3,000 people each. Before the firing on Fort Sumter, no two major cities in Alabama were linked directly and completely by rail, reflecting not only the state's lack of adequate funding for internal improvements but also the repeated failure of such cooperative ventures in the past. By 1860, there were less than 800 miles of tracks in operation in the state, and they were of uneven quality and assorted gauges, as the Confederate president-elect would discover in February 1861. Since there was likewise no railroad connecting Mississippi with Alabama, Jefferson Davis had to take a circuitous route from his plantation near Jackson through Tennessee and Georgia before finally rolling into Montgomery nearly four days later. The preferred mode of travel from the state capital to the Gulf Coast was by steamboat, a trip of some 331 miles down river. Indeed, because the Alabama, Coosa, and Tombigbee river valleys formed the cotton kingdom of the Black Belt, planters who lived in Central Alabama had closer economic ties with Mobile and, by extension, New Orleans, New York, and even Western Europe, than with the cotton planters and yeoman farmers of the Tennessee River Valley of North Alabama.

Early in 1860 there were five identifiable political groups in Alabama: old Whigs in the western and central parts of the state, who lacked a presidential candidate; moderate Southern Rights Opposition men in the southern and central areas, who supported John C. Breckinridge; old Jackson Democrats in North Alabama, who bickered with South Alabama Democrats over the bank question, among other issues; Stephen A. Douglas Democrats residing largely in Mobile, Montgomery, and Huntsville; and the extreme Southern Rights Democrats, who derived their strength from the Black Belt, which stretched from East Central to West Alabama. By the time of the Civil War, only about five percent of Alabama's approximately one million inhabitants resided in urban areas. Ever since statehood, politicians in Alabama had understood at least one crucial fact: their fortunes were invariably determined by catering to the needs of a rural people whose investments were in land and slaves. Since there was a higher concentration of slave holders in the Black Belt than in any other sub-region in the state, it is no surprise that secession was a South Alabama accomplishment, thanks to the actions and words of William Lowndes Yancey, an extreme Southern Rights Democrat agitator.

It often has been stated that without Yancey of Montgomery there would have been no secession, at least in Alabama. The Alabama Platform, written by Yancey in 1848, was his answer to the Wilmot Proviso. He had warned that Southern Democrats would not support a presidential candidate who sought to restrict slavery. Furthermore, he had rejected violently and spoken defiantly against the Compromise of 1850 and had urged immediate secession of the South, saying that it was "time to set the house in order." The tumultuous events of the 1850s—*Uncle Tom's Cabin*, Bleeding Kansas, the Dred Scott decision, the fight in Congress over the Fugitive Slave law, and especially John Brown's raid—had served to strengthen Yancey's position and to convince many moderates in Alabama that there could be no peace in the Union. Secession, or so Yancey and others like him had argued, was necessary for the preservation of the South's peculiar institution and the region's economic and social prosperity. And it was this same Alabama firebrand who had led the Southern delegations out of the Democratic Convention in Charleston, in April 1860, after Northern delegates, following the lead of Stephen A. Douglas, had refused to accept Yancey's extremist position. Thus, by the spring of 1860 Yancey's actions in South Carolina had changed Alabama politics. Now there were three parties: the Constitutional Unionists, which included among its leaders ex-Democrat Jeremiah Clemens (a Unionist from North Alabama) and former Whig Thomas Hill Watts (a moderate Southern Rights man); moderate and extreme Southern Rights Democrats, including Yancey, William F. Samford, and Leroy Pope Walker, who were strong supporters of Breckinridge; and Douglas and old Jackson Democrats in the rural areas of North Alabama and in the cities of Huntsville, Montgomery, and Mobile.

As important as Yancey's role was in arousing and prolonging secession sentiment, it is difficult to conceive that Yancey would have commanded as large a following as he did in the state had he not been able to win the support of moderates such as Thomas Hill Watts, who also represented the Alabama Black Belt-plantation constituency. On the eve of the war his combined estate in Montgomery County, worth nearly $500,000, included 179 slaves. But Watts held somewhat milder disunion beliefs than Yancey. While the two served in the state legislature for several years before Yancey won election to Congress in 1844, Watts zealously opposed a dissolution of the Union in 1850, though he stopped short of repudiating the doctrine of secession as a constitutional right. In fact, as the debate over the slavery question intensified throughout the 1850s, Watts came to believe as completely in the right of a state to secede from the Union as in the truth of the Christian religion. In a day when party affiliations were taken as seriously as professions of faith, he joined as early as 1856 the States Rights Opposition Movement in Alabama, a party which incorporated in its platform the same plank that Yancey had fashioned for his fellow Democrats; that is, the declaration that the election of a Black Republican as president of the United States would be sufficient grounds for the Southern states to withdraw from the Union.

So great had become secession excitement, and so fixed the determination of a majority of Alabamians, that in the winter of 1859-1860 the legislature provided for the calling of a state convention in the event of such an election. The resolutions were passed almost unanimously, and Governor Andrew B. Moore approved them on February 24, 1860. Although not members of the legislature, Watts had strongly endorsed the resolutions and Yancey had labored assiduously to effect their enactment. During the summer and fall of 1860, while Yancey campaigned for Breckinridge, Watts still sought to prevent disunion or to achieve a peaceable secession. Sincerely hoping that the North and South would agree on some national candidate, thus preserving the Constitution and the Union, Watts used his best efforts as an elector for John Bell of Tennessee to warn his fellow citizens from the stump and the press that a long and bloody war would follow secession.

In the end, Watts' efforts were sufficient for Bell to carry Butler County, his home county, and three other rural counties, and to garner 27,827 votes state-wide. But they were not enough to tilt the state in Bell's favor. Favoring a more aggressive and militant policy than Bell in dealing with the slavery question, Breckinridge won over one half of Alabama's fifty-two counties with a popular vote of 49,019, while Stephen A. Douglas polled only 13,657. Voter participation in the state on November 6, 1860, was unusually heavy, reaching nearly eighty percent. As expected, Douglas had taken Mobile and Huntsville, as well as Lauderdale, Lawrence, Madison, and Marshall counties, located in the Tennessee River Valley. But Breckinridge had won Montgomery (though only barely), thus breaking the traditional alliance between North and South Alabama Democrats. Moreover, Breckinridge's strength came largely from the Black Belt region, where the "typical" voter was a relatively young man (about forty-five years of age), who held on the average nineteen or more slaves, had a net worth of about $60,000, and had investments in land and cotton—an accurate reflection of Yancey's own socioeconomic profile. It was Abraham Lincoln who won the election on the national level, despite Breckinridge's victory and without help from Alabama.

If Yancey had paved the road to secession in Alabama, men such as Watts drove the state into the Confederacy and steered it throughout the war. Elected along with

Yancey to represent Montgomery County in the secession convention, Watts voted for the ordinance of secession. When the war commenced, he entered the army as colonel of the 17th Alabama, a regiment he raised and equipped himself. After serving seven months in the field, and while at the head of his regiment a month before Shiloh, Watts was appointed attorney general of the Confederate States. He continued in this office until October 1863, when he resigned to return to Alabama to serve as governor. Inaugurated on December 1, 1863, Watts continued in this capacity until the spring of 1865, when the presence of Federal forces near Montgomery prevented the further discharge of his duties.

By then, Yancey had long passed from the scene. Ironically, *he* had been offered the attorney general's slot, but declined it. Instead, Davis sent him on a special foreign mission, as the *Montgomery Post* said, into "honorable exile," to secure recognition and aid in Europe, where Alabama's Black Belt planters had built up credit before the war. Yancey resigned in disgust after less than a year and returned in March 1862 to New Orleans, where he told an audience that the South had "no friends in Europe," before continuing on to Richmond, where he served for about a year in the Confederate Senate as a critic of the administration.

As interesting as the parallels are between Yancey and Watts, there was another major figure who helped shape Alabama's secession history. Andrew B. Moore, a South Carolina-born attorney, was in the midst of his second term as governor in November 1859, when, in the aftermath of the raid on Harpers Ferry, the Alabama legislature received a communication from South Carolina suggesting that if a Republican were elected president, then all Southern states would hold a joint convention. The legislature rejected that suggestion in favor of a state convention, agreeing with Yancey and other Southern leaders that separate state action followed by cooperation was the proper legal recourse. In February 1860 the legislature passed joint resolutions requiring the governor, in the event of the election of a Republican president, to issue a proclamation immediately calling for every qualified voter in the state to elect delegates to a convention to consider exactly what the interests, honor, and future of the state of Alabama required to be done for its "protection." A Republican victory, or so it was argued, would "pervert" the whole machinery of government. Therefore, it was the state's responsibility to provide a means by which its people could escape such "peril and dishonor." In the meantime, the legislature appointed a committee to reorganize the militia system and establish military schools, passed a bill that encouraged the manufacture of firearms in the state, and in August 1860 appropriated $200,000 for purchasing muskets and cannon for Alabama's militiamen.

Once word concerning Lincoln's election had reached the state, there was an immediate cry from all quarters not to submit to Black Republican rule. In Montgomery, Breckinridge men proudly pinned blue cockades upon their lapels as emblems of "revolution and disunion," and urged the formation of Minutemen clubs throughout the state, with the motto "Resistance to Lincoln is obedience to God." In Selma and other parts of the Black Belt, vigilance committees awaited the governor's call to arms. "People [have] apparently gone crazy," remarked one observer in Greensboro, where "Union men, Douglas men, Breck men are all alike in their loud denunciation of submission to Lincoln's administration." James Mallory of Sylacauga observed that the people in his town were "determined to sell their liberties to satisfy their passions." Meanwhile, a grand jury in Montgomery declared the Federal government "worthless, impotent, and a nuisance."

Alabamians doubted whether Governor Moore would act immediately on the resolutions. Was he a secessionist, a cooperationist, or a conditional unionist? Would he do his constitutional duty and enforce the resolutions of the legislature despite his personal misgivings? Or would he (as some moderates hoped) call the legislature into special session, so that it could rescind its mandate for a state convention and provide instead that any action taken by the state would be submitted to a direct vote of the people? No one seemed to know, but there was reason to believe that Moore would move cautiously, in strict conformity to the law. Prior to being elected governor in August 1857, he had served as a circuit judge and had abstained from participating in the political discussions and excitement of the 1850s. He had opposed the doctrine of nullification in 1831-1832 and Yancey's call for Alabama to secede in 1850, and he had voted against Troup and Quitman, the candidates of the leading secessionists for president and vice-president in 1852. When he was first nominated for governor by the Democratic convention of Alabama, his nomination had been opposed by Yancey and other secessionists on the grounds that he was perceived as being too stringent regarding constitutional matters and too timid in asserting Southern rights. But Moore had won the nomination and run unopposed in 1857. In his second election, William F. Samford, a Democrat belonging to Yancey's extreme Southern Rights faction, was made to run against him but had lost. So there was a reason for people to be concerned about Moore's moderation.

At a meeting in Montgomery a few days after Lincoln's victory, Moore, now under pressure to reveal his intentions, indicated that he saw no course open to the South other than to secede from the Union and form a Southern confederacy for its future security. However, Moore said, he would wait to call a convention until after December 5, when all the electoral votes had been counted in Washington. As Yancey and other secession leaders rightly feared, the delay gave the "resistance men" time to organize. The governor received criticism not only from Yancey but also from conservatives such as Thomas Watts, who since the fall campaign had said that in the event of Lincoln's election he would advise immediate withdrawal. As Jeremiah Clemens, who still opposed immediate secession, explained, *"Time* is everything to us, & if we fail to gain that we are lost." Meanwhile, acceding to secessionists' pent-up demands, Moore appointed J. R. Powell as Alabama's agent to procure munitions and available arms for the state's militiamen. And early in December 1860, the governor named sixteen commissioners to advise and consult with other states contemplating withdrawing from the Union, a move which satisfied both the conservatives' hopes for cooperation and the secessionists' proddings for further action.

On December 6, after Lincoln's election had been confirmed by the electoral college, Moore, as promised, called for the election of 100 delegates to meet in a convention in Montgomery on January 7, 1861. The election of delegates that took place on December 24 revealed the various strengths and weaknesses, as well as the complexities and realities, of both the resistance and secessionist forces within Alabama. State-wide, the vote in favor of secession was fairly close, something like 36,000 to 27,000 or 33,000 to 24,000, depending upon which newspapers reported the results. Interestingly, secessionists won twenty-nine counties to their opponents' twenty-two, and resistance men carried only one county (Conecuh) in South Alabama, while secessionists likewise won only one county (Calhoun) in the northern part of the state, where the opposition was better organized. Moreover, the Black Belt region of Central Alabama elected seventy-two percent of the secessionist delegates, while ninety percent of the resistance men, or so-called cooperationist delegates, were from the Tennessee River Valley.

Being a cooperationist did not mean that a delegate was hostile to secession as such, but rather was undecided how it should be accomplished. Although he may have believed in the doctrine of secession, he also contended that safety demanded secession by blocs of states, that Alabama should try to cooperate with other states either within the Union or, as a last result, secede—but then only after the people of Alabama had been given a chance to ratify the convention's actions. Nevertheless, some men elected to Alabama's secession convention were staunch Unionists. For example, Jeremiah Clemens of North Alabama, a prominent opponent of hasty action, viewed Lincoln's election as an outrage but argued that secession was illegal and unconstitutional and urged compromise along the same lines as J. J. Crittenden of Kentucky, with whom Clemens frequently corresponded. Meanwhile, within the secession ranks there was little harmony, as revealed in Watts and Yancey, who were both elected as pro-secession delegates from Montgomery County. By his very nature Yancey tended to alienate both friend and foe, was prone to acts of rashness, and was more radical in his views than Watts, whom both "straight out" secessionists and cooperationists respected. While now fully agreeing with Yancey that secession was the right thing to do, Watts played the role of conciliator, which many interpreted as evidence of his somewhat milder disunion beliefs. At one point during the convention, after Yancey had given a long and violent harangue which he ended with a warning that anyone who dares oppose secession in Alabama "will become traitors—rebels against its authority, and will be dealt with as such," thereby causing some cooperationists to snap back at Yancey, Watts stepped in to try to heal the wounds and apologized for his colleague's angry tirade, saying that "this was not the time for exhibition of feeling or for utterance of denunciations." After all, Watts was a former Southern Black Belt Whig, who, like Henry Clay and his old national counterparts, had prided themselves on playing the role as compromisers.

During the two weeks between the election of delegates and their convening in Montgomery, all kinds of unsettling rumors only agitated matters more and convinced Alabamians that withdrawal from the Union was inevitable. There were shocking reports of slave revolts in Central Alabama and of Black Republicans rioting in the streets of New York City. One unconfirmed source claimed that Governor Henry A. Wise of Virginia had been assassinated by a deranged unionist, while another claimed that 7,000 abolitionists were marching on Washington, and still another that Andrew Johnson, that stubborn unionist senator from East Tennessee, had killed Jefferson Davis, the ardent secessionist from Mississippi, in a street fight in the nation's capital. On top of these rumors were the actual seizures and occupation of Federal Forts Morgan and Gaines, as well as the arsenal at Mount Vernon, by Alabama state troops (mostly members of the 1st Alabama Regiment) under orders of Governor Moore.

The military action had gone off without a hitch two days before the convention began. In his much-publicized letter to President James Buchanan, Moore explained on January 4, 1861, that he had directed the seizures and peaceful occupations of Federal property in order to prevent conflict and bloodshed which seemed imminent to him. In addition, Moore was certain that the convention which was scheduled to begin in a few days would withdraw the state from the Union and sanction his actions. Moore was right. The convention endorsed his actions and authorized him to send troops to Pensacola, as requested by Governor Madison Perry of Florida, an action which Moore had opposed.

As it turned out, the Alabama convention would go pretty much Yancey's way. On the first day they met, the delegates elected as their president William M. Brooks, a secessionist from Perry County, over Robert Jemison, Jr., a resistance man from Tuscaloosa, who also happened to be the wealthiest delegate in attendance, even more so than Watts. The test vote which resulted in Brooks' election reflected a fifty-four to forty-six alignment in favor of immediate secession, a ratio that was held on nearly all major issues during the eighteen days of the convention. The delegates then passed by unanimous vote a resolution vowing that Alabama would never submit to Republican rule, thus setting the tone for things to come. Before long Yancey got appointed to head a committee of thirteen to consider resolutions introduced by Michael J. Bulger, a Southern Rights Democrat and militia brigadier general from Tallapoosa County, who proposed that Alabama cooperate with other Southern states before contemplating secession. On January 10, Yancey presented a recommendation, signed by seven of the thirteen, that Alabama should withdraw immediately from the Union without prior consultation with her sister states. On the following day, January 11, 1861, the delegates voted sixty-one to thirty-nine to accept the committee's recommendation, thus becoming the fourth state to secede, though with by far the narrowest margin of any of the Deep South states. Upon the ordinance's passage President Brooks declared: "The people of Alabama are now independent; sink or swim, live or die, they will continue to be a free, sovereign, and independent state." Alabama had at last withdrawn. It was Yancey's finest hour. Later that afternoon a new flag celebrating the "Sovereign Republic of Alabama" was run up the staff on the Capitol dome proclaiming disunion between Alabama and the United States of America. Two months later, on March 13, Alabama formally joined the Confederacy it had helped to create.

Among the sixty-one delegates who voted for the ordinance were Jeremiah Clemens and a half dozen other cooperationists. As Clemens explained, "I am a son of Alabama; her destiny is mine; her people are mine; her enemies are mine." Yet Clemens' loyalty to the cause waned within a year and he resigned his major general's commission in the militia of the Republic of Alabama, before heading off to Washington and eventually Philadelphia, where he conducted a pamphlet campaign against the South. Meanwhile, eleven other delegates who originally had sided with Clemens and the minority changed their minds, though not involuntarily. Among them was David P. Lewis, a Virginia-born attorney, who, under special instructions from his constituents in Lawrence County, affixed his signature to the ordinance. Later chosen by the convention to serve along with Yancey as one of Alabama's nine representatives to the Provisional Congress, Lewis, who refused to sign the hastily written constitution, resigned his seat on February 8, saying that it would no longer be "convenient" for him to serve. After returning to his home, he organized a volunteer company that was never mustered into service, then dodged the Confederate conscript authorities—first by working as a judge, then as a miller—before defecting altogether from the Confederacy and making it safely behind Federal lines in Tennessee in advance of General John B. Hood's twin disasters in that state.

In addition to signing the ordinance, Alabama's secession delegates also agreed to propose a meeting of representatives from various states to convene for "consultation." The secession conventions of Florida, Georgia, Louisiana, Mississippi, and South Carolina accepted Alabama's invitation and sent delegates, who assembled in Montgomery on February 4. From that date until May 21, Montgomery served as the provisional capital of the Confederacy. Here, on February 9, the delegates took the oath of office as congressmen and immediately elected Jefferson Davis and Alexander Stephens as provisional president and vice president. On February 11 Stephens celebrated his forty-ninth birthday by taking his oath. A week later, on February 18, Jefferson Davis was inaugurated on the steps of the Alabama capitol while a crowd estimated at approximately 10,000 packed the town to witness the event. A salute of 100 guns was fired, church bells rang triumphantly, and the celebration with song, laughter, and prayer continued well into the night.

In the days ahead, Congress confirmed Davis' nominations for his cabinet, which included Leroy Pope Walker of Alabama as secretary of war. Both Yancey and former Senator Clement C. Clay, Jr., had recommended Walker for the post. A member of the Charleston Democratic Convention in 1860, he had announced Alabama's withdrawal from that body. Walker, while still in Montgomery, instructed General P. G. T. Beauregard on April 10, 1861, to demand the evacuation of Fort Sumter, and if the demand was refused, to "reduce it." On the evening of April 13, after the fort had been evacuated, Walker reportedly told a cheering crowd in Montgomery: "The flag" [a red, white, and blue banner that closely resembled the U.S. flag] "which now flaunts the breeze here" [having been hoisted on March 4 by the granddaughter of former President John Tyler to coincide with Lincoln's inauguration] "will float over the dome of the old capitol at Washington before the first of May."

As for Walker, he was merely the first among several who vainly tried to direct the Confederacy's war effort. In less than a year after taking office, he stepped down, sick, overburdened, criticized, and at odds with Davis. Meanwhile, he had overseen during the first six months of the war the mobilization of 200,000 men, of whom more than ten percent (27,000) were Alabamians. Even before Alabama had seceded formally, people everywhere had turned out to prepare for war. Local bodies of militia organized and drilled. In Marion, Alabama, a typical Black Belt community, two companies of cavalry and two companies of infantry were formed. One company, the Marion Rifles, went to Fort Morgan early in January on orders from Governor Moore. When it returned to Marion, the unit was mustered into the 4th Alabama Infantry, a regiment commanded by Colonel Egbert J. Jones, who died of wounds later that summer at Orange Court House, Virginia. When war came, companies of volunteers formed in practically every part of the state. Most outfits were named for the places where the men lived: the Auburn Guards, the Tuskegee Light Infantry, the Montgomery True Blues, the Suggsville Grays, the Coffee (County) Rangers, the Coosa Independents, the Raccoon Roughs, the Opelika Volunteers, the Morgan County Magnolia Rifles, the Wilcox Dragoons, and the Paint Rock Sharpshooters. There were elaborate preparations for sending the companies off to war; receptions, festivities, flag presentations, amid the singing of "Dixie" and "The Bonnie Blue Flag" far into the night, until finally the departure from home--an emotional scene replayed all over Alabama and the South in the spring of 1861. Formed in Greenville, Sylacauga, Tuscaloosa, Mobile, or Montgomery, the companies marched off to war to gather at Dalton, Georgia, where they were mustered into Confederate service and in May sent in boxcars to the Virginia front, where things were about to explode. Filled with hope and eager for fame, the young soldiers: "Hasten to the crimson field, There the glittering bayonets wield! There confront the cannons mouth, Fearless champions of the South!" [A. B. Meek, *What the Bugles Say* (1862)]

By the end of the war as many as 89,678 men had served in Alabama military regiments on the side of the Confederacy. Alabama troops were engaged in nearly every battle of the war, and, consequently, many soldiers never returned home. The "Fighting" 4th, comprised of men from the Black Belt counties of Dallas, Macon, Perry, and Marengo, and the counties of Madison, Lauderdale, and Jackson in the Tennessee River Valley, lost thirty-eight killed and 208 wounded out of 750 engaged at First Manassas, a thirty-three percent casualty rate. During the war 1,422 men appeared on its rolls. It surrendered 202 men at Appomattox. On May 31, 1862, Robert E. Rodes of Tuscaloosa led his brigade of 2,200 Alabama troops into their first battle at Seven Pines. By nightfall half of Rodes' Brigade was either dead or wounded, reduced to sixty percent of its effective strength. The 27th Alabama left home in December 1861 with men who were exclusively from North Alabama: Franklin, Lawrence, Lauderdale, Madison, and Morgan counties. After Fort Donelson, where it was captured, imprisoned, and exchanged in September 1862, the regiment saw action at Port Hudson, and later in Dalton and Atlanta, before accompanying Hood on his fateful march into Tennessee. By December 1864 there were only seventeen rank and file remaining, including Private J. P Cannon, who was the only enlisted man left in Company C, commanded by two lieutenants.

The battle of Shiloh proved to be the most decisive battle for Alabama. The battle's proximity to the state accounts for the large number of its troops engaged, in all about 6,000, or as many as thirteen regiments, and most had heavy casualty lists. The 22nd Infantry, comprised of west and east-central Alabamians, was reduced from 709 to 123. Receiving much praise in official reports, the 19th Alabama, comprised of men from northeast Alabama, sustained an appalling "baptism of blood," losing 110 killed and 240 wounded of 650 men. The regiment was commanded by Joseph Wheeler, a West Point man and Georgia resident, who would move to the Tennessee River Valley after the war. On July 18, 1862, at age twenty-six, he was appointed to command all of the cavalry of the Army of Tennessee, with the rank of major general. The 17th Alabama, the Black Belt regiment raised and commanded by Thomas H. Watts before he was called to Richmond to serve in Davis' cabinet, was battered at Shiloh, losing 125 killed and wounded.

With the withdrawal of Southern troops from the field at Shiloh to Corinth, all of northern Alabama lay open to invasion by the spring of 1862. To the Federals, North Alabama was a Confederate base of supply—one Federal commander called it the "garden spot of Alabama"—and had a large Union element which could be encouraged. For example, Colonel Abel D. Streight, commander of the 51st Indiana, learned early in 1862 that a large number of citizens in hill counties of Morgan, Blount, Marion, Fayette, Jefferson, and Winston, a "no man's land" which separated Federal forces in the Tennessee River Valley from Confederate forces in central Alabama, were willing to "fight for Abe Lincoln before they will fight for Jeff Davis." Streight received permission to go on a recruiting mission in the area. Among those he found was C. C. Sheets, of Winston County, a secessionist opponent who had been expelled from the Alabama legislature for disloyalty to the Confederacy. Working with Sheets and other unionist leaders, Streight succeeded in raising more than 2,500 men to serve in the Federal army. On another raid the following spring, Streight would not be so lucky, as he and his entire force were captured by Forrest's troopers following a mad dash across northern Alabama, from Decatur to Rome, Georgia.

When Alabama joined the Confederacy in 1861, no one expected to experience an invasion by Federal troops. The war was supposed to have been over by then. Besides, Alabama was protected on all sides by her sister Confederate states. One wonders whether, had the Confederate capital remained in Montgomery, the state would have been better prepared than it was. Certainly there were valid reasons for moving the capital to Virginia. William Howard Russell, a correspondent for the London *Times,* declared that "Montgomery had little claims to be called a capital. The streets are very hot, unpleasant, and uninteresting. I have rarely seen a more dull and lifeless place: it looks like a small Russian town in the interior." The excessive heat in the summer, poor food, overcrowding, and the lack of comfortable accommodations at the Exchange and two other lesser hotels, not to mention the mosquitoes—all proved to be weighty arguments against the capital's remaining in Montgomery. Moreover, from a military standpoint, President Davis had perceived the need for protecting Virginia's borders and perhaps for taking command of the military forces. As put forth by Douglas Southall Freeman and others, the removal to Virginia proved to be a tragic mistake, for it placed the capital nearer the front, focused attention on the Eastern Theatre of operations, and led to the neglect of the West. From Alabama's viewpoint, if Montgomery had remained as the capital, it would have been the center of the fiercest struggles of the war, and many of its men would have died on their own "sacred soil" rather than on a distant battlefield near an obscure Virginia town. As it turned out, with removal there were very few battles fought in Alabama.

Federal military operations in the state may be divided into three geographical areas, each with its own characteristics. North Alabama was the scene of extensive operations and frequent skirmishes but no major battles. Central Alabama, a Confederate stronghold, was spared during most of the war until mid-1864 and early 1865, when three separate Union forays penetrated here. South Alabama, except for naval operations in Mobile Bay, was virtually untouched by the war. Ironically, it was here, in and around Mobile, that most of Alabama's defenses were located. During the first year of the war, Governor Moore did little toward planning for the defense of the state; instead he concentrated on supplying the Confederate army with men and material. With the enemy's capture and occupation of New Orleans and Pensacola early in 1862, Moore's successor, John Gill Shorter, a fiery secessionist, former commissioner to Georgia's secession convention, member of the provisional Confederate Congress, and leader of one of the state's most powerful oligarchies, the "Eufaula Regency," focused his attention on fortifying Mobile "to repel invasion" and called on every Alabamian to "labor, and if need be die for the advancement of the glorious cause." It was Shorter who, in addition to supervising normal state affairs, also was faced with the problems of organizing and mobilizing the state militia, of dealing with the unpopular Confederate military conscription act, and of levying taxes to support the Confederate government. By late summer 1862, Mobile's defenses and the Gulf Coast region of the state were almost impregnable, but it did not seem to matter. North Alabama always was vulnerable to attack.

On April 11, 1862, four days after Shiloh, a detachment of Don Carlos Buell's army under General O. M. "Old Stars" Mitchel captured Huntsville, severing at that spot the strategic Memphis & Charleston Railroad, the only main artery that traversed the state. Leroy Pope Walker had referred to the line as the "vertebrae of the Confederacy." From then until the end of the war, the enemy intermittently occupied and continuously placed demands upon the resources of northern Alabama, which was devastated quickly. The Federal expeditions which moved into the Tennessee River Valley discovered a prosperous farming district with considerable Union sympathies but divided loyalties. The first invasion had occurred a few months earlier, when Federal raiders under Colonel A. H. Foote sailed up the Tennessee River and landed at Florence. That expedition, in addition to the capture of Huntsville, greatly alarmed the public. Most Confederate troops from Alabama were on the Virginia front or with the western army, so the main burden of defense of northern Alabama fell upon home guard units of cavalry under Generals Joseph H. Wheeler, Nathan Bedford Forrest, and Phillip D. Roddey, the so-called "Swamp Fox of the Tennessee Valley." These outmanned troops were unable to drive the enemy away or permanently occupy the strategic area. The Confederate military had to concentrate its men at key points and lacked effective manpower to guard against a raid that would penetrate the long line across Alabama. Certainly after July 1863, following David S. Stanley's raid on Huntsville, the Union army was in almost undisputed control of Alabama's Tennessee River Valley area, except for a brief period after the fall of Atlanta in September 1864, when John Bell Hood moved his forces through the area on his ill-fated mission into Tennessee. The remains of thirty infantry and five batteries of Alabama troops accompanied Hood.

The year 1863 proved to be a decisive one for Alabamians. There was, of course, the surrender at Vicksburg and the defeat at Gettysburg. Moreover, William Lowndes Yancey died of kidney infection in Montgomery on July 28 of that same year. Thus, the man whom the *New York World* had dubbed the "high priest of secession" did not live to see the war end. At his death many Northern writers took pleasure in finding out that Yancey had lived long enough to learn about the disasters at Gettysburg and Vicksburg. From a strategic point of view, Gettysburg was far less important than Vicksburg, which cleared the Mississippi and cut the Confederacy into two parts. Alabama had sixteen regiments at Gettysburg, all of which were badly beaten under the commands of Generals E. McIver Law, E. A. O'Neal, C. M. Wilcox, and James J. Archer. Alabama had thirteen regiments and three batteries at Vicksburg, where its losses were not so heavy as at Gettysburg. Those captured were later paroled and permitted to return home, many of them never to take up arms again. Moreover, in August 1863, Governor Shorter, who gradually had lost popular support as the fortunes of war turned against the Confederacy, lost his bid for re-election. With Union troops in northern Alabama and the blockade of Mobile under way, causing scarcity and hardships in many areas further north in the heartland of Alabama, Shorter was defeated by a three-to-one margin by Thomas Hill Watts, who carried every county in the state except Jackson, Madison, Marion, and St. Clair, all in northern Alabama. Elected along with Watts were a number of peace-party men, consisting of old North Alabama cooperationists. In addition, the legislature refused to send Clement C. Clay, Jr., an ardent secessionist, back to the Confederate Senate, and chose instead Robert Jemison, a prominent cooperationist. Along with Jemison, six pacifists were sent to Richmond, including one who had defeated Jabez L. M. Curry, a strong Davis ally in the Confederate Congress.

Watts took office in December 1863 but did not lessen the war effort, thereby putting to rest the belief that when elected he would go soft on the war and negotiate some kind of peace on the basis of the old Union. On a speaking tour of the northern and middle parts of the state, a tour he made to correct the "erroneous impression" that he was for reunion, he said that anyone who advocated peace now was a "traitor in his heart to the state . . . and deserves a traitor's doom." Rather than unite with such people, he said, "I would see the Confederate states desolated with fire and sword." Although Watts never became a Joseph E. Brown of Georgia or a Zebulon Vance of North Carolina, who were noted for their opposition to Davis, he did disagree with Davis and refused to cooperate with the authorities in Richmond over such unpopular measures as impressment, conscription, tax-in-kind, and suspension of the writ. Whenever there was a conflict between the Confederacy and the state, the former Confederate attorney general-turned-governor was prepared to interpret the laws in the favor of the state. Such a policy, however, did nothing to improve Alabama's defenses.

With the fall of Vicksburg, and with northern Alabama firmly in Federal hands, central Alabama was open to invasion. If the Tennessee River Valley was the state's breadbasket (which was entirely devastated after two years of warfare), then the central portion of Alabama was its arsenal. Indeed, the region was a major supplier of Confederate ordnance. As a matter of fact, Selma was perhaps the greatest ordnance center in the entire Confederacy, second only to Richmond. Along with the government-owned factory at Tallassee, Selma made arms and ammunition. Owing to its proximity to iron and coal fields in Bibb and Shelby counties, its rail connections, its deep water channel to Mobile, and the abundance of food and forage in the Black Belt, Selma early in the war had been chosen by the Confederate government to become a manufacturing center. As many as 10,000 workmen were employed there, where everything from ironclads, heavy ordnance, swords, carbines, pistols, and percussion caps were produced. Arguably the best cannon in America were cast there. One other advantage to Selma's location was its apparent inaccessibility to Federal raids. But that would change by the summer of 1864.

The first sign of trouble came in the form of Federal troops under the command of Lovell H. Rousseau. Directed by Sherman to do all "mischief possible," Rousseau aimed his raid at deep Alabama with the objective of cutting one of the main arteries which led into Atlanta from the west, Alabama's second most strategic railroad, the West Point & Montgomery. Rousseau's force of some 2,300 cavalry not only wrecked the railroad near and around Opelika and knocked it out for a month, but also severed an important Confederate line of communication, the Chattahoochee River, particularly threatening the Columbus, Georgia, area, where there was a large industrial center and naval works. In so doing, the raid demonstrated the weakness of Alabama's defenses. Rousseau met resistance by a small brigade and later fought a trainload of home guards, cadets, conscripts, militia, and exempts, about 500 strong, whom he routed and then ignored. News of the raid caused concern and panic in Montgomery and Selma. The success also demonstrated the ease with which Central Alabama could be invaded. As the *Montgomery Advertiser* declared in its issue of August 4, 1864: "We doubt that any other raid . . . comprised of so many men, has penetrated so far, done so much damage, and escaped with so little loss."

The attack on Mobile began that same month, in August 1864. With Mobile's fall the Alabama River could be used as another avenue of invasion into Alabama's heartland. On the gulf, Mobile was first in importance for the Confederacy after New Orleans, which had fallen in April 1862. The enemy had threatened Mobile many times before the real attack came. In November 1862 Alabama's legislators declared that Mobile would "never be surrendered: that it shall be defended from street to street, from house to house, and inch to inch, until if taken, the victors' spoils shall be alone a heap of ashes." Its defensive works had been planned and directed by Major Danville Leadbetter, a skillful Confederate officer who became, in October 1863, General Braxton Bragg's chief engineer, and thousands of Alabama slaves had been hired and impressed to work there. In February 1864, Governor Watts showed no sign of defeatism and vowed that "Alabama must, it shall be defended."

Admiral David Farragut's victory over Confederate forces in Mobile Bay on September 4, 1864, was almost as disastrous to Alabamians as the fall of Atlanta, which occurred on September 2. By this time the whole economy of the Confederacy nearly had collapsed, and the military situation was desperate. Among other worries were bread riots in Mobile and a draft riot in Randolph County, where the army was called out to keep the peace. Meanwhile, large numbers of Alabamians in the north and in the Wiregrass resisted the draft. After July 1863 Alabama had raised only eight regiments of infantry. Desertion and disaffection remained an unsolved problem. Another concern were the peace advocates, who had appeared in northern Alabama as early as April 1862, and in central and southern Alabama by the following spring. By the fall of 1864 the "glorious cause" had become a hopeless cause.

The bitter end began in March 1865, when Federal forces under James H. Wilson swooped down from northern Alabama upon Selma, which fell on April 2, the same day as Richmond, and then moved on through the heart of Alabama to Montgomery and later into Georgia, where they captured Jefferson Davis. Montgomery, the Cradle of the Confederacy, surrendered on April 12, 1865, without a fight from its few defenders of reserves, conscripts, and a company of boys, exactly four years to the day that the firing on Fort Sumter had begun, on orders from Montgomery. Before the city fell and the thousands of cotton bales which were stored there were ordered burned by its defenders, Governor Watts left and went southeast with the intent of moving the state government to Eufaula. Mobile surrendered on April 12, and General Richard Taylor, Jefferson Davis' former brother-in-law, commanding the Department of Alabama, Mississippi, and East Louisiana, surrendered all troops under his command to General Edward R. S. Canby at Cuba Station, Alabama, on May 8, becoming the last organized Confederate force to surrender east of the Mississippi River.

With war's end came another world for Alabamians such as Clement C. Clay, Jr., John A. Campbell, Joseph H. Wheeler, and others, who were all arrested. Each man appealed to President Andrew Johnson for executive clemency, and they were ultimately released from custody and allowed to return to their homes. For committing his high offense (he termed it "self-defense") against the United States by ordering the taking of Forts Morgan and Gaines and other Federal property, Andrew B. Moore was arrested by the Federals at his home in Perry County and confined in Fort Pulaski, Georgia, for several months. In feeble health, impoverished, and deeply distressed, in August 1865 Moore was given an "indefinite parole" to return to Alabama, where his wife languished in a lunatic asylum. In his application for pardon, Alpheus Baker, a former member of Alabama's secession convention from the Black Belt, who had entered the army as a private in February 1861 and had risen to the rank of brigadier general before his surrender with Joseph E. Johnston's army, seemed to reflect the spirits of Alabamians after defeat. With little property and a wife and two children to support, Baker made no bones about being broke. He admitted that he had voted for the ordinance of secession, which he had viewed since his youth as a "constitutional right." Like many others, he did not think that secession would have led to war, rather that the "two sections," North and South, could "live apart in amity and prosperity." But these hopes were "doomed to a bloody disappointment," he said. Baker did all that he could to secure the triumph of his cause, but "God [had] disposed it otherwise. The South was overcome, & that destruction of Slavery which I hoped to avert by Secession, was accelerated—accomplished by the war it produced." "It is gone forever," Baker lamented, "and with it, the motive which prompted me to desire separation." The Alabama general was pardoned by Johnson, as were thousands of other Alabamians excepted from the general amnesty proclamation of May 29, 1865, including ex-Governors Shorter and Watts. Ahead of them lay the challenge of rebuilding and the process of getting on with the rest of their lives and of trying to forget the past.

SUGGESTED READING

William L. Barney, *The Secessionist Impulse: Alabama and Mississippi in 1860* (Princeton University Press: Princeton, 1974).

Willis Brewer, *Alabama: Her History. Resources. War Record. and Public Men, From 1540 to 1872* (Willo Publishing Company reprint of an 1872 edition: Tuscaloosa, 1964).

Clarence P. Denman, *The Secession Movement in Alabama* (Alabama State Department of History and Archives: Montgomery, 1933).

Leavy Dorman, *Party Politics in Alabama from 1850 to 1860* (Wetumpka Printing Company: Wetumpka, 1935).

Walter L. Fleming, *Civil War and Reconstruction in Alabama* (Columbia University Press: New York, 1905).

Malcolm McMillan, *The Disintegration of a Confederate State: Three Governors and Alabama's Wartime Home Front, 1861-1865* (Mercer University Press: Macon, 1986) .

Joseph Wheeler, *"Alabama"* in *Confederate Military History; a library of Confederate States History* (Confederate Publishing Company: Atlanta, 1899).

LOUISIANA

by
Charles Edmund Vetter

The Republican Party's nomination of Abraham Lincoln for president in July 1860 produced mild concern among the citizens of Louisiana. The state was in a period of economic prosperity that insulated it from potential political crisis. The winter of 1860-1861 held promise of even greater prosperity. Crops were large and cotton and sugar sold at top prices. New Orleans was experiencing growth in business, wealth, improvements, and population. The streets were full, planters had begun to gather in the hotels of the city, and the salons were filled with Southern Belles. The wharves had been extended to handle the increase in shipping and the debts of the city for 1860 had been paid. Newspapers were filled with advertisements of sail and steamboat departures to all points of the globe. Overall, Louisiana was poised for a prosperous future, and the thought of disunion over a presidential election was not uppermost in the minds of its citizens.

Louisiana had a unionist history. Ten years earlier the legislature had refused to participate in the Nashville Convention, an effort to create increased Southern sectional awareness and political cooperation. The Compromise of 1850 had been endorsed by a majority of Whigs and Democrats in the state, a compromise most believed would end sectional disputes. The only opposition to the Compromise came from a group of Democrats led by Senator Pierre Soule and a few fire-eating emigrants from South Carolina. The efforts failed and even Soule, after criticizing the Compromise, reaffirmed his allegiance to the Union. Old Democrats such as Senator Solomon Downs had little toleration for Southern extremists. New Democrats such as Senator John Slidell knew that extremist talk and activity was unpopular, so he and his followers proclaimed their loyalty to the United States. Union sentiment was a strong tradition among non-slave holding farmers and much of the population of New Orleans. Merchants and bankers had strong economic ties to the North, particularly with the upper Mississippi Valley and New York. The city's business leaders had little sympathy with the proponents of state's rights. New Orleans also had a sizable European-immigrant population that had no enthusiasm for secession. Even the slave holding minority in the state, specifically the sugar planters, held firm ties to the Union. They were the dominant class in south Louisiana and had the most to lose from a Republican victory. They appreciated the protection that came from a Federal tariff and knew such protection would not continue under a Southern confederation or under an independent Louisiana. Louisianians had always advocated protection; to lose it would mean devastation to a major part of their economy. Even where the secessionists' cause had the greatest support—the cotton parishes along the Mississippi and Red rivers, areas dominated by large plantations with a heavy concentration of slaves—talk of secession was not widespread.

Thus, Louisiana, because of its history, economy, and geography, seemingly, was the least likely of the lower Southern states to secede from the Union.

But Louisiana was a Southern state. It was as much a part of the Southern subculture as South Carolina, Mississippi, or Georgia. Louisianians identified more with the agricultural Deep South than with the industrialized North. In spite of the reasons for remaining in the Union, there was a fear that power could be wrenched from them and the result would be the end of a cherished way of life. Unionists they were, but their unionism was conditional. Citizens held to the right of a state to secede and if enough pressure was applied, if convinced that all alternatives were exhausted, their unionism would crumble.

As the election drew near, the pressures began to build and the mild concern displayed in July turned to alarm. People lost their faith in the Compromise of 1850. Memories of past "abuses" were still alive, but the greatest fears came from what the Republicans might do if they gained control of the presidency. Some renewed old wounds by condemning the personal liberty laws of the Northern states which were viewed as attacks on slavery. Others condemned *Uncle Tom's Cabin*, anti-slavery activities in Kansas, the appeal to a "higher law" by Senator William H. Seward of New York, and John Brown's raid on Harpers Ferry. By election day the stage was set for a struggle that would lead Louisiana out of the Union.

Instead of simplifying the situation, the election complicated matters. Louisiana voters failed to register a decisive vote either for or against secession. John C. Breckinridge, the candidate for the Constitutional Democratic Party, received the state's electoral vote but won less than half the popular vote. John Bell of the Constitutional Union Party and Stephen A. Douglas of the National Democratic Party carried more than fifty-five percent of the popular vote. Lincoln did not receive a vote in the entire state. Breckinridge's vote was a vote for secession. Most, if not all, of the state's disunionists voted for him. A vote for Bell or Douglas was a unionist vote, but "the vote of a qualified and shrinking unionism." Although the voting did not indicate a victory for or against secession, it did do two things: it put into motion the machinery that would take Louisiana out of the Union; and it made clear the conditional nature of Louisiana's unionism.

In October 1860, Governor William H. Gist of South Carolina inquired of Governor Thomas O. Moore what course Louisiana would take if Lincoln won the election. Governor Moore replied; "I shall not advise the secession of my state," and added, "I do not think the people of Louisiana will ultimately decide in favor of that course." This was political rhetoric. Moore was a planter, a slave holder, and a believer in the doctrine of state's rights. He was a puppet of Slidell, the real political power in the state and an advocate of secession.

Then came the Lincoln victory, and the culmination of years of attempts to settle the problems of slavery and sectionalism through compromise. To secessionists and unionists in Louisiana this meant that the power of the national government had been placed in the hands of a man and a party who were enemies of their most sacred economic and social institutions. On November 19, Governor Moore took action. Sensing the changing mood of his state and urged by secessionist forces, he issued a call for a special legislative session to determine what course the state should take.

Discussion concerning the election, the special session, and secession reached a new high across the state. Newspapers took the lead. Some advocated immediate secession. Most, however, were cautious. They recognized the seriousness of the crisis, but urged salvation of the Union if possible. Thus, early in December, the press was divided along two lines: conservatives advocated concurrent state action and the more aggressive journals advocated separate state action.

The press reflected the sentiments of their editors, as well as the debate going on throughout the state. All agreed that the governor's call for a special session had but one purpose—to consider calling a convention to secede from the United States. All also agreed that secession would come, but there was no agreement on how to achieve it. Two interesting discourses emerged during the discussions prior to the convening of the special session. One appeared in the *Daily True Delta* in a series of articles signed "Jefferson," and the other was a sermon presented by Dr. Benjamin Morgan Palmer, pastor of the First Presbyterian Church of New Orleans. Both represented views that were widespread throughout the state.

The "Jefferson" articles criticized the governor's call for a special session because the convention would lack constitutional authority. Therefore, if a convention was called, "Jefferson" continued, "it would be with the view either that the convention shall amend the existing constitution of the state, or adopt some measure or ordinance by which the people will declare their will with regard to the event declared by the governor in his proclamation...." Many moderates throughout the state felt there was a lack of understanding of the consequences of secession.

"Jefferson" addressed those consequences in an editorial titled "Regard all the Consequences." He stated, "It is utterly impossible to have a peaceable dismemberment of the confederacy;" that upon separation, Louisiana "must either relinquish all pretension, all claim, all right to participate equally in the national property, public domain, improvements of all kinds, army, navy and appurtenances, etc., or prepare herself to vindicate her demands by a resort to force." Questions of importance must be considered: "Will the free states abandon the supremacy they now claim over the territorial property of the Union? And can they be made to do so otherwise than by force successfully invoked?" He was convinced that the answer to such questions was civil war. "A peaceful destruction of this government never can take place...," he concluded.

Palmer's sermon had a much greater influence on the outcome of the debate. Palmer was the most popular minister in New Orleans and was known throughout the state. People respected his word and most accepted it as truth. The subject of his sermon was relations between the North and South. The sermon was a passionate defense of slavery and the South. Palmer claimed that God demanded the preservation and transmitting of "our existing system of domestic servitude." This must be done, even "in the face of the worst possible peril." Concerning the possibility of war, he said, "Though war be the aggregation of all evils,...we will not shrink even from the baptism of fire." Turning to Lincoln's victory, he left no doubt in the minds of his listeners that a sectional candidate had been elected and a sectional party had gained control of the government. For Palmer the outcome was clear. "Let the people in all the Southern States in solemn council assembled, reclaim the powers they have delegated." Secession for Louisiana was the only honorable avenue to follow, for "If she will arise in her majority,... she will back for all time the curse that is upon her. If she succumbs, she transmits that curse as a heirloom to posterity...."

Palmer's sermon had an impact all over the state. Although criticized among conservatives, the sermon succeeded in crystallizing sentiment on the issue of secession. Since the election in November, the citizens of Louisiana had vacillated between cooperation, secession, and conditional unionism. By December 10, 1860, the issues had been narrowed to secession and cooperation. Citizens, no matter what their position, were in favor of doing something, if nothing more than to settle the slavery dispute once and for all.

On December 10 the legislature met in Baton Rouge with twenty-three Senators and sixty-one Representatives present. Moore told the gathering of lawmakers, "The election of Mr. Lincoln by the Northern people...shows that the Northern mind is poisoned against us, and that it no longer respects our rights, or their obligations." He added, "I do not think it comports with the honor and respect of Louisiana, as a slave holding state, to live under the government of a Black Republican President."

A joint committee of the senate and house was considered along with bills providing for a state convention, the organization of the military, sending commissioners to the various Southern states for consultation, and participation in a convention of all the Southern states. The next day, the committee made its report and the legislature acted immediately. A convention bill passed on December 12. It stipulated that the members of the convention were to be elected by popular vote on January 7, 1861. The delegates were to be chosen according to representative and senatorial apportionment just as if they were candidates for the state legislature. No distinction was made between the two categories of delegates at the convention. Delegates were to assemble in Baton Rouge on January 23. The legislature also passed bills calling for the reorganization of the militia and favoring a convention of the Southern states. Before adjourning, a resolution requested the governor to communicate with the governors of other states concerning secession. The work of the special session completed, the governor, senators, and representatives, having violated the constitution of Louisiana by refusing to submit the question of a convention to a popular referendum, traveled to their respective districts to participate in a campaign to elect delegates. In doing so they took the first illegal step toward secession.

Although the deliberations of the special session were characterized as harmonious, the passage of the bill requiring a state convention was met with opposition. The *Picayune* warned its readers that immediate secession could lead to serious consequences and raised a number of questions it felt Moore and the legislators had not considered. In an editorial published on December 12 the *Picayune* asked, "If to-day Louisiana was declared out of the Union, and consequently her custom-houses closed, how is a bale of cotton to leave our port? Or how can a hogshead of sugar, or a tierce of rice, or any of the millions of dollars worth of fruits of the earth now in storehouses be exported?" On December 14 the *Daily True Delta* ran an editorial entitled, "Everybody breathes easier." With sarcasm the editorial told its readers that the "great events of the day have come and passed into history.... The enlightened body known as the general assembly of the sovereign state of Louisiana has had its extra session, its whiskey, its mileage, its *per diem* and its important display...." But such sentiments were from a decreasing minority. Public opinion rapidly stabilized and citizens saw that the issue was between secession or cooperation.

From mid-December until the eve of the election Louisiana found itself in the middle of a regular political campaign. The newspapers were devoted to editorials for and against secession, and organized political clubs held meetings behind closed doors. Political leaders in the state—Slidell, Judah P. Benjamin, Soule, Randell Hunt, Jacob Barker, Thomas J. Durant—schemed to assure victory for their delegates. Everywhere the election was the topic of discussion.

After approximately two weeks, the *Picayune* concluded that the prospective delegates could be divided into three groups. The Immediate Secessionists, the most radical, advocated prompt, unqualified withdrawal from the Union. They wanted to follow the course of South Carolina and were organized as part of the political machine operated by Slidell. The second group, the Cooperationists, was composed of "those who, despairing of obtaining in the Union a formal and satisfactory recognition of Southern rights, are, therefore, inclined in favor of secession, but by united Southern action." This group was intent on preventing immediate secession and hoped to delay action by supporting a program of joint secession of all the slave states. They did not deny the right of secession, but they viewed it as a last resort. The third group was the Conditional Unionists. It included "those who...are in favor of a Convention of the slaveholding States to consult and decide upon, and submit to the Northern States the just requirements of the South." If the North refused to meet their demands, then secession should follow. The Conditional Unionists were fewer in number than the other groups. They were closer to the Cooperationist philosophically, and joined this group in an attempt to defeat the Immediate Secessionists. The *Picayune* failed to mention a fourth group, the Unconditional Unionists. They were the smallest in number and were avid supporters of continued allegiance to the Union. They opposed secession under any circumstances. Since they had no power they campaigned under the Cooperationist standard, if they campaigned at all. Because the Conditional and Unconditional Unionists joined forces with the Cooperationists, the Immediate Secessionists referred to the Cooperationists as Submissionists.

The Cooperationists' cause was trumpeted by "Jefferson," who, in addition to calling for calm deliberation, raised the issue of suffrage. "Should Louisiana secede," he wrote, "there would be no longer any citizens of the United States within her limits. Who, then, would be voters and qualified to elect officers?" He quoted the criteria of the state constitution for suffrage, emphasizing the requirement that a voter must be a citizen of the United States. If Louisiana seceded, he concluded, it would leave the state without a legally qualified voter. Another concern of the Cooperationists was the Mississippi River. Louisiana's wealth depended, in large measure, upon the navigation and commerce of this river. After secession, what would be the state's status regarding this waterway? If free navigation was guaranteed to all states bordering the Mississippi, would this not open Louisiana to attack from Northern forces? The other alternative, denial of the rights of transit, also was not acceptable. Would not such denial bankrupt the state by cutting off trade? In still another area, Randell Hunt, an Old Line Whig, questioned the legality of the state convention. The legislature should have placed the question of a convention to the people for a popular vote. He opposed separate state action. In other quarters the Cooperationists argued that New Orleans already had lost millions of dollars as a result of the possibility of secession. They wanted to know from the Immediate Secessionists how such losses would be regained. Soule, another Cooperationist, called for sending "discreet and experienced commissioners" to cooperate with the other states, and Durant advocated conditional solutions. To Durant, "Nothing could be gained by separate state secession, but all might be lost by it." Through the *Picayune*, a Cooperationist asked the Immediate Secessionists to explain the benefits of disunion. What would be done about the tariff on sugar? What was going to happen to the state's manufactures? Will the slave trade be re-opened? The *Gazette* and the *Comet* submitted that secession had been tried in 1832 and had failed. This attempt also would fail. The *Picayune* wanted to know if secession was to be permanent or temporary. The main question they left with their readers was, "After secession-what then?"

The efforts of the speeches, letters, and editorials of the Cooperationists were in vain. The Immediate Secessionists were organized by a powerful political machine controlled by Slidell. For years he had been the undisputed leader of Louisiana, and he was in no mood for rational debate. In November 1860 he had put himself on record as being a secessionist. In a letter to President James Buchanan he said, "Louisiana will act with her sister States of the South," and "I see no probability of preserving the Union, nor indeed do I consider it desirable to do so if we could." With the backing of other prominent secessionists, the use of propaganda, indoctrination, and coercion, Slidell played on "the emotional hysteria of sectional patriotism" and led the state out of the Union. He was assisted by political clubs, newspapers, and the clergy. In addition, he could count on emissaries from other Southern states and the activities of vigilance committees.

Despite the efforts of the Immediate Secessionists, and mounting evidence of increased secessionist sentiment in most parts of the state, a sentiment that was enhanced significantly after the secession of South Carolina, the Cooperationists remained optimistic. The results of the November election indicated that the forces of compromise had been strong. There was still, they argued, a chance they might win a majority in the January election of delegates. They pressed for a Southern Convention, and assured the electorate of a choice between a radical, Immediate Secessionist platform and a more moderate, conservative platform based on delay and possible compromise.

Their hope was not to be. The election on January 7 resulted in a victory for the Immediate Secessionists. They won by a majority vote of 1,763 votes, or 52.3 percent.

On January 23 the legislature convened in regular session in Baton Rouge. After speaking of the healthy condition of the state treasury, Governor Moore addressed them on the themes of secession and that war was inevitable. He said that "the vote of the people has confirmed the faith of the executive...that the individual sentiment of the state is for immediate and effective resistance...." He urged unity, stating that "a people with one heart and one mind...cannot be subdued." There was no reason, he concluded "to forestall the action of the State Convention...."

Before adjourning the legislature passed acts which transferred the regular military forces of the state to the Confederacy, established military companies, and provided for the expenses of the state. It passed a joint resolution stating that secession was a legitimate right and that "any attempts to coerce or force a sovereign State will be viewed...as a hostile invasion and resisted to the utmost extent."

On the same day, the state convention assembled at the capital. In less than three months, from the election of Lincoln in November to the meeting of the delegates in January, the state had experienced a whirlwind that had put it on a direct course to secession and war. Three months earlier the state was undecided as to its future; now it was a certainty that Louisiana would join the other seceded states. What had happened to cause such a rapid crystallization toward secession? First, in spite of the strength of Cooperationist sentiment, their cooperation ideology was mixed with a heavy dose of secession. They were Cooperationists, not Unionists, conditional or unconditional. When the hope for compromise died they chose the only alternative, secession. Their "cooperation" was narrow and limited. If cooperation failed, then secession was selected; their ideology gave them no other choice. Second, people became aware that efforts to achieve sectional compromise collapsed with the election of Lincoln. They grew apprehensive about what the North might do, and had to be prepared for the worst. Third, the secession of South Carolina and other Southern states created excitement and caused many to make the break with the Union more easily and comfortably. Louisiana must not be part of Southern division, but must follow the path to Southern unity. Fourth, the aggressive energy of the younger generation had an influence. Many of the younger slaveholders had lost hope in receiving justice from the Union. They were convinced that staying in the Union would mean losing their slaves and the basic social institutions so important to their way of life. They were a minority and decided that strength could be found by joining the Immediate Secessionists. The older generation of slaveholders might continue to speak of the days of Jackson, but that era had ended. The new one was to be built on the doctrine of secession. Fifth, the news of Beauregard's victory at Fort Sumter and the excitement of war played on the minds of many and pushed them into the Immediate Secessionist camp. Sixth, as Charles Roland has stated, the "force of propaganda, indoctrination, and coercion at the command of the radical secessionists" had a tremendous influence. The organization of "boss" Slidell created great pressure on the general public which, in turn, influenced attitudes toward secession.

Following the election of officers the first important matters that engaged the attention of the delegates included reading communications from the state's national delegation, reception of the South Carolina and Alabama commissioners, and appointment of a Committee of Fifteen to draft an ordinance of secession. On January 24, Governor Moore sent the convention a copy of his annual message to the legislature and called for approval of his confiscation of Federal property in the state. Immediately, a motion was passed approving the governor's seizure of forts, arsenals, and other Federal property. The same day the Committee of Fifteen reported an ordinance of secession. Although secession sentiment ruled the convention, it did not prevent two Cooperationist substitutes from being offered. The first, by Joseph A. Rozier of New Orleans, called for delay and urged that a convention be held in Nashville, Tennessee, of representatives from the slave states to propose amendments to the United States Constitution that would insure the protection of slavery. He also wanted to empower the Nashville meeting to enact secession of all the slaveholding states if the amendment effort failed. Rozier's motion was defeated. The second motion came from James O. Fuqua of East Feliciana Parish. His motion called for an Alabama convention of slaveholding states to cooperate in establishing a confederacy. This motion was defeated. Both votes were indicative of the declining interest in cooperation, especially the Rozier vote, which demonstrated that the Cooperationists had ceased being Cooperationist. The Fuqua motion was less of a Cooperationist measure than a conditional secessionist one. The defeat evidenced the decline in cooperation sentiment.

The final attempt to delay Louisiana secession came from Charles Bienvenu of New Orleans. His motion provided that once an ordinance of secession was adopted it should be "ratified by the vote of the majority of the people at the ballot box." The Bienvenu motion was defeated.

On January 26 the convention adopted the ordinance of secession by a vote of 113 to seventeen. All but seven of the delegates, probably Unconditional Unionists, signed the document.

News of the passage of the ordinance was received with general excitement, approval, and a sense of relief. "The deed has been done," wrote the *Picayune*.

Secession led to war and both devastated Louisiana. Militarily Louisiana contributed a costly share to the Confederacy. Approximately 56,000 men served in the rebel forces. Beginning in the early months of 1861, they rushed to arms to be part of the war for freedom. A year later their enthusiasm began to wane. In April 1862, New Orleans was captured by Admiral David Farragut and garrisoned by General Benjamin Butler. A base was established from which the Federals could reconquer Louisiana. Then in 1863, Vicksburg fell and General Nathaniel P. Banks led his forces against Port Hudson. The Confederate commander, General Franklin Gardner, surrendered when he learned of the fall at Vicksburg. The loss of Vicksburg and Port Hudson gave the Union control of the Mississippi from its source to the Gulf. This left only north-central and northwestern Louisiana under Confederate control. In an attempt to take this region, General Banks, in 1864, drove up the Red River toward Shreveport. He was defeated at Mansfield and Pleasant Hill by forces under General Richard Taylor. This campaign was the last major military encounter in the state. The war was all but over nationally and *was* over in Louisiana.

Of the 56,000 men who participated, 11,000 died. Louisiana had lost approximately one-fifth of its male population. As a result of the abolition of slavery, the state lost most of its wealth. An estimated $170,000,000 had disappeared. Consequently, the plantations were ruined. The planters were left prostrate. The sugar and cotton industry was devastated. The countryside was desolate, levees had crumbled, and land values dropped. The banking system was ruined and many of the mercantile firms were bankrupt. Over half the wealth of the state had been lost. Finally, the state lost its future leadership, a loss that was to plague the state for over two generations.

SUGGESTED READING

Official Journal of the Proceedings of the Convention of the State of Louisiana (J. O. Nixon: New Orleans, 1861).

Ordinances Passed by the Convention of the State of Louisiana (J.O. Nixon: New Orleans, 1861).

Willie Melvin Caskey, *Secession and Restoration of Louisiana* (Louisiana State University Press: Baton Rouge, 1938).

Roger W. Shugg, *Origins of Class Struggle in Louisiana* (Louisiana State University Press: Baton Rouge, 1966).

Charles B. Dew, "Who Won the Secession Election in Louisiana?" *Journal of Southern History*, 36 (No. 1, February, 1970), pp. 18-32.

James Kimmins Greer, "Louisiana Politics, 1845-1861" *Louisiana Historical Quarterly*, 13 (No. 4, October, 1933), pp. 617-654.

Lane Carter Kendall, "The Interregnum in Louisiana in 1861" *Louisiana Historical Quarterly*, 16 (No. 2, April, 1933), pp. 172-208.

Charles P. Roland, "Louisiana and Secession" *Louisiana History*, 19 (No. 4, Fall, 1978), pp. 389-399.

Roger W. Shugg, "A Suppressed Co-operationist Protest Against Secession" *Louisiana Historical Quarterly,* 19 (No. 1, January, 1936), pp. 199-203.

GEORGIA

by
Anne J. Bailey

No Southern state epitomizes the American Civil War better than Georgia, and no city personifies the tragedy of the conflict more than Atlanta. When Margaret Mitchell created Scarlett O'Hara and Rhett Butler, she assured that Georgia's red clay would be burned into the memory of people worldwide. Georgia was Mitchell's home, but it was also the perfect setting for her novel. Nestled in the Deep South with five Confederate states to the west and the remaining five denying easy access from other directions, Georgia seemed one of the most geographically secure. Moreover, as Georgia matured in the decades before the Civil War, it rightfully claimed the sobriquet, "Empire State of the South." When war tore the nation apart, it was only fitting that Georgians would take a leading role in the development of the nascent Confederate nation. Nonetheless, few Southerners would have believed that before the conflict ended some of the war's most dramatic events would take place amid the state's pine woods.

That Georgians would play a prominent role in the Confederacy was not surprising because in the years before the Civil War they had become active in national politics. As sectional differences intensified in the late *antebellum* period, Georgia's political leaders carefully monitored the national scene. When trouble erupted in 1850, Howell Cobb, leader of Georgia's unionist Democrats, served as speaker of the U.S. House of Representatives. With Alexander H. Stephens and Robert Toombs, these three—known as the Georgia Triumvirate—advocated moderation, and threw their support behind the Compromise of 1850. Georgians had taken part in creating the nation almost seventy-five years before, and with this in mind, the state's leaders counseled moderation. In the Georgia Platform of 1850 they accepted the compromise but warned that Georgians would resist if the North violated its promises. Most Georgians supported moderation, and elected unionist Howell Cobb governor the following year in the hope that the compromise would provide the needed solution to the nation's woes. But Georgians quickly became cynical as they watched the country move from one crisis to another, and increasingly disillusioned with a Federal government that did not seem able to solve the nation's problems.

Georgia was a state in transition; it had grown rapidly, and small towns dotted the landscape. With over one million people, Georgia ranked third in total population among the eleven states that joined the Confederacy, although forty-four percent of the people were slaves. The economy flourished in the decade prior to the war; for example, railroad routes more than doubled to over 1,400 miles of track, second only to Virginia. Industry also prospered, but agriculture remained the mainstay of the economy, and ninety percent of the population was rural. It was the yeoman farmer who elected the popular Joseph E. Brown governor in 1857, and then re-elected him for three more terms, until he was removed from office by an occupying Union army in 1865. Brown, a Jacksonian Democrat from the northern hill country, was an extreme reflection of the South's state's rights stand. As sectional differences increased, he became increasingly critical of the direction taken by the Federal government. The press and the wealthy planter class opposed Brown, but he had the support of the common people. Nevertheless, while many farmers advocated moderation in the political tumult surrounding the presidential campaigns in the summer and fall of 1860, Brown was an outspoken critic of the national government.

The presidential election fractured the hopes of the moderates. Northern Democrat Stephen A. Douglas had a former Georgia governor, Herschel V. Johnson, on his ticket and the backing of Alexander H. Stephens, but even this was not enough to overcome his popular-sovereignty platform and strong stand against secession. Although Constitutional Union candidate John Bell had the support of numerous newspapers, Democrat John C. Breckinridge proved to be the most popular with the electorate. Governor Brown, along with Howell Cobb and Robert Toombs, gave him their endorsement. When Georgians turned out in record number to cast their ballots in the presidential election in November, the results attested to the lack of consensus among the voters. Breckinridge garnered 51,893 votes, Bell was second with 42,886, and Douglas claimed 11,580. The conservative candidates, Bell and Douglas, had a majority, but with no clear winner the election was thrown into the state legislature where the radicals dominated. Therefore, Breckinridge, the choice of the extremists, won all ten of Georgia's electoral votes.

Although all the states of the Deep South threw their support to Breckinridge, this was not enough to keep Abraham Lincoln from victory. The news of Lincoln's election brought an immediate response from vocal secessionists, and quick action from Georgia's governor. Fearing a Republican victory, Brown asked the state legislature for $1 million for state defense and called for 10,000 volunteers. Just a few days after the election, future Confederate Quartermaster General Abraham C. Myers wrote his father-in-law, Georgian David Twiggs, the commander of United States forces in Texas during the crisis: "Secession seems to progress. Georgia has raised the colonial flag.... We must have trouble." Indeed, many former unionists now advocated secession, and among those whose voices rang loudest were Brown, Robert Toombs, Howell Cobb, and his brother, Thomas R. R. Cobb. Moreover, they had the support of men from the major slaveholding counties and many residents in the state's urban areas.

On the other side were the cooperationists who continued to oppose immediate action. Alexander Stephens had been a unionist in 1850, and he, along with his half-brother Linton Stephens, Benjamin H. Hill, and Herschel V. Johnson, pled for patience and perhaps another sectional compromise. North Georgia farmers continued to show little interest in national politics, and tended to oppose leaving the Union. But the radicals had the upper hand, and in an election on January 2 voters chose to send delegates to a state secession convention by a margin of 50,243 to 37,123.

The men who assembled in the capital at Milledgeville two weeks later quickly decided to follow South Carolina, Mississippi, Florida, and Alabama out of the Union. But even before Georgia made an official move to secede, Governor Brown already had taken steps to confiscate Federal property within the state. Fort Pulaski, guarding the entrance to the Savannah River, was seized by state forces on January 3. The Ordinance of Secession was adopted by the delegates on January 19 by a vote of 208 to 89, and five days later state troops occupied the U.S. Arsenal at Augusta. On January 26, Georgians took control of Oglethorpe Barracks and Fort Jackson at Savannah. The Federal mint at Dahlonega also fell to state forces.

As military matters progressed, the convention authorized the raising of two regiments and selected representatives to travel to Montgomery. Among the ten Georgians present at the birth of the Confederate nation were the Cobb brothers, Toombs, and Stephens. Howell Cobb served as president of the Montgomery convention while Toombs and T. R. R. Cobb worked on the document that became the Confederate constitution. When the new government began operation, Stephens was selected vice-president of the Confederate States of America, and Toombs became secretary of state. On March 7, the Georgia convention reconvened in order to approve the work done in Montgomery and to transfer state operations to the new national government.

Although many Georgians had opposed secession, most followed their leaders out of the Union without resistance. Even recalcitrant northern Georgia farmers were willing to follow Joe Brown to war. Like other Southerners, Georgians were confident that the Confederacy would prevail; indeed, Robert Toombs sarcastically predicted there would be no war. Nevertheless, the first company of Georgia soldiers joined the army on March 5, and the response was overwhelming after the war began the following month in Charleston harbor, just a short distance up the coast from Savannah. By May, Brown had organized six regiments and two battalions; one month later, the Cobb brothers and Toombs accepted commissions in the Confederate army. Before the war ended, some 120,000 Georgians had taken up arms for the South.

Even before Georgia seceded in January, it was clear that Governor Brown had his own agenda. Prior to the war's outbreak he had expressed concern for Georgia's coastal waters, the state's only vulnerable region in 1861. Georgia's approximately one-hundred-mile-long Atlantic shoreline is anchored to the north by the Savannah River, with the city of Savannah less than twenty miles upriver. Looking southward down the coast, Brown worried about defending St. Simon's Island, the entrance to Brunswick Harbor. Too many Georgia soldiers, he believed, were marching to distant battlefields and leaving their state open to invasion. To appease Brown, Georgian Alexander R. Lawton was appointed to a brigadier generalship and given command of the coast with authority to raise 600 volunteers, but in July Lawton complained that his men had few arms. Although Brown had made it illegal for men to carry weapons out of Georgia in May, he had to appeal to the people for rifles to cover the shortage.

The defense of the coast was a prime concern, and Brown tried many schemes to protect coastal counties. To alleviate the scarcity of weapons, he raised a battalion which he armed with pikes, superciliously known as "Joe Brown Pikes." Over 12,000 were manufactured and distributed to troops in Augusta, Savannah, and to the quartermaster at Chattanooga, but they were never used. In addition, Brown authorized the creation of a fleet. In the summer of 1861, Josiah Tattnall employed four tugs and a river steamer in patrolling the waters from South Carolina to Florida. When this "Mosquito Fleet" met Federal vessels at Port Royal Sound in the fall, Tattnall was forced to withdraw to inland waters. Union forces took Tybee Island at the mouth of the Savannah River in November, and Tattnall's little fleet retreated upstream. As Brown protested to President Jefferson Davis about the Confederate government's lack of response to the crisis, planters along the coast relocated in the state's interior.

Brown's contentious stance foreshadowed the beginning of a turbulent relationship between the governor and Confederate authorities. Although some Georgians denounced Brown's policies, he easily won a third term in November 1861 by a vote of 46,493 to 32,802. Nevertheless, his extreme state's rights stand caused dissension with some state leaders. When he denounced the Conscription Act in 1862 as unconstitutional and despotic, the state supreme court forced him to yield; moreover, the state legislature gave him only unenthusiastic backing in his battles with Richmond. To overcome the loss of men to the draft, Brown created a state force composed of those too young or too old for Confederate military service; to opponents of his policies, these men earned the label of "Joe Brown's Pets." Throughout the war Brown disbanded and reorganized his state militia in order to circumvent changing provisions in the draft. In June 1864, one of Howell Cobb's sons wrote to his wife: "Joe Brown is in Atlanta with his pets the militia officers and says he will lead them in the fight when the time comes. I hope the time will soon come, and that his time may come at the same time. I think his death would be a blessing to the country."

Brown's myopic state's rights stance hindered his participation in the central-ized war effort, and he was not alone in his acrimonious attacks on the Confederate government. Vice-President Stephens spent much of his time at his Georgia home complaining about President Jefferson Davis and making sure his brother Linton repeated this sentiment in the state senate. These men were joined by Robert Toombs, who, after resigning from both the cabinet and the army in rapid succession, returned home to voice his displeasure with Richmond. Herschel V. Johnson also disapproved of some Confederate measures. Johnson, a former governor and vice-presidential candidate, was not as radical as Brown, the Stephenses, or Toombs, but he joined in opposition to the Conscription Act. Johnson believed it was "odious" because the law "*compelled* men to fight for liberty" and "enslaved them under the pretext of making them free."

Brown's critics, however, could not overcome his loyal support from the masses. Unfortunately, the best known of those who opposed his measures, Brigadier General Howell Cobb and Confederate Senator Benjamin H. Hill, were seldom in the state to promote active resistance to his policies. Brown remained popular with the people, and it was the average Georgian who gave him a fourth term in November 1863. Although the voter turn-out was low, with less than 65,000 votes cast, Brown received 36,558.

From the perspective of white Georgians, Brown did much for the state and its people. He raised money to aid needy soldiers and supplied them with clothing and shoes. He worked to relieve the shortage of salt, tried to curtail the production of whiskey by urging farmers to use their grain for food, and limited the amount of cotton grown so that wealthy planters would be forced to grow edible crops. In 1862 the state legislature voted $2,500,000 in relief for the families of soldiers whose property value was less than $1,000. A $100 bounty for needy families was to be financed from the net proceeds of the state-owned railroad and a tax on the net incomes of speculators. In 1863 the amount appropriated was $5,000,000, and during the last two years of the war, the legislature voted $6,000,000 for this purpose. While assisting the soldiers' families, Brown also worked for an increase in the soldier's pay. Opponents claimed he was trying to start a class war; that he "slanders the rich for the simple reason that the poor have more votes." T. Conn Bryan, historian of Confederate Georgia, noted: "Until the end of the war, Brown towered over the legislature and dominated the state almost as though he were the sovereign of an independent republic."

Despite such acquisitions, Georgia's businessmen and aspiring entrepreneurs benefited most from the war. When the Confederacy began plans for arsenals and ordnance manufacturing works, location was of prime importance. Although it was logical to establish these centers at pre-existing facilities, it was also important that they be sheltered from the war and thus located far from the front. Moreover, these facilities needed to be near water or railroads in order to transport supplies to the armies. Georgia provided the perfect location and abundant natural resources. Furthermore, it had men ready to take advantage of the economic advantages offered by the war.

The cities of Atlanta, Augusta, Columbus, and Macon seemed ready for this opportunity. In northern Georgia the rail center of Atlanta became a headquarters for the quartermaster and commissary, as well as a supply depot. Colonel Marcus H. Wright, commander of the Atlanta Arsenal, received many weapons through contracts with local firms. Atlanta's industry included a rolling mill which produced cannon, armor plates, and rails, and by 1862 the city hosted a pistol factory. In western Georgia, Columbus, on the Chattahoochee River, was an important manufacturing center, and boasted the largest sword factory in the South. After the navy took over the Columbus Iron Works, production increased and one authority claimed that three ships and approximately seventy brass Napoleons were manufactured there. Located on Georgia's eastern border, Savannah was the site of an arsenal, but after the Union occupied the coast the arsenal was removed to Macon where it manufactured cannon, shot, shells, and other ordnance. In addition, small war-related industries could be found in Athens, Rome, and Dalton. As the war drew manpower from the state, women replaced their husbands and fathers in the factories.

The Augusta Powder Works, completed in April 1862, was one of the most productive of Georgia's war-time industries. Augusta was not only on the Savannah River, it had a rail link to Charleston and points east as well as proximity to the Augusta Canal. Under the capable command of George Washington Rains, the factory produced approximately three million pounds of powder during the war. In a history of the arsenal, Rains claimed its daily production was 30,000 rounds of small-arms ammunition and 125 to 150 rounds of field-artillery ammunition. From 1863 until 1865 this arsenal produced 110 twelve-pound Napoleon field guns, 174 gun carriages, 115 caissons, 10,535 powder boxes, 85,800 rounds of fixed ammunition, 476,207 pounds of artillery projectiles, 4,626,000 lead balls, and 10,760,000 small arms cartridges. Late in the war women workers kept the factory producing, and Major General William T. Sherman's failure to destroy the facility in 1864 was one of his rare miscalculations. Augusta prospered from the wartime activity, and an English visitor noted in June 1863: "No place that I have seen in the Southern States shows so little traces of the war...."

Indeed, for the first two years of the war, Georgians living in the interior had little reason to worry about military invasion. Robert E. Lee took command of coastal defenses from South Carolina to Florida in November 1861. His concern for Savannah prompted him to pull troops from the sea islands; therefore, by March 1862 Union forces controlled much of the coast, and were ready to move up the Savannah River.

As 1862 opened, Union troops isolated the Confederate bastion of Fort Pulaski, situated on Cockspur Island at the mouth of the Savannah River. In the midst of this crisis, President Davis summoned Lee to Richmond, leaving the coastal defenses to Major General John C. Pemberton, who was assigned to temporary, then permanent, command of the Department of South Carolina and Georgia. On April 11, Fort Pulaski surrendered, leaving the fate of Savannah uncertain. An attack on the city did not materialize, although Federal troops did raid up and down the coast. The best known of these forays was the burning of the town of Darien in July 1863, an event dramatically depicted in the movie *Glory* which premiered in December 1989. Pemberton's inability to defend the coast led one diarist to write, "as he is a Pennsylvanian.... Everybody has lost confidence in [him] and many even suspect treachery, although it cannot be proved of course." The public outcry, however, forced his removal in August, and General P. G. T. Beauregard assumed command in September.

The only other Georgians threatened by invasion were those living in the northern part of the state. Two Union raiding parties tried to cut the Western and Atlantic Railroad between Atlanta and Chattanooga. The first, in April 1862, was a group of twenty Federals led by a spy, James J. Andrews. Dressed as civilians, they made it to Big Shanty, seven miles north of Marietta, where they stole a steam engine, the *General,* and three box cars, then headed north. Andrews' Raiders were able to foil pursuing Confederates by obstructing the track, but between Kingston and Adairsville Southerners stopped a southbound train, took the engine, the *Texas,* and resumed the chase by running the engine in reverse. The Raiders were captured when their fuel gave out, and Andrews and seven others were executed in the summer of 1862. The event terrified Georgians, who thus far had been immune to the violence of war.

The second attempt to destroy the railroad occurred one year later in April 1863, when Colonel Abel D. Streight, who commanded approximately 1,600 cavalrymen, received orders to break the line south of Dalton. This action would disrupt supplies for Braxton Bragg's army at Tullahoma, Tennessee. Cutting through northern Alabama, the Union horsemen entered Georgia near Rome, but believing the city fortified, retreated. Pursued by Brigadier General Nathan Bedford Forrest and 600 cavalrymen, the rebels found-Steight between Gadsden and Rome. Forrest deceived Streight into believing that he was outnumbered, and the Federals surrendered on May 3, prompting residents of Rome to form military organizations "for repelling the thieving, house burning, and vandal foe that may venture upon our soil."

Nevertheless, just a few months later Union forces were back on Georgia soil. In August, Major General William S. Rosecrans marched the Army of the Cumberland toward Chattanooga, an important rail center located just above the Tennessee-Georgia border. Bragg, who had retreated from Tullahoma to Chattanooga, pulled the Army of Tennessee out on September 8 and moved to LaFayette, Georgia, approximately twenty-five miles directly south of Chattanooga. Rosecrans pursued the Confederates but unwisely divided his army, giving Bragg two excellent opportunities to strike the isolated Union corps. When both attempts failed, Bragg planned to move his army between Rosecrans and Chattanooga, but Rosecrans, realizing his vulnerability, pulled his army together and headed north toward Chattanooga. He hoped to keep the Confederates from getting between the Army of the Cumberland and Rossville, a small town located just across the Tennessee line.

In the meantime, reinforcements from the Army of Northern Virginia were on their way to join Bragg. By the afternoon of September 18, five of nine brigades under Lieutenant General James Longstreet had arrived at Ringgold; these troops would bring Bragg's army to more than 66,000 men to face Rosecrans' approximately 58,000 men. The two sides met on September 19 in the thick woods between Chickamauga Creek and the LaFayette Road, a north-south route between Chattanooga and LaFayette. During the night, while Rosecrans strengthened his position, Longstreet arrived on the field and Bragg reorganized his five infantry corps into two wings, the right under Lieutenant General Leonidas Polk and the left under Longstreet. Bragg planned to hit the Federal left near the LaFayette Road; he would outflank the Federals and drive them away from Chattanooga.

Although the Confederate attack was slow in developing, fortune smiled on the Southerners. Because of a mix-up, a gap developed in the Federal line and Major General John Bell Hood's Confederates quickly poured through the hole. Both sides of the Union army broke and fled toward the rear, leaving Major General George

Thomas to rally remnants of the army on Horseshoe Ridge, or Snodgrass Hill, northwest of the break. Thomas held all afternoon before retreating to Rossville; his stand saved the Union army, and earned him the sobriquet, "Rock of Chickamauga."

Chickamauga was the largest Southern victory in the Western Theatre, and the largest battle in Georgia, but it did not produce the hoped for results. Casualties were high on both sides—approximately 16,000 for the Union and 18,000 for the Confederates. In addition, Rosecrans was safe in Chattanooga, where he had wanted to go in the first place, and Bragg had not been able to shake the Union control of Tennessee. Bragg's failure to retake Chattanooga further eroded Confederate confidence in his ability, and his loss in the Battle of Chattanooga on November 24-25 forced his withdrawal into northern Georgia. One month later, while the Confederate army recuperated in winter quarters at Dalton, Bragg was replaced by General Joseph E. Johnston.

As 1864 opened, Georgians waited for the next scene of the drama unfolding along their northern border. When Lincoln promoted U.S. Grant to lieutenant general and appointed him general-in-chief, a new phase of the war began. Grant determined that to win, all the Union armies must move at the same time. For Georgia this meant that Major General William T. Sherman, commander of the Military Division of the Mississippi, would push south into the heart of the state. Grant's orders to Sherman were to attack Johnston's army, "break it up, and get into the interior of the enemy's country as far as you can, inflicting all the damage you can on their war resources." To do this, Sherman put together an army of around 100,000 men and over 250 pieces of artillery. This force included Major General George H. Thomas' Army of the Cumberland, Major General James B. McPherson's Army of the Tennessee, and Major General John M. Schofield's Army of the Ohio. Moreover, Sherman claimed an added advantage. He believed that he knew "more of Georgia than the rebels did" because he had become familiar with the area while stationed near Atlanta in the 1840s as a young artillery lieutenant. In preparation for the campaign, Sherman carefully studied maps, tax documents, and census reports for every county.

On May 4 the Union armies began to move. To oppose Sherman in Georgia, Johnston built up a force of approximately 65,000 men, including reinforcements that arrived from Mississippi under Major General Leonidus Polk. Sherman used his superior numbers to maneuver Johnston out of Dalton, forcing the Confederates to retreat along the Western and Atlantic Railroad. Although the two sides fought continually as Johnston followed the rails south, there was never the sustained fighting such as that going on in Virginia. By early June the armies neared Marietta, and on June 14, Polk was killed. From mid-June until early July, the two sides dug in around Kennesaw Mountain, a long ridge over two miles long. On June 27, frustrated with the inactivity, Sherman unwisely attacked the Confederate position. The assault cost Sherman approximately 3,000 men, while the Confederates lost only one-third that number, and convinced him to return to flanking maneuvers that forced Johnston to fall back in order to protect the rail line to Atlanta.

Georgians responded to the threat. Governor Brown called out the militia and ordered it to join Johnston. Atlanta's Mayor James M. Calhoun, watching his city swell from 12,000 to 20,000 with the flood of refugees, asked every able bodied male to take up arms, and in late June Brown requested that President Davis send reinforcements to the city. When Davis refused on the grounds that he had no troops to spare, Brown answered bitterly that there were troops scattered from Pennsylvania to Texas. Nevertheless, when he was unable to secure help from Richmond, Brown issued a proclamation calling for the very young and very old, including teenagers sixteen and seventeen years of age and every man between fifty and fifty-five, to report to Atlanta. Work details composed of impressed slaves built extensive fortifications around the city, and the state militia of around 10,000 men under Major General Gustavus W. Smith, with Robert Toombs as chief-of-staff, moved into the trenches.

As Confederates struggled to make Atlanta impregnable, Sherman ordered part of his cavalry to move around the city, cut the railroad, and advance to the Confederate prison at Andersonville. Brigadier General George Stoneman, with approximately 5,000 men, made it to the Ocmulgee River before encountering serious resistance. At Macon Howell Cobb assembled a force that stopped Stoneman from crossing the river. The Federals turned back, and on July 29, Stoneman and 700 of his men were captured by Confederate cavalry under Brigadier General Alfred Iverson.

One target of Stoneman's raid had been the prison at Andersonville, or Camp Sumter, located in an isolated region of southwestern Georgia northeast of Americus. The first Union captives arrived there in February 1864, and by the time Stoneman tried to liberate them, over 30,000 men crowded an area designed to hold only 10,000. The prison, originally covering 16.5 acres, was enlarged to 26.5 acres in June. Disease, resulting from the poor sanitation caused by overcrowding, took a heavy toll. Moreover, with the need to concentrate available resources on its own armies, the Confederacy was unable to provide sufficient food or medical care. A shortage of clothing magnified by the Confederacy's rapidly weakening economy forced the prisoners to suffer from exposure. Of the 45,000 soldiers confined in Camp Sumter during its fourteen months of operation, almost 13,000 died from various causes. The largest number incarcerated at any one time was 32,000, and that occurred in August. As Sherman neared Atlanta, however, Confederate authorities moved the prisoners to more secure locations.

Sherman outflanked the Confederate army, and by mid-July Johnston abandoned the Chattahoochee line, the last significant Confederate defense before Atlanta. Nevertheless, the city appeared prepared, and Sherman observed: "Atlanta presented a bold front at all points, with fortified lines that defied a direct assault." Johnston, however, gave no indication how he planned to stop Sherman, and a frustrated President Davis removed him from command on July 17. John Bell Hood, who privately had criticized Johnston for his lack of action, was promoted to temporary full general and given the monumental task of stopping Sherman. Known as a fighter, Hood wasted no time in reinforcing this reputation. In scarcely over a week he attacked three times. The first battle came July 20 when he struck Thomas north of the city at Peachtree Creek. Two days later Hood hit east of Atlanta (where McPherson was killed), and finally west of the city at Ezra Church on July 28. Each time Hood was repulsed, and the three battles exhausted his army. Hood lost approximately 12,500 men while Sherman counted half that number.

Sherman then began a forty-day siege of Atlanta, saying that he intended to "make the inside of Atlanta too hot to be endured." A constant bombardment forced the 10,000 people who stayed in the city into cellars and "bombproofs"—holes dug in the ground covered with wooden planks and dirt. On August 9 over 5,000 shells hit Atlanta and killed at least six people. But Sherman, who admitted he was "too impatient for a siege," did not want a military stalemate. Late in August he began a movement around the city to cut the rail lines. This action culminated in a Confederate defeat at the Battle of Jonesboro, and Hood was forced to evacuate Atlanta on September 1. The Union army occupied the city the following day. After Sherman arrived, he informed Mayor Calhoun that all civilians must leave. Hood bitterly accused Sherman of "barbarous cruelty," but between 1,600 and 1,700 residents packed up all the possessions they could cram into wagons and headed for Hood's army at Rough and Ready or destinations to the north.

Governor Brown was angered with the turn of events. No longer willing to assist the Confederate army, he gave the Georgia militia a thirty-day furlough. Sherman, hoping to capitalize on Brown's discontent, began talking with Georgia unionists and even offered to spare the state if Brown would throw his support behind a peace effort. Brown declined, saying he had no authority to discuss such matters, but talk of peace persisted throughout the state and people even held meetings to discuss the possibility. Alarmed by such actions, President Davis traveled to Georgia where he tried to bolster sinking morale in the army and in the state.

After Sherman failed in his efforts to convince Georgians to forsake the Confederacy, he made bold plans to punish the state. In November he gave orders to destroy the railroad depots, warehouses, machine shops, and other public buildings in Atlanta in preparation for a march to the coast. "Unless we can repopulate Georgia, it is useless for us to occupy it," wrote Sherman, "but the utter destruction of its roads, houses and people will cripple their military resources.... I can make the march, and make Georgia howl!" Hood had moved northward into Tennessee, so there was no force opposing Sherman except cavalry under Major General Joseph Wheeler and Gustavus W. Smith's Georgia militia—together they numbered only around 13,000 to Sherman's 60,000. Sherman divided his army into two wings. The right, under Major General Oliver O. Howard, moved through Jonesboro and Gordon with only a feint toward Macon. The left, under Major General Henry W. Slocum, moved by Decatur, Covington, and Madison toward the state capital at Milledgeville. On November 17 Governor Brown told members of the state legislature that Sherman was on his way, then visited the penitentiary, where he offered pardons to all who would join the militia; only four of the 126 prisoners refused. As the Union army approached, residents of the capital fled south along with state officials and legislators. Union soldiers arrived in Milledgeville on November 22 and marched out two days later, but before they left they held a mock session of the legislature in which they nullified the secession ordinance. As Sherman continued his relentless move through the state, it soon became evident that Savannah was his intended target. Major General William Hardee, with approximately 10,000 men, evacuated Savannah on the night of December 20, and Sherman's troops rode into the abandoned city the next day.

Even before the Union army cut a path of destruction across southeastern Georgia, war weariness had spread through the state. Many Georgians claimed that the Union soldiers were no worse than the predatory bands of Confederate deserters and renegades preying on defenseless citizens. In fact, Sherman barely had left Atlanta before predators flocked to the city to join in the plunder. Moreover, guerrilla bands plagued northern Georgia; some preyed on Unionists, others on families with Southern sympathies. Lawlessness became so widespread that some families were forced to leave their homes. Wheeler's cavalry came in for its share of criticism, and Kate Cummings wrote from northern Georgia: "Our Cavalry behave very badly, taking everything they can lay their hands on." Even after the Southern cavalry had left the area, mounted deserters claiming to be Texans terrorized civilians.

By the time Sherman left Savannah for his march through the Carolinas early in 1865, Georgia was in a state of frantic disorder, and many people clamored for peace. Food riots increased, and inflation was rampant; one Columbus woman saw her rent rise from $800 in 1864 to $3,000 in 1865. In mid-April Major General James H. Wilson and 13,000 Union cavalrymen cut into Georgia, captured Columbus, then moved on to Macon. Howell Cobb surrendered that city on April 20. Georgians were tired of war, and early in May Governor Brown likewise surrendered to Wilson.

As the Confederacy began to dissolve, President Davis and his entourage left Richmond for the Trans-Mississippi where he hoped to join the forces of General Edmund Kirby Smith. Davis was captured at Irwinville in southwestern Georgia on May 10, and transported to Augusta where he was incarcerated with Vice-President Stephens. Governor Brown, Benjamin Hill, and Howell Cobb also were imprisoned briefly, but Toombs escaped to Europe. Only Henry Wirz, the commandant at Andersonville, was punished by an angry northern public; he was executed for war crimes in November. Radical determination to find a scapegoat was perhaps influenced by the actions of Clara Barton, who worked at the prison throughout the summer identifying and marking the graves of the Union dead.

The Confederate government had collapsed, but in the last months of 1865 few Georgians worried about its replacement. While Sherman's march had left the region physically impoverished, the psychological damage that came with the Union armies had rapidly spread statewide. Disorder prevailed as army stragglers and local looters pillaged at will. Citizens in Augusta rioted when bread became difficult to buy, and the U.S. Army had to move into Wilkes County to restore order. But Georgians refused to accept the inevitable, and in November the state legislature selected Alexander H. Stephens, the former Confederate vice-president, and Herschel V. Johnson, a former Confederate senator, as United States senators. Their rejection in Washington left Georgians bitter; Stephens eventually would become governor, as would former Confederate generals Alfred Holt Colquitt and John B. Gordon. In fact, the so-called "Bourbon Triumvirate" of Colquitt, Gordon, and the indefatigable Joseph E. Brown, proved a strong influence in the postwar years. Nonetheless, when the capital moved to Atlanta in 1868, businessmen, industrialists, and large farmers replaced *antebellum* planters and lawyers on the political scene, and the city began to recover from wartime destruction. When Margaret Mitchell wrote *Gone With the Wind* at her Atlanta home in 1936, she may have exaggerated the genteel life of the plantation aristocracy and embroidered the worse aspects of Reconstruction, but she ably conveyed the dramatic changes that the war brought to Georgia and the legacy of bitterness it left behind.

SUGGESTED READING

T. Conn Bryan, *Confederate Georgia* (University of Georgia Press: Athens, 1953).

Albert Castel, *Decision in the West: The Atlanta Campaign of 1864* (University Press of Kansas: Lawrence, 1992).

Peter Cozzens, *This Terrible Sound: The Battle of Chickamauga* (University of Illinois Press: Urbana, 1992).

Mary A. DeCredico, *Patriotism for Profit: Georgia's Urban Entrepreneurs and the Confederate War Effort* (University of North Carolina Press: Chapel Hill, 1990).

Joseph T. Glatthaar, *The March to the Sea and Beyond: Sherman's Troops in the Georgia and Carolina Campaigns* (New York University Press: New York and London, 1985).

A. A. Hoehling, *Last Train from Atlanta* (Thomas Yoseloff: New York and London, 1958).

Michael P. Johnson, *Toward a Patriarchal Republic: The Secession of Georgia* (Louisiana State University Press: Baton Rouge, 1977).

James P. Jones, *Yankee Blitzkrieg: Wilson's Raid Through Alabama and Georgia* (University of Georgia Press: Athens, 1976).

Robert Manson Myers, ed., *The Children of Pride: A True Story of Georgia and the Civil War* (Yale University Press: New Haven, 1972).

Joseph H. Parks, *Joseph E. Brown of Georgia* (Louisiana State University Press: Baton Rouge, 1977).

Thomas E. Schott, *Alexander H. Stephens of Georgia: A Biography* (Louisiana State University Press: Baton Rouge, 1988).

Richard M. McMurry, "The Atlanta Campaign: December 23, 1863 to July 18, 1864" (doctoral dissertation, Emory University, 1967).

Errol McGregor Clauss, "The Atlanta Campaign, 18 July-2 September 1864" (doctoral dissertation, Emory University, 1965).

TEXAS

by
Archie P. McDonald

Union with the United States lost its luster for many Texans during the decade of the 1850s. Against the backdrop of such separating wedges as disagreement with the enforcement of the Compromise of 1850 and resulting disenchantment over their loss of so much western land, the strident activity of abolitionists, and especially the violence in Kansas, many Texans reflected their Southern heritage by affirming their belief in state's rights, especially as that related to slavery, and their acceptance of the principle of secession as the ultimate expression of that right. Hardin R. Runnells' victory over Sam Houston in the governor's race in 1857 can be traced to this feeling, but Houston's victory in 1859 came despite it. The legislature's selection of Louis T. Wigfall, an ardent fire eater and secession advocate, to Houston's seat in the Senate signifies the mood of the majority more than does the election of Old Sam to the governorship. He won that office with hard campaigning which invoked memories of his past leadership, but he never masked his true feelings — he was first and last a Union man.

The presidential election of 1860 crystallized Texans into a secession posture. Texas delegates to the Democratic convention in Charleston, South Carolina, including Runnells, Francis R. Lubbock, Guy M. Bryan, R. B. Hubbard, and Tom Ochiltree, joined other Southerners in a demand for a party platform embracing slavery and opposing Stephen A. Douglas' majority position on popular sovereignty. Since the Dred Scott decision confirmed the right of slave owners to take their property into the territories, Southerners assumed that slavery should be secured forever. But the election of 1860 alarmed them; the prospect of a victory by the new and radical Republican Party, a single-issue group demanding an end to slavery in the territories and eventually an end to it in the states, seemed real. Douglas was nominated by the mainstream Democrats at a second convention in Baltimore, and John Cabell Breckenridge of Kentucky received the nomination of still another group of Democrats meeting at Richmond, Virginia. Most Texans supported Breckenridge and joined other Southerners in the threat to leave the Union in the event of a victory by the Republican Party and its nominee, Abraham Lincoln.

The Constitutional Union Party entered the contest, hoping to block an electoral majority and force the election into the House of representatives where a compromise candidate might be selected. Sam Houston tried for the nomination of this party and outdrew Bell on the first ballot, fifty-seven to 68.5 votes, and when John Bell of Tennessee was nominated, he even thought of running as an independent candidate but finally decided against such a move. In November, Texans voted for Breckenridge by a margin of three to one, emphasizing the secessionists' threat to leave the Union in the event of a Lincoln victory. Breckenridge received 47,548 votes to Bell's 15,463; Douglas received only 410 votes. Lincoln's name was not on the Texas ballot.

In response to the election, South Carolina made good its threat to secede from the American Union on December 20. Georgia, Florida, Alabama, Mississippi, and Louisiana followed by the end of January, and Texas was expected to become the seventh state to secede. It did so over the political corpse of Sam Houston.

Houston attempted to ignore the popular clamor for a secession convention that began as soon as news of South Carolina's action reached the state. When secessionist leaders became convinced that Houston would not call the legislature to consider withdrawal from the Union, they usurped his powers by calling for elections within each judicial district on January 8, 1861, to select delegates for an *ad hoc* secession convention. Houston then summoned the legislature into session, hoping to steal the thunder of the secessionists. His legislature would meet on January 21, a week before the convention's delegates met on January 28. Houston hoped the legislature would prevent the convention from gathering, but many legislators were also members of the convention, and a majority of the remainder endorsed it.

The convention met in Austin on January 28. Delegates elected Oran M. Roberts to preside, and on the second day they voted 152 to six to separate Texas from the Union, subject to popular approval. They later approved a resolution on February 1 that disavowed the action of the legislature in 1845 accepting membership in the Union. They submitted the resolution to the voters for approval in an election to be held on February 23.

The vote on February 1 was conducted in a tense session, and when J. W. Throckmorton cast a negative vote, hisses and boos rained from the gallery. Throckmorton's courageous response, "Mr. President, when the rabble hiss, well may patriots tremble," gave testimony that Houston did not stand completely alone.

The convention's declaration of causes for its action for the people's consideration included criticism of the government's administration of commonly held territories to the exclusion of Southerners, provocative activity in Kansas, failure to protect Texans from the Indians adequately, Northern hostility to the South and its systems (slavery), the South's minority status within the Union, and the election of a president committed to the elimination of slavery. With these considerations, the convention adjourned until March 2 to await the result of the election.

The argument between secessionists and unionists was bitter. The *Galveston News* and the *Texas Republican* backed the secessionists, while the *Southerner Intelligencer* and the *Bastrop Advertiser* attacked them, but the outcome was inevitable: 46,129 in support of secession, with only 14,697 opposed. Ten central Texas counties, a few in north Texas along the Red River, and Angelina County in East Texas, isolated in a sea of secessionism, voted no. Every other county voted affirmatively.

The convention met again in Austin on March 2, Texas Independence Day, and within three days confirmed not only separation from the Union, but also Texas' affiliation with the Confederate States of America, newly organized at Montgomery, Alabama. The Texas convention had sent unofficial delegates to the Montgomery meeting, and when official word of the secession vote arrived from Texas, the Confederate group voted their acceptance even before a formal request for admission was received.

The convention's work continued. On March 16, they summoned all elected officials to take an oath of loyalty to the new government. Houston agonized the entire night of March 15, and the next day, although present in the capitol, sat silently and heard his name called three times to take the oath, then heard his office vacated and his lieutenant governor, Edward Clark, sworn in to complete his term. Lincoln had offered Houston the use of 2,700 Federal troops in Texas under the command of General David Twiggs, but Houston refused. He had fought for Texas, he stated, and even when Texas was wrong, he would not fight against her. This romantic pledge paralleled a more substantial reason—Houston's desire to avoid bloodshed.

The presence of Twiggs' command bothered many Texans, and they made an immediate demand for the Union commander to surrender his troops and all Federal property. Twiggs sympathized with the secessionists, but he tried to avoid betraying his oath to the United States by resignation. Before Twiggs was relieved, Ben McCulloch led an armed group to army headquarters in San Antonio and demanded surrender. Twiggs complied to avoid a fight, and his entire command, representing more than ten percent of all Union forces at the time, in effect became prisoners of war, although war did not then technically exist. Most were exchanged before the war began in earnest.

The convention also prepared for elections under Confederate statehood. Party activity, present but weak in the 1850s, ceased; the secessionists controlled the state's affairs completely. Francis R. Lubbock defeated Edward Clark by only 124 votes to become Texas' first Confederate governor, and John M. Crockett, mayor of Dallas, won the lieutenant governor's post.

Lubbock's administration supported the Confederate government enthusiastically, but he left after only one term to serve President Jefferson Davis in other capacities. His successor was Pendleton Murrah of Harrison County, who defeated T. J. Chambers by 17,501 to 12,455 votes in 1863. John Henry Reagan became Texas' highest ranking Confederate civilian official when he received appointment as postmaster general in Davis' cabinet. Louis T. Wigfall and W. S. Oldham represented Texas in the Confederate Senate.

Lubbock's job became largely the work of continuing domestic policies of the Houston-Clark administrations where war conditions permitted, and grappling with new difficulties posed by the conflict. He supported the war effort and the Confederate administration without reservation, organized home guards to fight against Indians on the frontier, mustered soldiers for fighting outside the state, and mobilized the legislature to provide for the state's needs. Through a Military Board, consisting of the governor, comptroller, and treasurer, Lubbock tried to establish a proper priority: win the war without undue domestic suffering. The Board attempted to dispose of bonds of the United States held in Texas to purchase needed military supplies; they also suspended debtor laws because so many of the state's workers served in the military, raised local revenue for the support of the military units in the field, and expended Confederate treasury warrants on state needs.

Murrah inherited a working state government, but one that suffered the same decline as did its parent government. Lubbock's administration had doubled state taxes, a heavy blow since so many taxes had been remanded during the 1850s, but still the war demanded more revenue, and needy families of soldiers also increased their demands on the government. Cotton cards were purchased by the state as a relief measure for homemakers to card, spin, and weave their own cloth. A portion of local tax revenues was designated for the relief of the destitute. Murrah remained a thorough Confederate until the end of the war and he presided over the steady decline of the economic productivity of his state while the public debt increased. War's end coincided with a near-collapse of the state's economy.

Texas performed much better in fielding men for military service. Lubbock organized military districts and organized the militia for action under the state's initial commander, General Earl Van Dorn. General Paul Octave Hebert soon replaced Van Dorn and was himself replaced in November 1862, following a dispute over the conscription laws, by General John Bankhead Magruder. Texas had no need for conscription in 1861. The census of 1860 revealed over 90,000 men between the ages of eighteen and forty-five, and of these an estimated 60,000 to 70,000 served in the military. Over 20,000 volunteered in the first year of the war. Usually a person of wealth organized a unit, financed its first operation, and often was elected as its initial commander. Later conscription added increased numbers of Texans to the army. The first draft selected men between the ages of eighteen and thirty-five, but this was later expanded to include youths of seventeen and older men of forty-five and fifty. Texas' most prominent soldier, Albert Sidney Johnston, commanded the Western Theatre of the Confederate Army until his death at the battle of Shiloh in April 1862. Other general officers from Texas included Felix Huston Robertson, the only native-born Texan to achieve such rank.

Most Texans served outside the state. Lubbock raised thirty-two companies in 1862, calling them the Texas Brigade. They were joined by their first commander, John Bell Hood of Kentucky, later supplemented with units from Arkansas and North Carolina, and fought principally in the Eastern Theatre under the command of Robert E. Lee. "My Texans," as Lee called them, learned that his affection often placed them at the center of his battles. Over 4,000 men served in the unit, but less than 700 survived the war. Another notable unit, Terry's Texas Rangers, commanded by General B. F. Terry, fought primarily in the Western Theatre. And Lawrence Sullivan Ross' Brigade, organized later in the war, fought in the Western Theatre and in the Trans-Mississippi Department. This department was created in 1863 to provide a separate military organization for the area after the Union regained control of the Mississippi River, thus separating the far west of the Confederacy from its political and economic control center. General Edmund Kirby Smith commanded the Trans-Mississippi Department, including Texas, until the end of the war.

No major battles occurred within Texas, but many significant actions were fought along its borders. As early as May 1861, W. C. Young led volunteers from the Red River country into Oklahoma to attack Forts Arbuckle, Cobb, and Washita. In August, John R. Baylor led a group into southern New Mexico and proclaimed the territory as far west as Tucson as the Confederate territory of Arizona with himself as governor. And General H. H. Sibley, with General Tom Green along, successfully attacked Valverde with a force of nearly 4,000 men on February 2, 1862. In March, he met Union forces under Edward R. Canby at Glorietta and was repulsed. This effectively saved New Mexico and Arizona from all Confederate encroachment.

The Federal blockade became effective on the Texas coast in July 1861, and Union forces occupied Galveston in October 1862. Magruder attacked them on January 1, 1863, from a troop concentration at Virginia Point and with men on two flat-bottomed riverboats with cotton bales lining the decks for protection. He succeeded in retaking the island, and the Confederate Texans held it until 1865.

Texas' most memorable battle occurred at Sabine Pass, a narrow inlet from the Gulf of Mexico to Sabine Lake, a saltwater impoundment that received the waters of the Sabine and Neches rivers. Both rivers were navigable to rail lines. In September 1862, Federal naval personnel forced the Confederates to abandon Sabine Pass, but it was soon reoccupied by an artillery battery commanded by Lieutenant Dick Dowling, a Houston saloon keeper. When General Nathaniel Banks attempted to send 17 naval vessels and a force of over 1,500 soldiers through Sabine Pass to attack the interior on September 8, 1863, Dowling's guns disabled two vessels in the main channel, blocking the way for the remainder of the ships and preventing the disembarking of the Union soldiers. The battle of Sabine Pass was hailed by Jefferson Davis as the most significant action of the war at a time when he hungered for good news after defeats at Vicksburg and Gettysburg. The battle did have a negative effect on American credit in England.

Banks was more successful elsewhere. His forces succeeded in capturing or controlling every port from the Rio Grande to just below Galveston, including Corpus Christi, Aransas Pass, and Indianola.

Banks' last attempt to invade Texas occurred in 1864. He ascended the Red River, intending to rendezvous with forces under General Frederick Steele from Little Rock to capture North Texas. Steele was repulsed by Confederates under Van Dorn, and General Richard Taylor stopped Banks at Mansfield, Louisiana. Some East Texans fought in this action as civilians, some with pikes and clubs, to prevent the invasion of their state.

In a final action, John S. Ford led forces against black Union soldiers at Palmito Ranch near Brownsville in May 1865, nearly a month after most other Confederate forces had surrendered.

Serious fighting took place between the Texans and Indians. Texans expected the Confederate army to police Indians as the American army had before the war, but the high command in far off Virginia had too many Union soldiers on their hands to worry about Texas Indians. Governor Lubbock organized state troops under James M. Norris for this service. Norris attempted regular patrols in the Indian country, but these proved easy for the Indians to evade, so his successor, J. E.

McCord, substituted irregular scouting expeditions. As men organized for Indian service, they were repeatedly transferred to the regular army and service outside the state. Finally, J. W. Throckmorton organized a force which included many like himself who would fight Indians but not Union soldiers. The most significant Indian action was at Adobe Walls, where Union and Confederate soldiers combined to fight Comanches, and the most unsuccessful occurred at Dove Creek in January 1864, when 370 state troops attacked 1,400 Kickapoo enroute to Mexico from Indian Territory. The Texans' heavy losses made them regret the attack.

Texans who remained at home did not suffer the ravages of war as did their fellow Confederates in Virginia and Tennessee; still, they had problems. Some Texans did not like the Confederate affiliation. Some, like Houston, remained relatively quiet; others, such as financier S. M. Swenson, left the state, depriving Texas of needed leadership both during and after the war; and some, such as E. J. Davis, organized Union forces to fight in Texas. Many Germans disliked the Confederacy because they favored Union nationalism and disliked slavery; often they refused to volunteer or to be conscripted, and some tried to escape to Mexico. One such group was apprehended and massacred. Other Germans did serve in the Confederate army. In 1862 a Peace Party, a secret society, was organized in northern Texas. It aroused fear in loyal Confederates who hanged over forty Peace Party members at Gainesville and other places. In 1864 the area also became a gathering place for army deserters and ne'er-do-wells and posed a police problem for the state.

In 1863 a conference of western state representatives at Marshall produced a plan to exchange Confederate cotton in Mexico for needed war materials. The plan called for the Confederate government to take over the trade by purchasing half of each planter's cotton and exempting the rest from impressment, to make sure the South's major economic resource would contribute to the war effort. Murrah's government devised an alternate "state plan," which called for the Texas government to transport cotton to the border, return half to the owner, and secure the remainder with state bonds. The Confederate Congress pre-empted the state's power in this area with a specific act, irritating some Texans.

Cotton production declined steadily during the war years as more and more men entered the military services. Women, minors, draft exemptors, and some objectors continued to work and produce as best they could. But as state revenue dwindled, and Confederate currency inflated, their lot was often difficult. Such necessities as salt became scarce, and people had to return to their pioneer ways to survive. They used corncob ashes as a substitute for soda; parched rye, okra, or acorns for coffee; and they made their own cloth. Murrah was inaugurated in a homespun suit partially to indicate its acceptability and partially because of availability. And paper grew scarce, forcing some newspapers to cease operations.

Texas had little industry before the war but developed it from necessity. Arms works were established at Austin, and Tyler; Marshall supported new factories; iron works functioned in East Texas; and the state penitentiary became a leading producer of cloth.

Texas became a haven for refugees from other Southern states and a shipping point for slaves whose owners sought to move them from threatened territory. Both migrations provided additional problems for the Texans, and many immigrants were not happy with their new home. Kate Stone, of Brokenburn Plantation in Louisiana, came to Tyler during the Vicksburg campaign and called her haven "the dark corner of the Confederacy." This assessment is perhaps too harsh; Texas functioned well considering its many difficulties, but its war problems were only preliminaries for greater difficulties during Reconstruction.

The war ended for Texans at different times. For the survivors of Hood's Brigade and other Texans in the Army of Northern Virginia, the end came with Lee's surrender to General U. S. Grant at Appomattox on April 9, 1865; for Terry's Texas Rangers and others with the Army of Tennessee, it concluded with General J. E. Johnston's surrender to General William T. Sherman at Bentonville, North Carolina, on April 19; and General Edmund Kirby Smith surrendered the Department of the Trans-Mississippi, including Texas, on June 2. But for most Texans, the day to remember was June 19. On that day, General Gordon Granger arrived in Galveston with 1,800 Federal troops to declare the war at an end and all war proclamations, including the end of African slavery, in effect. White and black Texans would one day view this as a day of liberation, but for decades most whites seethed with resentment and most blacks did not understand fully what it meant or have an opportunity to exercise their freedom. In time it became a day of celebration for blacks, a kind of Fourth-of-July of their own that has expanded to other states.

Texans had worked hard to join the Union during the period of the Republic of Texas, and just as eagerly attempted to leave it with sister Southern states in 1861. After four years of war, which cost the state much of its investment capital and human resources, Texans, like the citizens of other seceding states, found it necessary to acknowledge the error of their political and social ways and be pardoned, hat in hand, back into the Union of the United States. The cost of secession and affiliation with the Confederacy was high, but in the end Texas returned to the Union that Sam Houston and others had tried to convince them never to leave. Texas and the other states, North and South, grew stronger and better for the sacrifice, though the war-time and Reconstruction generations who mostly suffered it might have thought otherwise.

This paper was drafted from previous publications by the author, including a newspaper supplement that appeared in the *Dallas Times- Herald* on March 7, 1982, and in *Texas: All Hail The Mighty State,* published by Eakin Press of Austin, Texas, in 1983 and revised in 1991. Portions were presented to the Deep Delta Civil War Symposium in Hammond, Louisiana, in June 1990, and appeared in the *Journal of Confederate History*, VII (Southern Heritage Press: Murfreesboro, TN, 1991), pp. 33-50.

SUGGESTED READING

Walter L. Buenger, *Secession and the Union in Texas* (University of Texas Press: Austin, 1984).

James Alex Baggett, "The Constitutional Union Party in Texas" *Southwestern Historical Quarterly*, 82 (January 1979), pp. 233-264.

Robin E. Baker and Dale Baum, "The Texas Voter and the Crisis of the Union, 1859-1861" *Journal of Southern History*, (August 1987), pp. 395-420.

Walter L. Buenger, "Texas and the Riddle of Secession" *Southwestern Historical Quarterly*, 87 (October 1983), pp. 151-182.

James A. Marten, *Texas Divided: Loyalty and Dissent in the Lone Star State* (University of Kentucky Press: Lexington, 1990).

Anna Irene Sandbo, "Beginnings of the Secession Movement in Texas" *Southwestern Historical Quarterly*, 18 (October 1914), pp. 41-73.

Joe E. Timmons, "The Referendum in Texas on the Ordinance of Secession, February 23, 1861: The Vote" *East Texas Historical Journal*, (Fall 1973), pp. 12-28.

Joe T. Timmons, "Texas on the Road to Secession" (doctoral dissertation, University of Chicago, 1973).

Billy Don Ledbetter, "Slavery, Fear, and Disunion in the Lone Star S t a t e : Texans' Attitude Toward Secession and the Union, 1846-1861" (doctoral dissertation, North Texas State University, 1972).

Robert K. Peters, "Texas: Annexation to Secession" (doctoral dissertation, University of Texas, 1977).

VIRGINIA

by
Brandon Beck

The walls of Richmond's Battle Abbey glow with the heroic mural paintings known as "The Four Seasons of the Confederacy." Virginians endured all the war's seasons, contributing greatly, suffering much, and surviving final defeat.

The most northerly of the Confederate states, Virginia was among the last to secede, hesitating on the edge until April 17, 1861. In the end, ties with the deeper South pulled the Old Dominion out of the old Union. Once in the Confederacy, its geography and resources destined Virginia as a battleground for the duration of the conflict. The long familiar names of battlefields, railroad junctions, rivers, and entire areas of the state still evoke instant and emotional memories. Virginia provided sixty-three regiments of infantry, twenty-six of cavalry and many batteries of artillery to the Confederate military. Today, stone soldiers and iron markers stand across the state on the sites of what James Robertson has called "the bitterest and bloodiest fighting in the history of the Western hemisphere."

Virginia was the most populous Confederate state, both in white inhabitants and slaves, and its secession broadened the expanse of the Confederacy from the Atlantic to the Ohio. Even with the loss of the western counties and the formation of the separate state of West Virginia, Virginia's inclusion, with Tennessee, meant that the Confederacy's northern frontier stretched from the Tidewater to the Mississippi. Within her borders, but mostly in central and eastern Virginia, ran close to one fifth of all Confederate railway mileage. The state's modest industry produced more than one third of the iron manufactured in the Confederacy. Richard McMurry has pointed out that Virginia's iron production had increased by 194% in the decade *before* secession. Also, late in the decade, the General Assembly followed the lead of Governor Henry A. Wise and provided large sums for the state militia, further burnishing what was "certainly the strongest military tradition of any southern state."

Although Wise was an ardent "champion of southern rights," pro-secession sentiment grew slowly in Virginia. John Brown's raid on Harpers Ferry in 1859, on slavery's border, recalled Nat Turner's Rebellion only twenty-eight years earlier. In October 1859, however, most Virginians were satisfied with the Federal government's swift reaction. Brown's capture and trial on charges of treason against Virginia led to his hanging on December 2. In the presidential election held the following year, Virginia, with Kentucky and Tennessee, supported the moderate Constitutional Union Party's candidate, John Bell. While sentiment for secession was strong enough for the state to call elections to a secession convention, in February 1861, newly elected Governor John Letcher helped organize the Washington Peace Commission (February 4-27). Daniel Crofts has shown that in the convention, secessionists won majorities only in "high slaveholding Democratic counties." In the case of Virginia, Letcher Moderates outnumbered secessionists in the convention by 106 to forty-six. The convention deliberated during March and early April until on April 13, guns in Richmond boomed the state's salute to General P. G. T. Beauregard and South Carolina. On April 17, after President Abraham Lincoln's call for volunteers, Virginia committed herself to Southern independence: the convention passed an ordinance of secession by a vote of eighty-eight to fifty-five. Simultaneously, the plans of former Governor Henry Wise to seize both Harpers Ferry and the Gosport (Norfolk) Navy Yard were executed successfully.

On May 23 Governor Letcher appointed Robert E. Lee commander of Virginia's armed forces. Virginia voters, meantime, approved the convention's ordinance of secession by a margin of 128,884 to 32,134.

In the next weeks Virginia lost effective political control of fifty of its most westerly counties, where opposition to secession predominated. In no county west of Frederick, located in the Lower Valley, were either slavery or secession of political significance. While western Virginians served in both armies, the loss of these counties was almost foregone. They joined the Union as West Virginia in 1863.

Beyond the Blue Ridge, in a different political and military world, Richmond became the capital of the Confederacy in May 1861. The transfer from Montgomery, Alabama, was the result of negotiations begun while Virginia remained in the Union. It was a bold, even defiant step, and one much criticized later.

Robert E. Lee's responsibilities in the spring of 1861 were vast. Douglas Southall Freeman enumerated them as: (1) finding a means to neutralize Federal sea power at the mouths of Virginia's rivers; (2) occupying Norfolk and Harpers Ferry, and making the best use of the navy yard, arsenal, the B & O Railroad, and the C & O Canal; (3) finding capable officers for field commands; (4) assembling a staff; (5) mobilizing and training the militia and new recruits; (6) finding arms and equipment for the men; and (7) placing state forces at the most threatened points on Virginia's borders, particularly at Manassas, at the junction of the Orange and Alexandria and Manassas Gap railroads. An additional task would be to transfer Virginia's forces into those of the Confederacy. On May 10 the Confederate Congress placed Lee in charge of all Confederate forces in Virginia. The transfer to Confederate authority went smoothly early in June. Virginia was the first state to make this transition. Lee, by then a brigadier general in the Confederate Army, placed forces at Manassas, Harpers Ferry, and Norfolk. Lee understood that Virginia's role might well determine the outcome of the war, and was concerned with the danger and the opportunity in the southeast, the northeast, and in the Lower Valley of the state. In the southeast, Norfolk and Gosport were almost indefensible with the Union navy in Hampton Roads, and fell in May 1862. In the northwest, Harpers Ferry was dominated by Maryland Heights, Loudoun Heights, and Bolivar Heights and scarcely could be defended. Joseph E. Johnston, Valley District commander, abandoned the town in June 1861 in favor of Winchester. Its proximity to Manassas, by way of the Manassas Gap Railroad at Piedmont Station, meant that Confederates could move quickly from the Valley across the Blue Ridge and Bull Run Mountains down to Manassas. Johnston's ability to reinforce Beauregard at Manassas along this internal line of communication underlay the great Confederate victory on the Henry House Hill on July 21.

War came late to Virginia in 1861 and its stay was short; east of the mountains, the state seemed little touched by the war. In 1862, by contrast, war's season commenced with an early spring and gained in ferocity throughout the summer. Increasing in August, the war returned to Manassas, by way of Culpeper Court House and Cedar Mountain, before it crested beyond Virginia's borders in September. It subsided only in the last frozen days of the year at Fredericksburg.

In the spring of 1862 it was evident that Virginia's defenses lay well behind her frontiers. The new Federal commander, George B. McClellan, who earlier had detached northwestern Virginia from the Confederacy, now sought to approach Richmond from the far southeast. On March 17 he began to transfer his force of about 100,000 men to the tip of the peninsula formed by the James and York rivers. The beginning of his Peninsula Campaign meant that neither Manassas nor Winchester could be held.

Winchester was the key to the Lower Shenandoah Valley. Through it ran the macadamized Valley Pike leading north to the Potomac River at Williamsport. Rich in grain as well as in strategic options, and linked by rail to the east at Staunton and Lynchburg, the Valley of Virginia paid rich dividends to the Confederacy until 1864. Well could General T. J. Jackson say in 1862, that "if the Valley is lost, Virginia is lost." Compelled to withdraw from Winchester on March 12, and then defeated just above Winchester at Kernstown on March 23, Stonewall Jackson could as yet do little for the Valley of Virginia. Johnston evacuated Manassas and arrived at Yorktown on April 10. There he contained McClellan until May. On May 9, however, Norfolk was abandoned, forcing the Confederates to scuttle the ironclad *CSS Virginia*, opening the James to Federal gunboats as far as Drewry's Bluff. By mid-May the question had arisen of whether even Richmond could be held. Johnston thought it might be, but only if the Confederates continued to concentrate most of their forces there. Lee, now Confederate President Jefferson Davis' primary military advisor, disagreed. In the next weeks his tact, deference, and strategic vision, combined with McClellan's own weaknesses and hesitancies, cleared the way for Jackson's brilliant diversionary campaign in the Shenandoah Valley. Jackson's impressive victory at the first battle of Winchester on May 25 meant that the reinforcements McClellan expected and believed he needed never came. Instead General Irvin McDowell's corps initially was held at Fredericksburg and then sent west—to the Valley. Jackson soon joined Lee, in command at Richmond after May 31, for the Seven Days battles.

Freeman believed that at no time before Five Forks, in 1865, were Union forces closer to decisive victory in Virginia than in the spring of 1862. Between March and early July 1862, however, Lee and Jackson saved the Confederacy by their bold actions. James McPherson has observed a great historical irony in the emergence of the partnership between Lee and Jackson: the Confederacy would survive—until 1865, when a vastly different Union had come into being.

The terrific bloodshed in Virginia in 1862 surpassed anything in previous American history. The Seven Days battles made the battles of 1861 seem small by comparison. McPherson has pointed out that the casualties for the Seven Days battles—30,000 killed and wounded—equaled those of *all* battles in the Confederate west for the first half of 1862.

Virginia's greatest defensive asset, her southeastward flowing rivers, had not yet figured in heavy fighting, but it was clear that Lee could not yet stand on the defensive in Virginia. Instead, the Union's newly created Army of Virginia was already in position south of Manassas and east of the Blue Ridge to threaten the important railroad junction at Gordonsville. It was imperative for Lee to destroy this threat to his communications with central Virginia before McClellan's force could be moved from its base on the James and combined with General John Pope's new command. With both Gordonsville and Manassas under their control, the Federals could force a passage over the Rappahannock upstream from Fredericksburg without fear of any Confederate diversion in the Valley.

On July 12, Lee sent Jackson's two divisions to hold Gordonsville. The Second Manassas Campaign (August 26-September 1) which followed, stands out as Lee's greatest strategic masterpiece. With McClellan in transit away from Richmond to the Potomac, Jackson was able to check Pope's vanguard under General N. P. Banks on August 9 at Cedar Mountain. Four days later Lee put James Longstreet's wing of his army in motion to combine forces with Jackson in the heavily wooded country north and west of Gordonsville. If Pope could be trapped in the angle formed by the confluence of the Rappahannock and Rapidan rivers west of Rappahannock Station on the Orange and Alexandria Railroad, he might be annihilated. When Pope retreated north of the river on August 24, however, Lee divided his forces again, sending Jackson up stream to cross and disappear behind the Bull Run Mountains. Jackson reached the Manassas Gap Railroad at Salem and marched east through Thoroughfare Gap to reach Pope's base of supplies at Manassas Junction. Longstreet joined Jackson north and west of Manassas Junction on August 29, to crush Pope on August 30.

The great victory of Second Manassas, won at a cost of some 9,000 casualties, took the strategic initiative away from the Federals. The resulting military, political, and diplomatic situation yields the second great irony of 1862: in the aftermath of victory, with the strategic initiative now Lee's, there were as many justifications for a defensive strategy in Virginia as for an offensive beyond the Potomac. Losses, even in victory, had been particularly high among divisional and brigadier generals and company- and field-grade officers. Lee, it must be remembered, had replaced Johnston only three months previously, and the army could not yet be said to have been Lee's "own." The army was close to exhaustion, and straggling might cripple its strength.

Yet, as Confederates in the west eyed Kentucky, Lee looked to Maryland. From there Lee believed operations against Harrisburg or points farther north beckoned. If a battle were to be fought in Maryland, Lee would fight on ground of his own choosing, well to the west of Washington and close to his own line of communication with the Valley. Most compelling of all, however, and finally decisive, was the opportunity to draw the war away from Virginia and to reinforce and provision his army beyond the Potomac in a state thought to have strong Confederate sympathies. Whether the Confederate crossing became an invasion or a great "raid" would depend on the Federal response. In either case, the necessity of feeding the army in Maryland as crops were harvested in Virginia was paramount in Lee's mind. He crossed over at White's Ford, above Leesburg, on September 4-5, 1862.

The days in Maryland were few, crowded with the occupation of Frederick, the loss of General Orders #191, the battle of South Mountain, the fall of Harpers Ferry, and the battle of Sharpsburg (Antietam). The preliminary draft of the Emancipation Proclamation soon followed. Justifiably, Lee regarded the drawn battle of Sharpsburg as his soldiers' most heroic fight, but there was no further thought of "Maryland, My Maryland" as the army returned to Virginia. The stakes of war had changed.

War returned to Virginia as the old year ran to its end. The third Union "on to Richmond" offensive receded in blood on the slopes of Marye's Heights at Fredericksburg. The bloody repulse of General Ambrose Burnside on the high south bank of the Rappahannock River produced a tragically ironic end to the grim year of war in Virginia. Burnside missed the chance to cross the Rappahannock unopposed on November 17, and so gave the Confederates time to concentrate in an ideal defensive position. Nevertheless, Stonewall Jackson would have preferred that the army fall back to the North Anna, where a victory might have led to Burnside's annihilation.

The Confederates could not follow up their victory. Protected from Confederate counter-attack by artillery posted on Stafford Heights along the north bank of the Rappahannock, Burnside could not be destroyed. The most significant result of the battle was its impact on Confederate morale: after the near defeat and terrible losses in the rolling, smoky terrain of Sharpsburg, victory at Fredericksburg was practically inevitable. A sergeant serving in the Third Arkansas, C. S. Pruit, wrote to a lady friend in Winchester: "Gen. Lee informed [Burnside] if he crossed the river he would give them a whipping this is what you may rest assured will be there (sic) fate." Moreover, the victory was stunningly visible to every soldier in Lee's Army. The army was now Lee's "own." Sergeant Pruit added, "we will not stay here long if B's crossed over we will fight him out and then go somewhere else. I am proud to say that all of our troops are well clothed and fit for this winter."

The summer of 1863 was the most decisive season and dramatic period in Civil War history. For the Army of Northern Virginia the year began with its greatest victory at Chancellorsville and ended in the fall with two of its divisions serving in Tennessee during the Army of Tennessee's great victory at Chickamauga. But between the victories came the death of Jackson and the battle of Gettysburg. A new "on to Richmond" drive had begun in April under a new Federal commander, General Joseph "Fighting Joe" Hooker. Hooker crossed the Rappahannock above Fredericksburg beyond Lee's left, into the "Wilderness," an aptly named region stretching away from the Rappahannock down to Culpeper Court House. Its forests fed the furnaces of the local ironworks, and the Wilderness of 1863 was a boggy and dimly lit jungle of nearly impenetrable second growth. The cross roads of Chancellorsville lent its name to the smashing defeat of Hooker on May 2-3. Three scenes from the battle became permanently etched in the mind of Confederate Virginia; the last meeting between Lee and Jackson on May 1; the wounding of Jackson on May 2; and General Lee on Traveller, riding into the Chancellorsville clearing at dusk on May 3. The clearing was crowded with exultant soldiers, illuminated by the blazing inn and ringed with the darkening wilderness. Once again, however, the defeated Federals escaped total destruction. Confederate losses had been high, and this time they included Jackson. "Mighty Stonewall" died on May 10.

The strategic initiative again lay with Lee. There was opportunity either to reinforce Confederate forces in Tennessee or Mississippi, or as Lee argued in Richmond in mid-May, to strike a decisive blow beyond the Potomac. In 1862 the Confederates had advanced simultaneously into Maryland and Kentucky. The situation in 1863 was much less promising, with both Vicksburg and Chattanooga endangered. General Lee believed that an invasion of the North from Virginia could alter the strategic balance and transform the entire war. On June 3 the Confederate army left its Rappahannock camps for the Valley. In 1862 Lee had crossed the Potomac east of the Blue Ridge. Now, with Hooker inactive after Chancellorsville, Lee advanced west of the mountains, travelled down the Shenandoah Valley, crossed the Potomac at Williamsport and Shepherdstown and advanced down the Cumberland Valley. In 1862 the Federals had evacuated Winchester, but in 1863 the local Federal commander, General Robert H. Milroy, was spoiling for a fight. For the second time in the war the Lower Shenandoah saw the unfolding of grand strategy and felt the shock of battle. After the cavalry battle of Brandy Station just north of Culpeper Court House on June 9, the Pennsylvania campaign began in deadly earnest with the Second Battle of Winchester on June 13-15. General Richard S. Ewell's Second Corps of Lee's army methodically destroyed the Union force of 6,900 men at Winchester in a way that influenced Ewell's coming decisions on the first day at Gettysburg.

There are many explanations for the defeat of the Confederate Army that advanced into Pennsylvania "clanking with victory." For many in Virginia it would always be, in the words of William Faulkner, "not yet two o'clock on that July afternoon in 1863...the guns are laid and ready in the woods and the furled flags are already loosened to break out...waiting for Longstreet to give the word, and it's all in the balance...." When it was over on July 3, standing nearly alone in exhaustion and sorrow, General Lee said "We must now return to Virginia."

Virginia's Confederate experience now entered its final season. For all the months of war, but perhaps more so for the last, recent historians have noted historiographical gaps in the economic and social history of Confederate Virginia. There are ample sources for regional studies, such as for the Shenandoah Valley. Daniel Sutherland has called for county histories, pointing the way in an exemplary look at Culpeper County. Gary Gallagher has shown that the new "home front" approach is inseparable from military history. Virginians, as all Southerners, felt the impact of the disasters of 1863 at Vicksburg, Gettysburg, and Chattanooga. Furthermore, the casualties and the inconclusive results of the Bristoe and Mine Run campaigns in Virginia (October 9-22, November 26-December 2) only added to the feeling of despair many must have felt. "Bury these poor men and let us say no more about it," said Lee to A. P. Hill after his fiasco at Bristoe Station.

Many Virginia communities felt the disruptions and horrors of war. Pope, with his harsh policies against civilians, stayed east of the Blue Ridge, and the Valley was spared until Generals David Hunter and Philip Sheridan came in 1864. Elsewhere, Daniel Sutherland has drawn an unforgettable portrait of the impact of the Second Manassas campaign on Culpeper County. The fate of Fredericksburg's population in the winter of 1862-1863 further embittered Virginians. Southwestern Virginia was the scene of intermittent vicious fighting between small units throughout the war, as Federal forces tried unsuccessfully to cut the Virginia-Tennessee Railroad and to destroy the important lead, iron, and salt works of the region.

For Richmond's populace it had been one long season of war. A food riot in April 1863 threatened to become insurrection. Emory Thomas described Richmond the following spring: "Old and failing...precious little remained to be sacrificed." The Kilpatrick-Dahlgren cavalry raid in May 1864 frightened and infuriated the city's populace. Dahlgren had ridden to within five miles of the capital before being killed, and Richmond never doubted that he meant to release Union prisoners, set fire to the city, and kill the president and his cabinet. The strange disappearance of his body, until the end of the war, indicated the existence in Richmond of a small "Union underground."

In January 1864 a new governor came to the Virginia state house: Major General William Smith, who had left the army after Gettysburg. Smith, like his predecessors Wise and Letcher, "was reasonably cooperative with the Davis administration." Virginia's militia had been turned over to the Confederate authorities in February 1863 and although Smith raised new home-guard forces—13,072 men by September 1864—he did not withhold them from the Confederate government. His political conflicts were rather with the General Assembly, as he moved energetically ahead to see Virginia supplied with food and cotton for clothing.

Governor Smith tried to expedite both the government and the field commanders' requisitions for slave laborers. Unlike those Confederate states either wholly or largely occupied by Federal forces, slavery had not yet disappeared in Virginia. The flight of slaves towards Union armies, the demands of the government and of field officers for laborers, and the temptation for some owners to "refugee" south either with or without their slaves had done much to erode the institution. In March 1864, Smith joined the governors of South Carolina, North Carolina, Georgia, and Mississippi in urging the Confederate government to enact General Cleburne's proposal to arm the slaves. A year later, the Virginia General Assembly authorized Confederate authorities to call on Smith for slave-soldiers, and instructed the state's senators to support national legislation to the same end. This they did on March 16, 1865.

In 1864 the great Union offensive against what remained of the Confederacy aimed to destroy the only strategic advantage the South had ever had—her internal lines of communication. The new Union General-in-Chief, Lieutenant General U. S. Grant, would apply unrelenting pressure from eastern Texas to northern Virginia. Of his five most important offensives, three had Virginia targets. Grant would accompany the Army of the Potomac on what became its "Overland Campaign" (May 5-June 15), between the crossings of the Rappahannock and the James. He planned simultaneous operations for the Shenandoah Valley, where Franz Sigel's Union force of 6,500 men departed Winchester on May 2, and the Bermuda Hundred Peninsula, between the James and the Appomattox rivers, approximately seven miles north of Petersburg. Here Union General Benjamin Butler landed 39,000 men on May 5. Both Sigel and Butler met disaster. On May 15 a Confederate force that included 258 cadets from the Virginia Military Institute defeated Sigel at New Market. By the next day, Beauregard had succeeded in "bottling" Butler on the peninsula. But the collision in the Wilderness between Grant and Lee began the most terrific and sustained military clash of the war. Not until Grant broke off contact with Lee after Cold Harbor on June 1-3 and crossed the James on June 14 was there a brief respite. Between the battle of the Wilderness (May 5-7) and the butchery at Spotsylvania and Cold Harbor, Grant lost nearly 55,000 men, close to the number with which Lee began the campaign. Yet Lee's losses were proportionally close to Grant's. Some fabled units, such as the Stonewall Brigade, had ceased to exist. There were too few replacements or reserves—"none," Lee said to Postmaster General John H. Reagan during the fighting at Cold Harbor. Reagan also recalled the ceaseless Confederate volleys that sounded like sheets being torn apart; Grant's losses were over 7,000.

On June 14, Grant prepared to cross the James and strike at Petersburg from the south. Beauregard's heroic defense of Petersburg saved the town and its rail communications with Richmond. The arrival of Lee's army on June 17 led to ten months of stalemate and siege. Another 42,000 Union and 26,000 Confederate casualties followed, until Lee's lines finally broke a week before Appomattox.

Between Cold Harbor and the end of the war, the last Confederate hopes played out in the Valley of Virginia. After Cold Harbor Lee saw a chance to return the Second Corps to the Shenandoah. It was imperative to drive Sigel's successor, Hunter, away from the railhead at Lynchburg. Jubal Early's victory there on June 18 drove Hunter out of the Valley and created the opportunity for Early to march down the Valley and repeat the successes of Jackson in 1862. He reached Winchester on July 1, and his victories at Monocacy, Maryland, on July 9 and at Kernstown on July 24 awoke hope that saving the Valley and threatening the Potomac line might again save Virginia. The opponents of 1864, however, were not those of 1862. As the date for the presidential election in the Union neared, Sheridan's victories over Early at Winchester (September 19) and Cedar Creek (October 19) effectively ended the Confederate presence in the Valley. Soon columns of smoke from the "Great Burning" marked Virginia's encounter with what Georgia and South Carolina endured following the fall of Atlanta and Savannah.

As the Lower Valley burned, and A. P. Hill's men fought along the railroad lines west of Petersburg, only two acts remained in Virginia's Confederate history. Each colored the peace that followed. The Hampton Roads Conference on February 3, 1865 ended quickly with no movement beyond President Lincoln's stipulations of surrender, reunion, and emancipation. At Appomattox, the last act followed a harrowing week of retreat and pursuit from Richmond across the Southside, ended with honorable terms granted on Sunday, April 9. On the last evening before the surrender, Lee rejected suggestions that the army resort to partisan warfare, citing the effects this would have "on the country as a whole." The Army would neither disperse nor move beyond Appomattox.

The Commonwealth of Virginia gave herself to the cause of Southern independence. Virginia lived the tragedies and ironies of war as no other state could have. The only state to suffer permanent loss of territory as a result of the war, Virginia's state capital became the new nation's capital even as the western counties seceded from the Confederate authority. Apart from the Mississippi Valley and the Confederate "heart-land," the defense of Richmond and Northern Virginia became the defense of the Confederacy. Appomattox marked the death of the Confederacy, but Virginia survived to take her place in the new nation. Virginia embraced as a legacy from Robert E. Lee a memory of duty and hope for reconciliation that became imperishable bedrock in the foundation of the new nation.

SUGGESTED READING

James H. Brewer, *The Confederate Negro: Virginia's Craftsmen and Military Laborers, 1861-1865* (Duke University Press: Durham, 1969).

General C. G. Evans, ed., *Confederate Military History* (Morningside: Dayton, reprint 1975).

Richard McMurray, *Two Great Rebel Armies: An Essay in Confederate Military History* (University of North Carolina Press: Chapel Hill, 1989).

James I. Robertson, *Civil War Virginia* (University of Virginia Press: Charlottesville, 1991) .

Emory M. Thomas, *The Confederate Nation, 1861-1865* (Harper & Row: New York, 1979).

Emory Thomas, *The Confederate State of Richmond: A Biography of the Capital* (University of Texas Press: Austin, 1971) .

Alvin H. Fahrner, "William 'Extra Billy' Smith, Governor of Virginia, 1864-1865: A Pillar of the Confederacy," *Virginia Magazine of History and Biography*, 74 (1966), pp. 68-87.

Gary Gallagher, "Home Front and Battlefield: Some Recent Literature Relating to Virginia and the Confederacy" *The Virginia Magazine of History and Biography*, 98 (1990), pp. 135-168.

Daniel E. Sutherland, "Introduction to War: the Civilians of Culpeper County, Virginia," *Civil War History*, 37 (June 1991), pp. 120-137.

Letter from Sgt. Pruit, 3rd Arkansas, was found in 1991 under the a t t i c floorboards of the old Winchester jail. It is the property of the Winchester-Frederick County Historical Society.

ARKANSAS

by
Carl H. Moneyhon

Arkansas was one of the last Southern states to join the Confederacy. With other border states, it seceded only after the attack upon Fort Sumter and President Abraham Lincoln's call for volunteers to suppress the Southern insurrection. The initial reluctance of its people to follow Deep South states into the Confederacy was not reflective, however, of the commitment they brought to the Southern cause. Nevertheless, factors that undermined the war effort throughout the South were present early in Arkansas. The interplay of civilian and troop morale with internal conflicts, economic crises, governmental failure, and military disasters early produced conditions that doomed the Confederate attempt to gain independence.

Although linked fundamentally to slavery and to the plantation economy, Arkansas was differentiated geographically and economically from the Deep South. Arkansas' Ouachita and Ozark highlands and its position on the frontier created a complex political situation in the secession crisis. These factors produced social and economic interests unfavorable to disunion and caused the state's wait-and-see attitude in 1860 and 1861. Prominent secessionist leaders such as Governor Henry M. Rector, Senator Robert W. Johnson, and Congressman Thomas D. Hindman pushed for immediate action after South Carolina's leaders took that step in December 1860. Under pressure from them, the General Assembly called an election for a convention but the election campaign uncovered disagreement over the best course of action. Strong Unionist sentiment appeared across the state. Governor Rector may have instigated the seizure of the Federal arsenal at Little Rock on February 6 to counter the unionists and unite opinion before the election, but the peaceful surrender of the facility gave the secessionists no advantage.

A pro-Union majority, drawn particularly from western and mountain counties, appeared at the state convention in Little Rock on March 4, 1861. The unionists blocked all secessionist efforts for immediate action, although they agreed to a referendum on secession to be held in August and accepted a report mandating resistance to Federal coercion. Before they adjourned on March 21, they adopted resolutions proposing constitutional amendments to maintain the Union. The majority's support of the Union had limits, however. Most unionists sympathized with the Deep South, supported slavery, and were unwilling to have the national government coerce the seceding states back into the Union. When hostilities broke out in April, unionists shifted positions. Under the mandate to resist Federal coercion, the convention reassembled on May 6 and voted almost unanimously to secede and join the Southern Confederacy. Only one of the seventy delegates remained uncompromisingly unionist to the end.

United by events in support of the Confederacy, the delegates prepared the state for war. They enacted laws delaying the collection of debts, confiscating alien property, prohibiting payment of debts to Northerners, and imposing war taxes. They created a three-man Military Board consisting of the governor and two advisors, under whom was the Army of Arkansas that would muster troops and then turn them over to the Confederacy. The Board received an appropriation of $2 million for its work. Early cooperation, however, quickly gave way to factional strife.

Partisan and personal struggles among political leaders at the Little Rock convention could not be suppressed. In the election of members of Congress, unionists, moderate secessionists, and old Whigs combined to elect a delegation composed almost totally, except for Senator Johnson, of moderates. The convention outraged radicals when it elected Brigadier General N. Bart Pearce and Brigadier General Thomas H. Bradley, both unionists, as commanders of the state's two military divisions. The majority also clashed with the governor over numerous military matters, including his authority over state troops mustered. Rector retaliated and forced concessions from the convention by threatening to reconvene the legislature. The convention secured its own revenge on Rector by ordering a new gubernatorial election for October 1862, two years earlier than the governor's term normally would expire. These fights were ominous portents for Confederate unity and future cooperation.

When the convention adjourned on June 3, its quarrels spread to the military camps. Arkansas troops organizing near Memphis refused to accept the authority of General Bradley, accused him of cowardice, then tried to have him court-martialed. Objections to Bradley became so strong that the Board had to send General James Yell to take over the eastern division. Governor Rector argued with General Pearce over who ultimately commanded state forces. Soldiers of the western division charged Pearce with favoritism and nepotism in selecting land owned by his father-in-law for Camp Walker, their campsite in Benton County. These responses delayed the organization and training of the first Arkansas troops enlisted into service.

The political conflict that created the most immediate trouble was between Governor Rector and Confederate authorities over enlistment policy and authority over troops raised in the state. The governor initially argued that state troops should be turned over to the Confederacy quickly, then changed his mind and tried to maintain state control. His actions reflected his early concern with the Confederate government's resolve to defend the state as well as his protectiveness of the concept of state's rights. In June, when Brigadier General Ben McCulloch called for Confederate volunteers to enlist for three years or the duration of the war, Rector and the Military Board called for 10,000 men for one year's service to be limited to the state. Brigadier General William J. Hardee, named Confederate commander of the state on June 25, negotiated the transfer of state troops in the eastern division only after agreeing to give them the right to vote on the transfer. Such conflicts slowed mobilization and left many Confederate regiments short of recruits.

These problems were still to be resolved when the state's soldiers fought their first major battle at Wilson's Creek in southwestern Missouri on August 10, 1861. Arkansans served under General N. Bart Pearce, alongside General Sterling Price's Missourians and General Ben McCulloch's Confederates. Despite the organizational problems, the troops fought well and were victorious. Questions related to the soldiers' terms of service, however, prevented the commanders from following up their victory. Pearce's Arkansans refused to remain in Missouri. When they returned to Arkansas, the men voted against transfer into Confederate service, and Pearce disbanded the units. After three months of war Arkansas had only two authorized Confederate regiments in the field.

The conflict between state and national authorities continued after the battle at Wilson's Creek. To enlist more men, in August Confederate Secretary of War Leroy P. Walker authorized General McCulloch to recruit five regiments for three years or the duration of the war. At the same time he asked Rector for ten or twelve regiments, enrolled under the same terms. The governor gave Walker five regiments, enrolled for one year, and protested Confederate direct recruitment in the state. Rector demanded that troop requests be sent to the Military Board, contended that state units had the right to approve any transfer to Confederate service, and argued that arms provided by the state could not be taken out of the state. Walker refused to concede these points and the conflict continued until the imposition of conscription in the spring of 1862.

Most Arkansans were unaware of the controversy over authority that occupied political and military leaders. Many rushed to support the Confederate cause by joining state and Confederate regiments. One source estimated that by the end of 1861, 21,500 men had enlisted in Arkansas units, a number equal to nearly half of the voters of 1860. The state's congressional delegation believed 30,000 men had joined by the spring of 1862. Ultimately, conscription and enlistment pushed the total to 60,000 men by the end of the war. The state provided forty-six Confederate infantry regiments, seventeen cavalry regiments, and thirteen artillery batteries, as well as numerous other formations.

Confederate authorities in Richmond clearly believed that the center of war would be east of the Mississippi River and moved units raised in Arkansas to that theatre at the cost of the state's defense. In September, while General McCulloch tried to raise troops to defend northwestern Arkansas, General Hardee moved seven infantry regiments, one cavalry regiment, a cavalry battalion, and supporting artillery across the Mississippi for service in Kentucky. These actions confirmed Rector's fears and fanned the fires of conflict between him and the national government. As a result of the movements, the majority of soldiers raised in Arkansas served outside of the state.

Arkansans fought in almost every theatre of war. Thompson B. Flournoy organized the first regiment authorized for Confederate service, the First Arkansas Infantry, even before the state seceded. The First Arkansas rushed to Virginia but arrived too late for the first battle of Bull Run. Sent west, it joined Hardee's units at Shiloh and remained with the western armies through the rest of the war. Only one Arkansas unit, the Third Arkansas Infantry organized by Colonel Albert Rust, fought throughout the war with the Army of Northern Virginia. The majority of Arkansas troops fought in the west with the Army of Mississippi or the Army of Tennessee. In the latter army many were unified in an Arkansas division, commanded at one point by Major General Patrick R. Cleburne of Helena.

Recruitment proceeded in the summer of 1861 despite official squabbles, but the creation of a military command within the state and preparation for its defense stood at a standstill. No real effort was made until the Confederacy created the Trans-Mississippi Department No. 2, on January 10, 1862, and united Missouri, Arkansas west of the St. Francis River, Indian Territory, and northern Louisiana under Major General Earl Van Dorn. Van Dorn arrived just as General Samuel R. Curtis pushed his Union army into northwestern Arkansas. Van Dorn had little time to plan, but he responded immediately to the threat. Van Dorn had troops in the northwest, including those of McCulloch, Price, and an Indian force under General Albert Pike, but the three disagreed over command. As a result, Van Dorn assumed personal direction of the army. Military necessity thus delayed any serious effort at long-range planning of a defense.

Van Dorn concluded that he must use his army offensively against Curtis. His operations ultimately led to an attack on the Union position along Sugar Creek on March 6, 1862. Van Dorn began the battle of Pea Ridge by dividing his army in an attempt to flank Curtis. The plan was bold but implementation was faulty. Curtis withstood Van Dorn's assaults on March 6 and 7. Low on ammunition and unable to dislodge the Federals, the Confederates withdrew on March 8.

Tactically the battle of Pea Ridge was inconclusive, but the Confederate withdrawal was a strategic disaster for their cause in Arkansas because they lost control of most of the area north of the Arkansas River. This loss deprived the Confederacy of both men and supplies that could have been acquired from the area. In addition, the absence of authority allowed the development of a guerrilla war that seriously affected civilians and undermined morale in the area and throughout the rest of the state.

After Pea Ridge, Confederate authorities again jolted Arkansas by removing troops civil authorities considered essential for the state's defense. With little apparent concern for Arkansas, Van Dorn's army was ordered to Mississippi to reinforce General Albert Sidney Johnston. While Van Dorn's army was moving, a Federal invasion of the state already was underway. After Pea Ridge some Federal troops moved directly south to Van Buren, but Curtis' main army had relocated to the White River and marched along it into the state. The Federals found virtually no Confederate resistance. The state appeared to have been abandoned by the Confederate army.

General John S. Roane took command of the remaining Confederate forces in Arkansas when Van Dorn departed. Roane's problems were overwhelming and his military position was impossible. He faced a full-scale Union invasion and every unit recruited up to that time had been removed from the state. General Albert Pike, when called upon to provide troops from the Indian Territory, refused. Raising a new force was difficult because the first rush to the colors had waned. The number of volunteers had declined after 1861 and in the northwestern portion of the state many service-aged men had banded together in a peace society to oppose the war and resist Confederate service. The men available were equipped poorly, some only with pikes and lances, and the state had been stripped of military supplies.

Civilian support for the war also declined. Economic conditions spurred concerns. Shortages existed, caused by the interruption of trade with the North and by crop failures. Scarcity, combined with government fiscal policy and a lack of faith in Confederate paper money, produced an inflation of prices. Hard-to-get items such as salt climbed from $2 to $20 during the first year of the war. Less precious items such as flour increased from $6.50 to $20 per hundred pounds. Military and civil efforts at relief produced bickering among officials and did little to alleviate civilian suffering. The military situation offered no reason for optimism. Confederate troops appeared to have been defeated at Pea Ridge, northern Arkansas was indefensible, and all Confederate troops had been pulled out of the state. Even the civil government had lost all faith in the Confederate military, and the governor and other officials fled the capital at Little Rock, certain of its imminent capture, when Curtis reached Batesville in May, 1862.

On May 31, 1862, General P. G. T. Beauregard authorized Major General Thomas C. Hindman to take command in Arkansas. Hindman, an attorney from Helena, was an aggressive commander who seized civilian supplies necessary for defense, raised unauthorized military units, assumed command of Texas troops moving through the state for Mississippi, and destroyed cotton endangered by Federal advances. He used the Confederate conscription act of April 16 to mobilize the state's manpower and encouraged partisan bands to resist the Federal drive. Hindman's growing army harassed Curtis' column. In a battle at St. Charles on June 16, a single shot from a Confederate gun disabled the ironclad *Mound City* and turned back a Federal naval force moving up White River from the Mississippi River to reinforce Curtis. Military success and the falling water level on White River forced Curtis to cancel his proposed attack on Little Rock. Instead, he left Batesville and marched his army overland to Helena on the Mississippi.

Even before forcing Curtis' retreat to the Mississippi, Hindman realized the desperate situation within the state and the need to bolster civilian morale as well as strengthen the military. He acted decisively and on June 30 proclaimed martial law, divided the state into provost marshal districts, and authorized officers to purchase or impress arms, ammunition, and supplies, and to draft all eligible men. He also began a military factory system at Arkadelphia to produce small arms, percussion caps, and other goods to supplement the state penitentiary's production of clothing, shoes, wagons, harnesses, tents, knapsacks, cartridge boxes, and drums. He pushed existing facilities, such as the textile mills at Royston in Pike County, to increase output to meet the needs of soldiers and civilians alike.

Hindman's measures marshaled a larger force of men and began to solve some of the state's supply problems, but they provoked much criticism. Political leaders split into rival camps on the general's actions. One group, including C. C. Danley of the *Arkansas Gazette*, supported Hindman and the extraordinary measures as necessary for the state's survival. The other, led by Governor Rector, members of the congressional delegation, and General Albert Pike, condemned Hindman, his assumption of authority, and his suppression of individual liberties. While he may have saved Arkansas, Hindman created a political crisis that further undermined the war effort. Richmond ultimately caved in to the pressure and replaced him with General Theophilus Holmes.

Another casualty of the Hindman conflict was Governor Rector. The secession convention had provided for a general election in October 1862, but the governor and most other officials did not consider this provision binding and made no plans for the election. Rector's enemies, including supporters of Hindman, demanded an election. Rejected by the Pulaski County sheriff and the state circuit court, they ultimately received a supreme court decision ordering the election. Rector ran against Colonel Harris Flanagin of the Second Arkansas Mounted Rifles, a candidate put up by Rector's enemies. Flanagin, who did not know of his nomination and did not campaign within the state, easily defeated the incumbent.

Hindman was gone, but the centralization of authority in the hands of the army continued. The military, economic, and social crises within the state were too great for civil authorities to solve. When Holmes arrived in Arkansas in August, he found that Curtis remained a threat to eastern Arkansas and that a new Federal menace had appeared in the northwest. He learned that while Hindman had initiated solutions to many problems, shortages of manpower and supplies persisted. In addition, he discovered the state in practical rebellion against the Confederate government, particularly against the enforcement of conscription. Ultimately, Holmes agreed with Hindman's assessment of the situation and his measures. Holmes retained martial law, suspended the writ of *habeas corpus*, and actively enforced conscription by sending troops to round up resistors. Hindman's removal had not brought an end to the expansion of the military's power.

The active role by the military did not mean that civilian government ceased, although it played only a small role in subsequent events. The legislative session in the autumn of 1862 offered some help. Members appropriated $62,000 to buy corn to distribute in western Arkansas and $1,200,000 to provide relief for the needy and destitute families of soldiers. They also provided $300,000 for loans to companies producing salt, iron, or cotton cards. Given continued inflation and shortages of even essential food, these measures made little impact. The $5 per-family-per-month assistance for the needy did not relieve suffering. Few entrepreneurs took advantage of the state-backed loans for manufacturing.

Constant military pressure gave officials little time for dealing with non-military issues. Faced with a large Federal force operating in the northwest, Holmes had to keep Hindman in Arkansas. He ordered him into the Fayetteville area to recruit men and establish a defensive line. Hindman built a new army, but his protective line was so extended that it offered little defense against any campaign in force. As a result, the aggressive Hindman took the offensive and in the battle of Prairie Grove on December 7, 1862, met Federal troops under Generals James G. Blunt and Francis J. Herron. The battle was indecisive, but once again, Confederate commanders and soldiers showed themselves capable in the field. Hindman had inadequate supplies, however, and could not hold his position. His regiments, the men dressed in rags and many without shoes, fell apart as they marched out of the northwestern hills. Not only the army but most of its equipment was lost.

Holmes received another setback on January 10 and 11, 1863, when General John McClernand and a Federal force seized Fort Hindman, located near Arkansas Post at the mouth of the Arkansas River, a position intended to keep Federal gunboats from operating along it and the White River. McClernand's overwhelming superiority in force, in the battle of Arkansas Post, made short work of the Confederates, although Holmes had ordered it defended to the last man. The loss was another stunning blow, with 5,000 men captured along with all of their arms and equipment. Simply keeping an armed force in the field became the preoccupation of Confederate authorities.

The defeat at Prairie Grove and the fall of Arkansas Post created a serious crisis. Commanders in the field reported their soldiers practically had given up and had little fight in them and that civilian morale was low. Arkansans blamed bad generals and poor organization for their plight. President Jefferson Davis responded to complaints by removing Hindman from Arkansas on January 30, 1863. The government reorganized the Trans-Mississippi Department and named General E. Kirby Smith to command it on February 9. Smith's task was to restore support and rebuild the armies in the west. Even before Smith arrived, Holmes began the process of restoring faith in the Confederate cause. He sent expeditions into areas north of the Arkansas River to restore Confederate authority. He also struggled to rebuild the army, granting pardons to soldiers who had deserted and enforcing conscription. Smith's appointment and Holmes's actions produced a resurgence of confidence in the spring of 1863, but that was short-lived.

Confederate authorities stabilized the situation in Arkansas, but they were unable to reverse it. They did not command the resources to stop the Federals who were able to operate at will. The last major effort to try to drive a Federal force out of the state came in July 1863, when Holmes ordered an attack upon Helena. His design was to recapture that river city as well as provide relief for besieged Vicksburg. The campaign had little chance of accomplishing either goal. Holmes' force was not in position until July 4, the day that General John C. Pemberton surrendered Vicksburg. The battle itself involved little more than a frontal assault on a heavily fortified and entrenched position. The battle of Helena was short and decisive, with the Confederates losing over twenty-one percent of their troops. As they retreated to Little Rock, Holmes' army disintegrated, forcing Confederate officials to raise an army once again.

Holmes had little time to rebuild. After a period of inactivity, in September 1863, the Federals struck directly at Holmes with an invasion from the east and west. At Backbone Mountain on September 1, General James G. Blunt's troops defeated Confederates under General William L. Cabell and opened the way for the capture of Fort Smith. On September 10, General Frederick Steele's army marched victoriously into Little Rock. Holmes did not have enough men to stop them, and he gave way with almost no resistance. The Confederate state government and the army withdrew into remote southwestern Arkansas to try to salvage what they could.

Flanagin located the capital at Washington and the remnant of the Confederate army positioned itself around the city of Camden. Smith and Holmes tried to counterattack. Confederate troops carried out raids such as that staged by General John S. Marmaduke against Federals at Pine Bluff on October 25. As at Helena, the Confederates did not have enough strength to overcome a well-defended position. Looking for Federal weaknesses, they probed the Yankee defenses through the winter of 1863-1864. One such effort led to the capture by the Federals of seventeen-year-old David O. Dodd and his execution as a spy on January 8, 1864. Ultimately, the Confederate forces were not strong enough for a successful offensive and were relegated to the defensive.

The fall of Little Rock left Confederate Arkansas in disarray. Opposition to the Confederacy became stronger and many civilians openly expressed their desire for an end to the war. In the congressional election held in the autumn of 1863, Rufus K. Garland ran successfully against Felix Batson on an anti-government platform, arguing for increased state's rights or an end to the war. The Union army reported that in some areas of the state their scouts were welcomed by civilians ready for peace. In the areas occupied by the Federals, unionists reorganized a loyal government and many prominent ex-Confederates, including Colonel E. W. Gantt of the Twelfth Arkansas Infantry and Attorney General Sam Williams, returned to the fold. Further indicating the growing hostility to the Confederacy was the fact that some 5,000 citizens joined Union regiments organized in the state, adding to the 5,500 black Arkansans in the Union army. Unified support of the Confederacy among Arkansans clearly had died.

The decision by Union strategists to de-emphasize the war in the west prevented the complete collapse of Confederate Arkansas in 1863-1864. General Steele went on the defensive and gave the Confederates an opportunity once again to replenish their regiments with volunteers and conscripts. The officials of the Trans-Mississippi Department also expanded manufacturing and munitions facilities at Arkadelphia and created new ones at Camden and Washington to supply the army's needs. Slaves were conscripted as laborers to prepare resistance to any future Federal actions.

General Smith was successful at reassembling enough of a force to hold on to southwestern Arkansas and his resources in Louisiana and Texas. In the spring of 1864 the Federals struck into that area, encouraged by President Lincoln to make a presence felt in Texas and to warn France against its activities in Mexico. Federal columns were to strike at Shreveport, Louisiana, from New Orleans and Little Rock. In his part of this Red River campaign, Steele had about 13,000 men by the time he reached Prairie d'Ane near Washington on April 9. He faced only a small cavalry force because General Sterling Price, who had replaced Holmes the previous March, had sent most of his infantry to Shreveport to be used against the Federals moving up the Red River. The Confederates defeated General Nathaniel Banks' army at the battle of Mansfield on April 8.

Banks' defeat forced Steele to the defensive and presented the Confederates with their best opportunity for military success in the latter years of the war. Steele diverted his troops to Camden after skirmishing at Prairie d'Ane. Confederate cavalry victories at Poison Spring on April 17 and Mark's Mill on April 25 prevented Steele from opening up a supply line to Pine Bluff, and Smith hurried his infantry from Shreveport, hoping to bag Steele. The Federals abandoned Camden on April 26, 1864, before they could be cut off, and on April 27 Steele's rear guard crushed pursuing Confederate forces at the battle of Jenkins' Ferry. Steele could not be defeated on the defensive and his men retired to Little Rock and dug in. The Confederates had worked a miracle in rebuilding their force, but they were still not strong enough to drive the Federals out of Arkansas.

After the Red River Campaign, General Sterling Price was more aggressive than Holmes had been but he also proved unable to recover territory lost to the Union Army. Price ordered General Joseph Shelby into northern Arkansas to cut Steele off from his supply line to the Mississippi and to recruit men from the northern sections of the state. Shelby's operations on this mission included a particularly successful cavalry attach upon a Federal ironclad, *Queen City*, at Clarendon on June 24. Confederate cavalry, including that of General John S. Marmaduke, also operated along the Mississippi, striking at plantations leased by the Federal government and steamboat traffic on the Mississippi River. When faced with a strong Federal response, however, neither operation could be sustained. General E. A. Carr drove Shelby out of eastern Arkansas and an expedition under General Andrew J. Smith defeated General John S. Marmaduke's Confederates in southeastern Arkansas at Ditch Bayou on June 6.

Given the situation and relative strengths, it is unclear why Kirby Smith allowed Price to take most of the cavalry force remaining in the southwest on a raid into Missouri in August. Without achieving success, Price was driven back from Missouri with the loss of many men, his army suffering massive desertions as it retreated. Confederate military leaders in the department devoted themselves thereafter to building up their defense. Kirby Smith ordered General John B. Magruder to establish a defensive line along the Ouachita River, construct fortifications, warehouse supplies for the use of the defenders, and prepare for what they all feared would be the inevitable Federal assault.

The Federals never came, however. Union strategy increasingly devoted resources elsewhere and the Federals brought the war to an effective end at Appomatox Court House, Virginia, and in North Carolina, in April 1865. When word of General Robert E. Lee's and General Joseph E. Johnston's surrenders in the east reached the Trans-Mississippi, some government officials and military officers wanted to continue the fight. The majority of soldiers had had enough, however. Officers awakened each morning to find that their men had slipped away to their homes, anxious to repair the damages of four years of fighting. Smith recognized what his men already had accepted when he surrendered to General E. R. S. Canby, at New Orleans.

General Smith's surrender ended the Civil War in Arkansas and the dream of a separate Confederacy. The people of the state fought well. Despite serious problems of supply, they were able to keep their armies in the field until the end of the war. In Arkansas, however, early support of the war and the will for victory by soldiers and civilians died early. Problems unleashed by war created distress throughout the community and raised unanswered questions about the value of the conflict for all members of society. Those who remained in the areas controlled by the Confederacy kept on fighting, but Confederate officials faced a constant struggle to maintain their authority and the support of the people. Outside of Confederate lines, Arkansans readily embraced the old Union and an end to the war. In many ways, the Confederate loss in Arkansas resulted as much from this lack of undying support for the cause as from specific military or economic factors.

SUGGESTED READING

Michael B. Dougan, *Confederate Arkansas: The People and Policies of a Frontier State in Wartime* (University of Alabama Press: Tuscaloosa, 1976).

John M. Harrell, *"Arkansas,"* in Clement Anselm Evans, *Confederate Military History*, Vol. X (Confederate Publishing Company: Atlanta, 1899).

Carl H. Moneyhon, *The Impact of the Civil War and Reconstruction in Arkansas, 1850-1874: Persistence in the Midst of Ruin:* (Louisiana State University Press: Baton Rouge, 1994).

Bobby Roberts and Carl Moneyhon, *Portraits of Conflict: A Photographic History of Arkansas in the Civil War* (University of ArkansasPress: Fayetteville, 1987).

William L. Shea and Earl J. Hess, *Pea Ridge: Civil War Campaign in the West* (University of North Carolina Press: Chapel Hill, 1992).

David Y. Thomas, *Arkansas in War and Reconstruction. 1861-1874* (United Daughters of the Confederacy: Little Rock, 1926).

James M. Woods, *Rebellion and Realignment: Arkansas' Road to Secession* (University of Arkansas Press: Fayetteville, 1987).

Thomas A. Belser, "Military Operations in Missouri and Arkansas, 1 8 6 1 - 1865" (unpublished doctoral dissertation, Vanderbilt University, 1958) .

TENNESSEE

by
John McGlone

Tennessee in 1860 was a country with a proud heritage. Few men then could conceive of an abstraction that stretched from "sea to shining sea." When they spoke of "their country," they meant Tennessee and even more specifically the mountains of Claiborne County, the rolling fields of Rutherford, or the flat delta lands of Shelby County on the Mississippi River.

The people of the "Volunteer State" were a mixture of Southern aristocrats and slaves, two-fisted Westerners and free blacks, Jacksonian democrats and unionists in their mountain fastness. They loved their part of the Union in the shadow of Andrew Jackson and former Tennessee governor Sam Houston. Their ancestors had come across the mountains in a great surge about the time of the American Revolution. These buckskinned harbingers of civilization did not bring the family crystal with them, but rather the long rifle and hunting knife. These they handled well, so well, in fact, that their grandchildren often were able to live in luxury and lace. Many early Tennesseans were Scot-Irish while others claimed descent from the first families of Virginia. Some were North Carolina Revolutionary War veterans seeking bounty land; others came involuntarily as slaves. To this mixture must be added surviving Native Americans and Creoles from the South and adventurers of every persuasion who drifted through on their way to Arkansas, Texas, or a farther dream. Whatever their background or roots, early in their history Tennesseans acquired a taste for struggle, an independent streak, and the love of a fight.

By the time of the secession crisis, Tennessee had been a state for less than the lifetime of one man. In that short period, Tennesseans had fought the British, engaged hostile natives, Spaniards, Mexicans, and anyone else who would oblige them. When things got too civilized at home, they roamed far afield to satisfy their battle lust. In 1836, one contingent left Nashville to fight the Seminoles in Florida under the foreboding title of the "Tennessee Mounted Gunmen." When Texans declared their independence from Mexico, Tennesseans flocked to their colors. More men from Tennessee died defending the Alamo than from any other state or nation. By the time of the Mexican-American War, Tennessee had acquired the nickname of the "Volunteer State" as it supplied over twice as many volunteers as the government requested from Tennessee in the War of 1812 and again in the Mexican War. It was a name that would be perpetuated proudly in 1861.

Tennessee was among the last Southern states to join the Confederacy by a majority vote of her people, and was also the first Southern state to be reconstructed after the war. This "last to leave, first to return" scenario does not imply any lack of devotion to the Southern cause. Tennessee's reasons for seceding may have been different than those of other Confederate states of the Deep South; but, once the die was cast, Tennesseans served their cause with a vengeance. More battles were fought in Tennessee and more Tennesseans volunteered for the fight than members of any other Southern state, if East Tennessee unionists are included. Confederate numbers vary from the 115,000 tabulated by Union General Marcus Wright to 186,652 computed by the more recent *Tennesseans in the Civil War*. Union figures remain more precise at 31,092. Whichever figure is accepted, it is clear that Tennesseans volunteered for Confederate service over Union at a ratio of 4:1 to 6:1.

"Unreconstructed rebels" abhor the term "Civil War" as applied to the conflict. It makes it sound like a petty struggle for control of the presidential palace in some Central American country, and it trivializes the undeniable fact of Confederate nationhood. The term "Civil War," or at least "war within a war," could, however, be applied to the bitter struggle within Tennessee.

East Tennessee was mountainous, pro-Union, and largely non-slaveholding, while Middle and West Tennessee became Confederate bastions. Traditional differences between mountain people and "flatlanders" were exacerbated by differences in political philosophy and rivalries for control of the state. When war came, these rivalries surfaced and largely determined the color of the uniform one chose for the coming fight. Many East Tennesseans remained fiercely loyal to the Union, but their patriotism was augmented by a hatred of the "planters and aristocrats" of the lowlands. When an East Tennessee subsistence farmer opted for the Union, he struck a blow in a class struggle. Later, when Confederates executed "disloyal" bridgeburners in East Tennessee, when General Nathan Bedford Forrest's troopers killed "Tennessee Tories," or when Union cavalrymen murdered Confederate partisans by strangulation, there was a particular bitterness about it beyond the horror of the events. Soldiers were not just killing a blue or gray clad enemy, they were killing fellow Tennesseans.

The war was not only a blood feud between Tennesseans but a struggle for political control and power. While grand armies moved all over the state in the name of the Union or the Confederacy, smaller dramas were played out among Tennesseans. When the Confederates evacuated Nashville in February 1862, a Confederate home guard commander, Colonel Henry Claiborne, took care to evacuate not only bank assets and current state records but also less tangible documents which proved the state's, and by inference, the Confederacy's, claim to legitimacy. These included maps, early land grants, and Revolutionary War records. In a similar, if opposite vein, when Andrew Johnson was appointed military governor, he possessed not a shred of popular support in Confederate Middle Tennessee, but with the backing of Union bayonets, he quickly assumed control of that symbol of Tennessee statehood, the capitol in Nashville. The classical Greek revival building quickly became an armed fortress complete with stockade walls and cannon glaring from the steps as much to subdue Confederate Nashville as to repel any invader. Johnson confiscated property, levied taxes, imprisoned opponents, and generally made life miserable for Southerners in "occupied" Tennessee. Ironically, Confederate forces held the eastern part of the state, which was quite unionist. When Johnson became Lincoln's vice president and then president, he was replaced, again with little popular support, by William G. Brownlow. "Parson" Brownlow perpetuated venom, division, and a long-simmering hatred in the Volunteer State.

When the time finally came to choose sides, Tennesseans flocked to the Confederate colors in overwhelming numbers. Six out of every seven men who joined the fray did so in a Confederate uniform and thought they did so *for* their country, not *against* it. They believed they were the rightful heirs of those earlier American rebels, George Washington, Patrick Henry, and Thomas Jefferson. The North was the section that no longer venerated the Constitution and had become an unknown country to them. If anything, they perceived the North as the area that was "rebelling" against the original Constitution and values of the country. It was becoming urbanized, industrialized, and filled with immigrants, while the South remained agricultural, conservative, and patriotic to the original Union. Tennesseans believed in the Constitution their ancestors had helped to write. The old Southern domination of politics was disintegrating, as well as the ability of earlier statesmen to achieve compromise and maintain a balance between Northern and Southern interests. New political parties, especially "Black Republicans" and abolitionists, forced the South into an increasingly defensive and minority position. Southerners did not like losing political power and control. If they could not get equity within the system, they would leave. Their intention was not to "rebel" against the national government but to reestablish the proper relationship between that government and the sovereign states. They would fight, if necessary, a second American revolution for the government their forefathers had established. It was hoped that they would be allowed to depart in peace. Just as their sires had struggled for American independence, they would fight for Southern independence. Next to these considerations, slavery was an economic problem, not a *casus belli*. In the coming war, few Tennesseans would die "for" or "against" slavery. They would die for their strong political beliefs, their tradition of military service, and that most compelling of reasons, to protect hearth and home from an invader.

In the prosperous last decade before the war, Tennessee remained relatively free of conflict or secessionist sentiment. As early as 1832, South Carolina had taken a Southern rights position during the nullification crisis, but it was alone and had to deal with Andrew Jackson. One is tempted to speculate how the battle-scarred, steely-eyed Old Hickory would have dealt with the crisis of 1861, but Jackson was in his grave and lesser men filled his place. Although Tennesseans were not secessionists in the 1850s, some did take part in the Nashville Convention, an early attempt to assert Southern rights, and some participated in the conflict on the Kansas-Missouri border. They also shouldered arms in various "filibustering" expeditions to Central America in futile attempts to acquire new slave territories. The "gray-eyed man of destiny," William Walker of Nashville, died before a Nicaraguan firing squad, but Tennesseans generally were content to witness, argue, and debate these events of their time. They did not become emotionally involved in secession until it was almost upon them. The period of the 1850s was a complicated era of struggle between North and South, compromises, border warfare, strident propaganda, and endless tension, which for Tennesseans began to come to a flash point near the end of the decade. In October 1858, William H. Seward, a Republican leader in New York who later joined Abraham Lincoln's cabinet, had pronounced that war between the sections was inevitable. Reaction in Tennessee to this "irrepressible conflict" doctrine was anger and hostility. The state legislature branded the doctrine "infamous" while various editors railed against Seward and the abolitionists. In 1859, when John Brown led a raid on Harpers Ferry to incite servile insurrection, many Tennesseans blamed Seward in particular and black Republicans in general. They now perceived that the South was not only bombarded by hostile propaganda but also subject to armed attack. In reaction to Northern violence and extremism, some Tennesseans began to agree with the secessionist views of Governor Isham G. Harris. Early in 1860, Harris proclaimed the right of revolution, which was written into the original 1796 Tennessee state constitution, and said he feared that the right would be exercised if the "reckless fanatics of the North should secure control of the government." When Lincoln was elected, Southerners perceived that the "reckless fanatics" had indeed seized power since Lincoln had been placed in office by the minority vote of one section of the country. He was not even on the ballot in Southern states, including Tennessee.

The election of Abraham Lincoln in November 1860 was the immediate cause for secession in the Deep South. He did not represent the South, and he had not been elected by the South, but now he was to be their president. A few days after the election, the legislature of South Carolina called a convention that unanimously adopted an ordinance of secession on December 20, 1860. "UNION DISSOLVED," blared the headlines triumphantly. Southerners danced in the streets, played "The Marseillaise," and wore tri-colored badges of defiance. At last they were to be free of tyrannical, Republican, abolitionist Northerners who would destroy their way of life. The "fire eaters" of South Carolina were soon followed in secession by Georgia, Alabama, Florida, Mississippi, Louisiana, and Texas. The "Bonnie Blue Flag," a revolutionary white star on a blue field, was first flown in Jackson, Mississippi. Throughout the Deep South, a holiday air of jubilation prevailed. In February, representatives of six of the seven states met in Montgomery, Alabama, to create the government of the Confederate States of America.

All was not jubilation and fireworks in Tennessee. Some citizens of the Volunteer State, like their former governor, Sam Houston, in Texas, were saddened at the prospect of going "against the old flag." Others, such as Governor Harris, were already secessionists. But the vast majority were undecided. Although sympathizing with states of the Deep South, they were not yet ready for the fateful step of secession.

By the end of February 1861, as the Confederate government was being established in Montgomery, Tennesseans voted resoundingly *against* secession. Governor Harris had called a special session of the legislature and had taken the position that the presidency of the United States was now in the hands of a sectional (Northern) party that had sworn undying enmity to slavery and the South. Tennesseans remained unconvinced and when they went to the polls on February 9, they rejected the call for a secession convention by a vote of almost four to one. The vote for calling a secession convention was 24,749 while 91,303 were against it.

Tennesseans would watch and wait for the time being. As events moved toward war elsewhere, men of good conscience still tried to find a compromise solution. Andrew Johnson, still representing Tennessee in the United States Senate, proposed an amendment to the Constitution which provided for sectional alternation of the presidency and of the members of the Supreme Court. His plan also envisioned a permanent division of the territories into free and slave sections. Harris proposed that any Northern official who refused to return a fugitive slave as required by law would be assessed double the value of the runaway. Senator John J. Crittenden of Kentucky proposed a compromise that was considered seriously by some Congressional leaders but was thwarted by uncompromising Republicans. Tennessee even sent delegates to a last-ditch Washington Peace Conference called by Virginia and presided over by former President John Tyler of Virginia. Eleven of the twelve Tennessee delegates stood for compromise and moderation, but to no avail. The time for compromise had passed.

In his inaugural address, Lincoln made it clear that he thought secession illegal and that he would enforce the national will in all the states. This seemed reasonable to unionists and inflammatory to Southerners. Fort Sumter, located in the harbor of Charleston, South Carolina, presented an immediate problem. Garrisoned by a small military force, it quickly took on symbolic meaning for both sides. To the South, it was a bastion of hated Federal authority within the borders of sovereign South Carolina. To the North, it was an outpost of loyalty in the face of treason. There was little room for dialogue. Lincoln had been advised that any attempt to send relief to the garrison would be considered an act of war. South Carolinians were serious, as indicated by their earlier firing on an attempted relief ship, *The Star of the West*. Lincoln chose to disregard these warnings and, as some would say later, maneuvered the South into firing the first shot. A relief expedition was ordered by Lincoln. True to their promise, Confederate authorities decided to reduce the enemy outpost. On April 12, 1861, the batteries surrounding Fort Sumter opened fire, and the next day the garrison surrendered. The war was on.

Tennesseans were electrified by the news of the firing on Fort Sumter. The long years of vicious debate, wrangling, duels, and compromises that had plagued the nation had ended. Now all would be action.

It can be argued that Lincoln's reaction to the firing on Fort Sumter helped to bring about the secession of the remainder of the Confederate states of the Upper South. Lincoln's call for 75,000 volunteers on April 15, 1861, to "put down the rebellion," created a firestorm in Tennessee, Virginia, Arkansas, and North Carolina. Faced with the prospect of taking up arms against their brothers in the Deep South, many Tennesseans opted for the Confederacy.

Governor Harris' fiery response to Lincoln's call for volunteers was to telegraph the message to Washington that "Tennessee will not furnish a single man for coercion, but 50,000 if necessary for the defense of our rights and those of our Southern brothers." He called a special second session of the legislature to meet in Nashville on April 25 and proclaimed that "in such an unholy crusade, no gallant son of Tennessee will ever draw his sword." This set the tone for what happened in Middle Tennessee. East Tennessee was still unionist, and West Tennessee was "pro-secesh," but the change in Middle Tennessee was most dramatic. Confederate flags appeared, politicians "speechified," parades and demonstrations supported secession, and many agreed that Tennessee was "ripe for joining the Confederacy." Even moderate unionist John Bell, a presidential candidate in 1860, and ten other prominent conservatives issued a statement which supported Harris and condemned Lincoln. Governor Harris and the legislature would soon take Tennessee out of the Union, *de facto* if not *de jure*, before it was even confirmed by popular vote.

On April 25, 1861, the first night of their second special session, the Tennessee legislators, guided by Harris, met in secret session and passed a "Declaration of Independence and Ordinance Dissolving the Federal Relations Between the State of Tennessee and the United States of America." This was kept secret from the general public for eleven days, while secessionist sentiment grew. On May 6, 1861, the Declaration of Independence was made public with the provision, almost as an afterthought, that it was to be ratified or rejected by the voters in a special election on June 8. No one doubted the outcome of the referendum; and, in fact, steps were being taken that would make that vote superfluous.

The day after the Declaration was made public, Tennessee entered into a military alliance with the Confederacy. On May 7, 1861, three state senators, Washington Barrow, Gustavus Henry, and A. O. W. Totten, signed a "convention between the State of Tennessee and the Confederate States of America." Henry W. Hillard of Georgia signed on behalf of the Confederacy. Tennessee had formed a military league with the Confederacy and was now, for all practical purposes, a Confederate state.

Many Tennesseans already considered themselves to be Confederates and had not waited for the legal formalities. They joined Confederate units in neighboring states, drilled their militia under Confederate banners, and generally prepared for war. For some, however, Tennessee did not "go Confederate" fast enough. In Franklin County, in southern Middle Tennessee, hundreds had signed a petition to "secede" from Tennessee and join Confederate Alabama. Not content with mere rhetoric or political posturing, the people of that area raised and equipped a First Tennessee Infantry regiment and sent it off to the coming fight in Virginia. Later, after Tennessee legally seceded, another First Tennessee Infantry was raised in the Nashville area to serve in the western armies. Both regiments would acquit themselves with glory.

In the next few weeks, and still before the popular vote on secession, Tennesseans began to gird for war. In a reversal of the famous biblical prophecy, the Nashville Plow Works converted to the production of arms, and a river defense fleet was started on the Cumberland River waterfront. Rifles were ordered from New Orleans, but more men volunteered than could be armed or equipped. Men drilled with broomsticks in fear that the war would be over before they got their chance at "those people." Some carried shotguns or squirrel rifles. A few showed up with flintlock muskets from the War of 1812, in some cases carried by the gray-bearded veterans themselves. Politicians, with their mind more on prestige than strategy, offered the state capitol to the Confederacy as a seat for the government instead of Richmond. A local landmark, Belmont, was even suggested as the executive mansion for President Jefferson Davis. The suggestion came to naught, but it does reflect the spirit of the times. Tennessee may have been the last state to secede officially, but now Tennesseans would fight to the death for their country.

In the end, the popular vote on secession was almost anticlimactic. Predictably, Tennesseans voted overwhelmingly for secession. The June 8 balloting revealed 104,913 Tennesseans for secession and only 47,238 against. Of the latter number, 32,923 were cast in East Tennessee, leaving only 14,315 Union votes scattered throughout the rest of the state. The vote confirmed a division which already existed in the state and which would be manifested in the savage fighting that followed and for a century beyond. It took nine days to count the vote and to make the results public. The vote was symbolically confirmed on June 17, 1861, when the Stars and Bars was raised over the state capitol. Tennessee was now officially one of the Confederate States of America.

Governor Harris made predigious efforts to prepare Tennesseans for war. On July 2, he tendered to the Confederacy twenty-two regiments of infantry, two regiments of cavalry, ten companies of artillery, an engineer corps, and an ordinance bureau. Sadly, Tennesseans' enthusiasm to fight for the Confederacy was not matched by Confederate enthusiasm to defend Tennessee.

Gideon Pillow was appointed commander of Tennessee Forces. Pillow's questionable record in the Mexican War was overshadowed by political considerations. President Davis soon replaced Pillow with Leonidas Polk, the Episcopal bishop of Louisiana. Although Pillow was removed from command of state troops, he was retained in the army long enough to contribute to the disaster at Fort Donelson. Polk's appointment was hardly better. Polk had graduated from West Point, where he had been a roommate of Jefferson Davis, and upon graduation had resigned to pursue a clerical calling. He had spent his entire life in the service of his church and now found himself a general in command of vast armies. With more enthusiasm than tact, he violated Kentucky's declared neutrality and gave Federals an excuse to do the same. The eventual fall of Confederate Tennessee could be traced to the loss of Kentucky. Fortunately, in September 1861, Albert Sidney Johnston assumed command of the department. Johnston's new command, Department Number 2, consisted of a vast area of the west from the Appalachians to the Mississippi River and beyond, including Tennessee, Kentucky, Arkansas, parts of Missouri, Kansas, Mississippi, and Indian territory. The imaginary northern boundary of this "Line of the Cumberland" was thinly defended in the face of a strong Union build-up in Ohio, Indiana, Illinois, and northern Kentucky. Unlike Virginia, where the east-west rivers afforded natural defensives and the mountains narrowed the enemy front, Tennessee was wide open to the coming attack. In addition, the rivers in the west, the Mississippi, Cumberland, and Tennessee, provided natural avenues of attack for Northern forces. These river highways pierced the heart of Johnston's department and would be used to great advantage by the North.

In East Tennessee, strong unionist sentiment manifested itself in meetings in Knoxville and Greenville to discuss separation from the Confederate state of Tennessee and the establishment of a (Union) loyal state of East Tennessee. Brownlow and others had advocated this position as early as the 1840s. Confederate Tennessee viewed this position as disloyal "rebellion" and sent troops to the area to enforce the majority view on the malcontents. The Confederate forces that occupied East Tennessee were commanded by Nashville editor Felix Zollicoffer. His nearsightedness and lack of military experience cost him his life and provided a Confederate defeat that started an escalating process that unraveled Johnston's entire line defending Tennessee.

The inexperienced Zollicoffer moved his small army northwest from the Cumberland to a position in Kentucky near Beech Grove. With an unfordable river at his back after a week of pelting rain, the Confederates fought a battle variously known as Mill Springs, Logans Crossroads, Fishing Creek, or even Beech Grove. It was a disaster for the South.

The Union forces were commanded by General George H. Thomas. John C. Breckinridge, Zollicoffer's superior, had assumed overall command of the Confederate forces. At first successful, the wet, bedraggled Confederates, many armed with flintlocks which were inoperable in the rain, began to give way. Disaster struck when Zollicoffer lost his bearings in the rain and nearsightedly began to issue orders to a Federal colonel, who promptly shot him. The death of Zollicoffer caused a Confederate stampede which did not stop until the survivors were some sixty miles from Nashville. Johnston's right wing had been broken.

Hard upon the shocking defeat at Mill Springs came the Union attack upon Fort Henry and Fort Donelson which guarded the Tennessee and Cumberland river's entrance into the state. Fort Henry was battered into submission by Union naval forces. Fort Donelson was surrendered by the sheer stupidity and cowardice of its commanders. General John B. Floyd, a Virginia political appointment, commanded good men but apparently feared so much for his own life—he believed Federal Forces would execute him as a traitor for his real or imagined escapades as secretary of war in the 1850s—that he was willing to sacrifice his entire command to save his own skin. Union Forces had been beaten back from the fort and victory was within Floyd's grasp when he withdrew his troops from the one road left to escape to Nashville. With his forces bottled up in the fort, victory suddenly turned to defeat as Ulysses S. Grant pressed the attack and demanded "unconditional surrender." Floyd passed his command to Gideon J. Pillow, who was apparently made of the same stuff, for he passed the "hot potato" on to the third in command, Simon Boliver Buckner. Buckner, none too happily, stood by his command and surrendered the fort to his old friend Grant, while Floyd and Pillow fled for their lives. Cavalry Colonel Nathan Bedford Forrest claimed that he would "get out of this place . . . or bust hell wide open." Forrest led his mounted troops through saddle-deep, icy waters to safety, accompanied by infantrymen clinging to their stirrups.

While some 12,000 to 14,000 Confederate soldiers were herded north to prisons, Forrest retreated to Nashville. The Confederate state government of Tennessee was effectively destroyed with the fall of Nashville in February 1862, but it maintained a government-in-exile for almost three years. After the fall of Fort Henry and Fort Donelson, Forrest retreated to Nashville and made predigious efforts to evacuate supplies, ammunition, and machinery before the Federals could take possession of the capitol. Colonel Henry L. Claiborne, the home guard commander and chief clerk of the Bank of Tennessee, was assigned the task of saving bank records, assets, and other state records and documents. These valuables were evacuated by train, wagon, and in the personal carriage of Claiborne's wife, Lucy Steele Claiborne. Gold, bonds, and currency were even hidden in her petticoats and in the clothing of her children. A Masonic emblem given to Mrs. Claiborne by her husband allowed her safe passage past a Union patrol commanded by a Federal officer who was also a Mason. Nathan Bedford Forrest commended Colonel Claiborne for his services but omitted mention of his wife and children who were also serving the cause.

The state government, personified by Governor Harris and legitimized by possession of state records, archival holdings, and the Bank of Tennessee, now began a three-year odyssey following the fortunes of the Confederacy and the Army of Tennessee. State bank assets were used to pay the troops, buy supplies, and invest in English banking houses in Liverpool for European purchases. As Confederate fortunes waxed and waned, the Tennessee Confederate "government" moved to Murfreesboro, Tennessee; Corinth, Mississippi; Montgomery, Alabama; Winchester, Tennessee; and finally to various cities and towns in Georgia, ever avoiding Federal armies, cavalry patrols, and guerrillas. Once during a sojourn at Winchester, Tennessee, a convention was held to nominate and elect the next Confederate governor of Tennessee. Washington Barrow, the state senator who had signed the military alliance with the Confederacy in May 1861 and who had been imprisoned in the North and exchanged, was one of the candidates. Judge Caruthers of Lebanon was the final choice of the convention, but it came to naught since most of the electorate was in occupied Union territory—the votes came from the Army camps—and the legislature could not meet to validate the election. The end for the Tennessee state government came in Georgia in May 1865, when members were captured by the cavalry troopers of Union General James H. Wilson. Significantly, the then governor of Tennessee, unionist William Brownlow, made great fanfare of having the captured material brought by rail to Nashville and triumphantly carried up the hill to the state capitol.

General Johnston now abandoned Middle Tennessee and gathered his forces at Corinth in northern Mississippi before having another go at the enemy. When he learned the Federals were gathering near Pittsburg Landing on the Tennessee River, he set off after them with the promise that "tonight we will water our horses in the Tennessee."

The first day of the battle near a little country church called Shiloh would go to the Confederates, but at a fearful price. The much beloved Albert Sidney Johnston was wounded and slowly bled to death while his personal surgeon tended Union wounded. A tourniquet would have avoided the tragedy, but Johnston's wound was unknown to those around him until he reeled in the saddle, and by then it was too late. At his side, helping him to the ground, was Governor Harris. Harris was no bombastic politician. He had led his people to war and saw his duty at the front, but he could do little for Johnston. With the death of their commander and the arrival of Union reinforcements, the second day went to the Union. General P. G. T. Beauregard led the Confederate Forces in retreat back into Mississippi.

While the events at bloody Shiloh were unfolding, General Polk suffered a defeat at Island Number 10, which opened the Mississippi River for a Union attack on Memphis. That attack came in June when a strong armored Union fleet blew the wooden Confederate "cotton clads" out of the water in a river battle witnessed by Memphians.

In the space of one year after secession, Confederate forces were driven out of Middle Tennessee, Fort Henry and Fort Donelson had fallen, Nashville had been captured, Shiloh lost, and Memphis had been occupied. There was cause for Union jubilation, but the Union forces were in grave error if they thought the fighting was over. Confederate Tennesseans would be back.

Nathan Bedford Forrest and John Hunt Morgan harassed the Federal occupiers until the main army returned. In lightning raids on Gallatin, Hartsville, Murfreesboro, Lebanon, and the outskirts of Nashville, these cavalry leaders taught the world the meaning of guerrilla warfare as they captured horses and weapons, destroyed millions of dollars worth of supplies, and insured that the Union occupation of Tennessee was never effective beyond the range of Union guns.

In the fall of 1862, the Confederacy organized one of the few coordinated efforts to defeat the North. General Robert E. Lee led his Army of Northern Virginia on an invasion of Maryland while the new commander of the Army of Tennessee, General Braxton Bragg, supported by General E. Kirby Smith, led Confederate forces into Kentucky, and General Earl Van Dorn and General Sterling Price made a similar effort in Mississippi. This three-pronged effort to carry the war to the enemy was not to be. In Maryland, at Antietam Creek near Sharpsburg, Union General George B. McClellan was able to stop Lee. A drawn battle at Perryville discouraged the ever-cautious Bragg, who promptly retired to Middle Tennessee. Confederates were beginning to grumble that Bragg could snatch defeat from the jaws of victory. It would get worse. A similar fate befell the Confederates at Iuka and Corinth in Mississippi.

In an effort to bolster sagging Confederate fortunes in the West, President Davis visited Bragg's army in Murfreesboro, Tennessee. He reviewed the troops and pronounced them the finest he had seen. No one ever seriously questioned the fighting qualities of the Army of Tennessee, just the leadership. Davis also met with his quarreling officers and even had time to attend a storybook wedding of one of his cavalry generals, John Hunt Morgan.

William S. Rosencrans now commanded the Union forces in Nashville. On December 26, 1862, he began an advance toward Bragg at Murfreesboro. Since he was harassed by Confederate cavalry General Joseph Wheeler, it took Rosencrans four days to cover the thirty miles to Murfreesboro. Battle was opened with a Confederate attack on December 31, which drove the Union lines some four miles back hard upon itself at right angles. The day clearly had gone to the Confederates, and Bragg telegraphed the news of his victory to Richmond. It was premature. After a day of staring at each other, Bragg resumed the fight with a suicidal attack on the Confederate right led by General John C. Breckenridge. The doomed Confederate infantry futilely charged massed Union artillery, and 1,800 Confederates fell in some twenty minutes. The next day Bragg retreated south to Bedford and Coffee counties, leaving the Union in possession of the field, Murfreesboro, and a claim to victory. Some of Breckinridge's officers urged the Kentuckian to challenge Bragg to a duel. General Robert Hanson, who had fallen in the battle, said prior to his death that he could have solved the problem by shooting Bragg. Dissatisfaction with Bragg was rampant in the army and the general population. Bragg tried to shift the blame to some of his unruly subordinates, and General Joseph E. Johnston, in overall if ill-defined command, did not help matters when he further reported on the dissatisfaction with Bragg to his commander in chief, Jefferson Davis. Davis remained loyal to Bragg, not because of their pre-war friendship but because of Davis' perceptions of loyalty and consistency. The unhappy Army of Tennessee would be saddled with Braxton Bragg through yet another campaign and several defeats.

East Tennessee unionists were jubilant when General Ambrose Burnside occupied Knoxville and sealed his claim on East Tennessee by defeating General James Longstreet at Fort Sanders in November 1963. East Tennesseans had endured Confederate martial law and summary executions of "disloyal" bridgeburners by Confederate authorities. These unionist Tennesseans now resumed control of their part of the state, and with the help of Union bayonets soon controlled the entire Volunteer State.

While battles raged and armies marched back and forth over the entire state, the political and economic situation was chaotic at best. Union military governor Andrew Johnson controlled affairs from Nashville while Confederates yearned to recapture their capital. Confederate cavalry raided the outskirts of Nashville and pounded through the streets of Union-occupied Memphis. Vast areas in between these centers were disputed, raided, and burned by both armies, and loyalty to a particular cause was often determined by the proximity of a given army. Many Tennesseans in Middle and West Tennessee had sons, brothers, and fathers with the Confederate Army and suffered at the hands of Union occupiers, while the same happened in reverse in East Tennessee. Commerce, agriculture, and business all suffered during the war. In spite of these horrors, Tennesseans carried on to the bitter end.

After capturing Murfreesboro, Rosecrans allowed Bragg a six-month respite, leaving the Confederate army unmolested at Tullahoma. In June 1863, Rosecrans began a campaign of maneuvers which forced or allowed Bragg the excuse to retreat toward Chattanooga. This last Confederate stronghold in Tennessee was soon abandoned by Bragg, who retreated into northern Georgia. Rosecrans recklessly pursued him and was surprised to find the Confederates drawn up in line of battle near the Chickamauga River. The Confederates attached on September 19 and tore the Union army to pieces. A complete annihilation of Union forces was prevented only by the stand of General George H. Thomas, known thereafter as the "Rock of Chickamauga." Forrest exploited the victory, but once again Bragg managed to let the fruits of victory rot on the vine. Immediately following the battle, Confederate forces could have overrun the Union survivors who had fled to Chattanooga, but Bragg quarreled with his subordinates, dispersed his troops, and laid an ineffectual "siege" on Chattanooga. Union forces were down to slim rations, but their discomfiture was relieved by the "cracker line" up the Tennessee River and by the arrival of Generals U. S. Grant, W. T. Sherman, and Philip Sheridan with enough troops to dislodge Bragg and lift the siege.

The battle was opened on November 24, 1863, with a minor action at Lookout Mountain which became revered in Union legend as the "Battle Above the Clouds." The main Confederate army was entrenched farther south at Missionary Ridge, in a strong defensive position which should never have been captured by direct assault, but was. Union forces entrenched at the base of the steep heights became irritated by sniping Confederate fire and took it upon themselves to charge the mountain. Without orders from their generals, privates, sergeants, and young offices such as Arthur MacArthur—father of General Douglas MacArthur—surged forward in the face of withering Confederate fire. Soldiers of the Army of Tennessee, demoralized under Bragg, fled for their lives. Their erstwhile commander attempted to rally them with cries of, "Here is your commander!" to which they replied, "Here's your mule." Bragg was thankfully removed after the debacle at Missionary Ridge.

Joseph E. Johnston was placed in command of the Army of Tennessee. Johnston had the confidence of most of the men and officers of the army, if not of the commander in chief. The feud between Johnston and Davis went back to credit for the victory at First Manassas—some would say back to their West Point days in a quarrel over the attention of a young lady—and would seriously impair the effectiveness of the Army, but for the time being, new uniforms and battle flags, rations, and the end to capricious punishments put new life into the Army. That new spirit would be displayed in various actions such as Kennesaw Mountain where Tennesseans of the 1st/27th Regiment helped defeat the legions of W. T. Sherman.

Tennesseans, like the Kentucky Confederates, were now "orphans" fighting for their state which was overrun by Union forces. In Georgia, Sherman conducted a campaign of maneuver which gradually pushed the outnumbered Confederates toward Atlanta. Fearful that the important supply and rail center city would fall, Davis replaced Johnston with John Bell Hood. With Hood in command, many Tennesseans returned home to shallow graves.

General John Bell Hood was once a favorite of General Lee. As a regimental, brigade, and division commander, Hood had led his "gallant Texans" with such dash and bravery that he had lost a leg and the use of an arm. He clearly should have been assigned to a desk or rear echelon duty, but such were the fortunes and politics of the Confederacy that when Johnston was removed from command of the Army of Tennessee before Atlanta, he was replaced by Hood. It was said of Hood that, if he saw an idle bugler, he would order him to sound the charge. In the ensuing battles for Atlanta, Hood lived up to his reputation and lost thousands of men and the city of Atlanta.

With Federal forces in control of the city, and Sherman's supply line stretched from Chattanooga to Atlanta, Hood conceived of a plan to threaten Sherman's supply lines, invade Tennessee, and with a great amount of luck capture Nashville, push on to Louisville, Cincinnati, or even to Northern Virginia to aid Lee. Such were his dreams.

Leaving Sherman in Georgia, Hood struck out across Alabama and north to Tennessee. The resources of the Union were so great that Sherman left other armies to contend with Hood and moved across Georgia almost unopposed on his famous "march to the sea." Meanwhile, Hood's army marched from the south through Middle Tennessee toward Nashville. At Spring Hill, Tennessee, the Union Army of General John M. Schofield managed to slip by Hood's army in the night and reach Franklin, where the bluecoats hastily prepared for the assault they knew would come. Hood, "wrathy as a rattlesnake" at his army's failure to detect or stop Scholfield, ordered his men on toward Franklin. They arrived before the Union works late in the afternoon of November 30, and Hood ordered the assault. Without artillery support or reconnaissance, against the advice of his generals, and with forlorn hope, Hood threw his infantry against the Union works. In one of the most desperate and gallant charges of the war, six Confederate generals, including the irreplaceable Patrick R. Cleburne, and thousands of their men, fell. The fell so thickly that in some places the dead and wounded were piled four and five deep. In other areas, the dead, shoulder to shoulder, did not have room to fall over. The ghastly slaughter continued into the night until Schofield's army abandoned Franklin and began a retreat to Nashville. The next morning, Hood was in possession of the field and could technically claim a victory, but at a cost of the flower of his army. Hood later claimed that Franklin had proven that the Army of Tennessee would charge entrenched positions, as if that were ever a question.

The Confederate army then moved toward Nashville. Nashville had been occupied since 1862 and was the largest Union supply base and one of the most heavily fortified cities in America. The Union army, commanded by General George H. Thomas, reinforced by Schofield, and with a huge cavalry force under Wilson, gathered strength and prepared to meet the Confederates. In the first weeks of December, Hood's army was spread out thinly in the hills south of Nashville and immobilized due to severe weather and ice storms. Thomas and his army waited for a break in the weather. Grant, Lincoln, and the whole Union administration prodded Thomas to attack. Grant was actually on his way west to relieve Thomas when news came of the battle. Finally, on December 15, warming conditions had permitted a Union attack which overwhelmed the already shattered Army of Tennessee. In two days of fighting, the remnants of Hood's Army were destroyed. The battle of Nashville was the last major action in Tennessee. The Army of Tennessee had died on its home ground at Franklin and Nashville. The survivors, protected by the rear guard under Forrest, managed to escape to Alabama and Mississippi, and some of them eventually joined Johnston in North Carolina; but, in the main, the war was over in Tennessee.

The war in Tennessee was particularly bitter because of internal divisions within the state. East Tennessee was, in effect, a separate mountain state like West Virginia. Tennessee also became a major battleground and was overrun by Union forces fairly early in the war. No other state, save Virginia, was the scene of more battles and the scars left by the fighting and the bitter rivalry between Union East Tennessee and Confederate Middle and West Tennessee are apparent still. Although the vast majority of Tennesseans wore the gray, they did so not as "rebels" but as patriots fighting for their honor, their traditions, and their homes. As one bedraggled Confederate prisoner explained to his Union captors, he was fighting because "They were down here."

SUGGESTED READING

Belle Edmondson, *A Lost Heroine of the Confederacy: The Diaries and Letters of Belle Edmondson*(University Press of Mississippi: Jackson, 1990).

John Cimprich, *Slavery's End in Tennessee, 1861-65*(University of Alabama Press: 1985).

Jennie Starks McKee, *Throb of Drums in Tennessee, 1862-1865*(Durrance & Co., Philadelphia, 1973).

James Welch Patton, *Unionism and Reconstruction in Tennessee, 1860-1869*(Peter Smith: Gloucester, Mass, 1966).

Fred Arthur Bailey *Class and Tennessee's Confederate Generation*(University of North Carolina Press: Chapel Hill, 1987).

Christopher Losson *Tennessee's Forgotten Warriors: Frank Cheatham and his Confederate Division*(University of Tennessee Press: Knoxville, 1989).

NORTH CAROLINA

by
Alan C. Downs

On May 20, 1861, North Carolina seceded from the Union and cast its future with the infant Confederacy. Four years later, 40,275 of the state's volunteers, substitutes, and conscripts lay dead—a sacrifice of humanity greater than any other Confederate state. North Carolina's contribution to the Confederacy overshadowed its initial hesitation. With one-ninth of the Confederacy's population, the Old North State furnished one-seventh of its troops. Twenty-five percent of all Confederate soldiers killed in battle were from North Carolina. Eleven sizable battles and over seventy-three skirmishes were fought within the state's borders—including the largest naval bombardment ever experienced in North America. The Fayetteville Arsenal served as a haven for evacuated tooling and machinery from Harpers Ferry while Charlotte developed a navy yard following the arrival of ordnance and apparatus transferred from Norfolk. The city of Wilmington quickly emerged as the most important port of entry for import-laden blockade runners and by 1864 the Wilmington and Weldon Railroad served as the "lifeline of the Confederacy." After choosing the long road to disunion, North Carolina played a vital role in the Confederate war effort.

Few North Carolinians had thoughts of secession early in the 1850s, though agitation over the slavery issue polarized the nation. This was a decade of rapid growth within the state. Railroad construction, long neglected because of political battles over the propriety of using state funds for building projects, accelerated during the 1850s, resulting in the completion of the North Carolina Railroad running from Goldsboro to Charlotte. By 1860, 891 miles of iron rails spanned the state from Wilmington on the coast to Morganton near the foot of the Blue Ridge Mountains. Railroads directly contributed to the growth of new communities and the expansion of agriculture within the state—especially in the piedmont. New cotton mills were constructed as production of the cash crop doubled. Planting of bright-leaf tobacco also increased as the crop spread from the central to the eastern part of the state. But, North Carolina's population in 1860 remained primarily rural; only two percent of the state's residents lived in towns—the largest being Wilmington with over 9,500 inhabitants. The rural essence of North Carolina contributed to its slow cultural progress, one by-product of which was the state's dubious distinction of having one of the highest illiteracy rates in the nation.

The expansion of agriculture accompanied a continuing need for slave labor. Of the approximately one million people who lived in North Carolina in 1860, 331,000 were enslaved. The majority of this slave population lived and worked on small farms. Only twelve percent (or approximately 4,000) of the state's slaveholders owned twenty or more slaves—the number most often used to designate planters. While only a little over one-fourth (27.7 percent) of the state's white families owned slaves, the institution was in no danger of dying out. Slaves not only worked in cotton and tobacco fields, they were also used increasingly in nonagricultural pursuits such as mining. More than 30,000 free blacks also resided within the state's borders, a total second only to Virginia among the future Confederate states. The majority of the state's black population lived in the eastern counties where they composed forty-four percent of the population. It was in the east and in the piedmont that the loudest voices for the protection of slavery could be heard. Social control and the fear of slave rebellion harkened both slaveholders and non-slaveholders to the defense of the "peculiar institution."

When the ties holding the union together began to unravel during the 1850s, North Carolinians, like most Southerners, watched with mixed emotions. The crisis over California's admission to the union in 1850 triggered criticism from the state's leading newspapers. Both the *Raleigh Register* (Whig) and the *North Carolina Standard* (Democrat) railed against the designs of anti-slavery Northerners and spoke of separation from the union. Many bellicose Democrats demanded that the state send a representative to the Nashville convention of Southern states in June to join in the chorus of grievances and perhaps issue a call for secession. Cooler heads prevailed with the introduction of Henry Clay's "Omnibus Bill" in Congress, and the state's Democrats and Whigs saw the wisdom in approving at least most of the compromise provisions.

Anxiety over Northern noncompliance with the Fugitive Slave Act and the emergence of the anti-slavery Republican Party led North Carolinians to view the presidential election of 1856 with trepidation. William Woods Holden, editor of the *North Carolina Standard*, and other radical Democrats once again talked of secession in the event that the Republican candidate, John C. Fremont, won the election. Fears subsided, however, with Democrat James Buchanan's victory, but few believed that the Republican Party was dead. As the Buchanan Administration stumbled from one crisis to another, moderate North Carolinians struggled with mounting anti-abolitionist hysteria. A hostile response to the publication in 1857 of *The Impending Crisis of the South: How To Meet It*, an anti-slavery tract written by Rowan County native Hinton Rowan Helper, combined with fears of insurrections spawned by John Brown's October 1859 raid on Harpers Ferry, cast an ominous shadow upon the election of 1860.

Adding to the significance of the election in North Carolina was the resurgence of the state's Whig Party, which had been without effective organization since 1854. The party proved to be a powerful voice for moderation in both the gubernatorial and presidential elections. The threat of disunion resuscitated Whig leadership and supporters called for the preservation of the Union and the implementation of *ad valorem* taxation. John Pool, the Whig candidate for governor, ran a close race with his Democratic opponent, John W. Ellis. Ellis won, but Whigs succeeded in toning down radical demagoguery. North Carolina's delegates to the Democratic convention in Charleston did not join the Southern delegation in walking out of the party's nominating convention following the rejection of the pro-slavery Alabama Platform. They did, however, endorse John C. Breckinridge, who became the "official" candidate of the Southern wing of the Democratic Party. When the votes were counted, Breckinridge captured all of the state's electoral votes, while Whig candidate John Bell placed a strong second. Stephen A. Douglas, the candidate of the Northern wing of the Democratic Party, came in a distant third. Republican Abraham Lincoln was not included on the ballot. On the national level, however, the Republicans won a victory over a divided opposition.

North Carolina's immediate response to Lincoln's election was surprisingly phlegmatic—at least in relation to the states in the lower south. The impact of Whig rhetoric, combined with editorials from Holden urging restraint, steered the state away from the swift road to secession. Moderate Whigs and Democrats championed a "watch and wait" attitude, allowing the Lincoln Administration a trial run before resorting to other options. Governor Ellis, nevertheless, was not willing to endorse inaction. In his message to the General Assembly on November 20, 1860, Ellis called for an immediate state convention to chart a course for North Carolina during this time of national crisis. He also called for military preparations leading to a reorganized militia and an army of 10,000 volunteers armed with weapons purchased from Northern manufacturers.

While the General Assembly condoned the governor's defense proposals the matter of a state convention was less popular. Many conservatives and unionists feared that the meeting would be manipulated by secessionists. It was not until January, after the Christmas adjournment, that state legislators seriously considered a convention bill. With South Carolina already out of the union, four other Lower South states moving rapidly to follow suit, and Virginia approving a state-wide convention to discuss secession, many North Carolinians could see the necessity for action. On January 9, Forts Caswell and Johnston, located near the mouth of the Cape Fear, were seized by citizens from Wilmington who suspected the arrival of U. S. troops to establish a permanent garrison. The forts were returned to Federal authorities by order of Governor Ellis, but the excitement created by the incident, combined with effective lobbying of Raleigh's politicos by commissioners from seceded states, all but assured the passage of a convention bill.

Unionist legislators joined their secessionist counterparts in voting for the measure in the hope that a large number of conservatives in the convention could insure temperance in any debate. With the General Assembly's endorsement, the act required a statewide referendum, to be held on February 28, on the convention issue. Once approved, all decisions made at the convention would have to be ratified by North Carolina's electorate. The General Assembly also affirmed its commitment to moderation in February by sending commissioners to other Southern states to lobby for compromise, and dispatching Judge Thomas Ruffin, among others, to Washington to participate in a peace conference called by Virginia.

After four weeks of campaigning, North Carolinians voted down the call for a convention by a narrow margin of 47,323 to 46,672. A well-led Union movement, combined with a general fear that the delegation would follow the same course out of the Union as had others in the Lower South, contributed to the defeat, and Lincoln was given time to reveal his domestic policy and his intentions toward the seceded states. The president's refusal to recognize secession and his unwillingness to relinquish Federal property in states technically no longer under his control strengthened the arguments of North Carolina's secessionists. The final blow came on April 15 when Lincoln, responding to the firing on Fort Sumter three days earlier, called for 75,000 volunteers to suppress the "insurrection." Governor Ellis responded to Secretary of War Simon P. Cameron's request for two regiments from North Carolina by labeling the president's intentions as a "gross usurpation of power." He concluded, "I can be no party to this wicked violation of the laws of the country and to this war upon the liberties of a free people. You can get no troops from North Carolina."

With the backing of many former conservatives, Ellis ordered the seizure of all Federal property in the state and called for a special session of the General Assembly to consider another convention bill. The legislators met on May 1, approved the bill, and designated May 13 for the election of 120 delegates to a convention to be held one week later. The governor was authorized to organize ten regiments of state troops and call for 50,000 volunteers. On May 20, 1861, after some minor bickering over wording, the delegates unanimously adopted an ordinance of secession and ratified the Provisional Constitution of the Confederate States of America.

With all debate aside, North Carolina's policy-makers were united behind Governor Ellis. A $5,300,000 bond issue was approved to supply the swelling ranks of volunteers answering the state's call to arms. Training camps sprang up in the piedmont and eastern counties while new fortifications were erected on the coast. A small, five-vessel navy dubbed the "mosquito fleet" set sail to protect the state's rivers and sounds. Surgeon General Charles E. Johnson saw to it that hospitals were established at points around the state and even set up a nursing service. By the end of May, North Carolina had four infantry regiments serving in Virginia. Just three weeks after his state seceded from the Union, nineteen-year-old Henry Lawson Wyatt was killed in action near Big Bethel, Virginia, the first of many thousands of North Carolinians to die during the war. On July 21, three North Carolina regiments participated in the first major Confederate victory of the war—the defeat of Federal forces under Brigadier General Irwin McDowell at Manassas Junction, Virginia.

On the heels of this initial setback in northern Virginia, strategists in Washington contemplated a number of alternative avenues of operation against the Confederacy, including a combined land and sea operation aimed at coastal fortifications protecting North Carolina's inlets, sounds, and rivers. The first objective was to prevent Confederate raiders and privateers based in this safe-haven from preying upon United States vessels. A second, future goal was to establish a foothold in eastern North Carolina, making it possible eventually to cut the Wilmington and Weldon Railroad running northward with connections to Petersburg and Richmond. Forts Hatteras and Clark located on the Outer Banks guarding Hatteras Inlet emerged as the primary Federal targets in the summer of 1861. The offensive was led by Brigadier General Benjamin F. Butler and his 880 troops accompanied by Commodore Silas H. Stringham commanding a small fleet of warships and transports. Departing the Chesapeake Bay on August 26, the Federal force reached Hatteras Inlet the following day.

Even though authorities in Richmond and Raleigh recognized the strategic importance of North Carolina's shoreline, its defenses were incomplete and undermanned when the Federal operation materialized. Colonel J. C. Lamb and the defenders at Fort Clark were overwhelmed by a combined naval and land bombardment and withdrew on August 28. That same day Commodore Samuel Barron, chief of coastal defenses for Virginia and North Carolina, arrived at Fort Hatteras with 230 troops and assumed command. The fort's 700 defenders, however, broke under the weight of a three-hour naval bombardment and surrendered on August 29. Soon fortifications guarding Oregon and Ocracoke Inlets were evacuated. So by early September, access to the sea from Albemarle and Pamlico Sounds was largely controlled by Federal forces and the initial objective of the operation had been achieved. The North also could claim one of its first significant victories of the war.

Instructed to block the channel at Hatteras Inlet and return to Virginia, Butler chose to modify his orders and leave behind a contingent under Colonel Rush C.

Hawkins to serve as an occupying force. Having been successful in their military mission, the Federals now turned their attention to a political agenda in North Carolina. Revived unionist sentiment among the inhabitants of the Outer Banks led Hawkins to suggest to his superiors that a convention be held in Hatteras to begin the process of restoring a loyal government to the state. By his estimate, one-third of the state would gladly return to the Union fold. An assembly convened in November nullified the state's ordinance of secession and declared Reverend Marble Nash Taylor provisional governor of North Carolina. The convention also called for a congressional election that ultimately chose Charles H. Foster of Maine to represent the state in Congress. While Foster never took his seat in Washington and Taylor's reign was brief, the Union movement in the eastern part of the state was enough to seize the attention of both Federal and Confederate authorities.

Encouraged now to continue operations in North Carolina, Northern strategists planned for an offensive in January 1862 to capture Roanoke Island, which guarded the immediate entrance to Albemarle Sound. The plan, initially proposed by Hawkins, included securing the Pamlico and Neuse rivers as well as the coastal town of Beaufort. Once accomplished, Northern troops could move inland, gain control of the state's eastern counties, and disrupt Confederate communications with Virginia. They also would be available to cooperate with General George B. McClellan's planned operation to capture the Confederate capital from the east. On January 11, an expeditionary force consisting of an "amphibious division" of over 15,000 troops under Brigadier General Ambrose E. Burnside, commander of the newly-created Department of North Carolina, and a flotilla of eighty vessels of varying sizes under Commodore Louis M. Goldsborough, set out to sea from Fortress Monroe. The lead ships entered Hatteras Inlet two days later, but bad weather and keels too deep for the shallow inlet waters delayed the attack on Roanoke for three weeks.

Because of the work of busy informants, North Carolina and Confederate officials knew of the impending attack prior to the fleet's departure from Virginia. Brigadier General Henry Wise, commander of the Chowan District of the Department of Norfolk, made efforts to reinforce Colonel Henry Shaw's 1,435 men on Roanoke Island. While a few men and weapons trickled onto the island and to nearby batteries, Confederate forces were outmanned and outgunned when Goldsborough and Burnside began their assault on February 7. The "mosquito fleet" withered and withdrew in the face of superior naval firepower while Burnside's division outflanked and overran the island's defenders the following day. Shaw surrendered 2,580 men and gave the North its first significant battlefield victory of the war.

On February 10, a squadron of vessels from Goldsborough's flotilla destroyed the remnants of North Carolina's navy on the Pasquotank River. With Albemarle Sound open for navigation, Federal detachments entered Elizabeth City while infantry-laden gunboats steamed up the Chowan River with orders to destroy two railroad bridges and rally Union sympathizers. On February 20, Colonel Hawkins' Ninth New York Infantry set fire to the small town of Winton after a band of Confederate defenders contested the advance up the river. Other raids into Currituck Sound and up the Scuppernong River proved unfruitful. Burnside next turned his attention southward toward Pamlico Sound and the Neuse River—the latter running southeastwardly from Raleigh through Goldsboro, Kinston, and the old colonial capital of New Bern. Control of the Neuse would give Burnside a line of operation against the Wilmington and Weldon Railroad and the interior of the state.

Protecting New Bern and the lower Neuse River were seven forts—two still under construction—and two lines of breastworks and rifle pits, all under the supervision of Brigadier General Lawrence O'Bryan Branch, commander of the District of the Pamlico. With his headquarters at New Bern, Branch had at his disposal approximately 4,000 inexperienced troops. Burnside's operation began on March 13 when his division disembarked in pouring rain on the west bank of the Neuse River six miles away from the first line of Confederate defenses. With the aid of Commander Steven Rowan's gunboats, Federal troops advanced against Branch's position on March 14, split the Confederate line, and forced an evacuation of the city. By the end of the day Federal troops worked to restore order in New Bern and began an occupation that lasted for the remainder of the war.

With a base of operations firmly established on the Neuse River, Burnside moved to occupy Beaufort and Morehead City—the latter a deep-water port linked by rail to New Bern. He detached Brigadier General John G. Parke, who had the added responsibility of seizing Fort Macon, a pentagonal masonry fort overlooking the entrance to Morehead City's harbor. Unable to convince Colonel Moses J. White to surrender the fort without a fight, Parke settled into a siege that lasted over five weeks. After an eleven-hour bombardment on April 25, White handed over control of the fort to the Federals. Soon Morehead City developed into a port of entry for U. S. military supplies and a coaling station for the North Atlantic Blockading Squadron.

Burnside hoped for reinforcements that would enable him to operate inland toward Goldsboro and Raleigh, but they were in short supply. The commencement of McClellan's campaign in eastern Virginia, combined with concerns over the safety of Washington resulting from "Stonewall" Jackson's strike at Federal troops in the Shenandoah Valley, meant few regiments would be available for service in

North Carolina. When word arrived in New Bern of a large Confederate force under Major General Theophilus Hunter Holmes assembling thirty miles up river near Kinston, Burnside had little option but to remain on the defensive while ordering occasional raids on Plymouth, Washington, and other eastern towns. The largest of these raids, and the only failure of the entire expedition, occurred on April 19 at South Mills near the Virginia border. Owing to poor coordination and clashing personalities, the combined forces of Brigadier General Jesse L. Reno and Colonel Rush Hawkin were repulsed by Confederate defenders under the command of Colonel Ambrose R. Wright when they attempted to destroy the locks and embankments along both the Dismal Swamp and the Albemarle and Chesapeake Canals.

By May 1862, North Carolina's sounds and surrounding counties were under Federal control. Burnside and officials in Washington hoped that supporters of the Union would feel secure enough to condemn the state's Confederate policies openly. In a second attempt to establish a political agenda in the wake of military success, Abraham Lincoln appointed Edward Stanly, a former Whig congressman and native North Carolinian, military governor of the state. Stanly's brief tenure at his New Bern capital was controversial, but he did relieve Burnside of the burden of civilian administration. His inability to inspire widespread unionism, combined with an open antipathy for anti-slavery proponents, led to his resignation in January 1863 after the issuance of the Emancipation Proclamation. Following Stanly's departure, a fugitive slave colony was established on Roanoke Island under the supervision of the Reverend Horace James.

At the beginning of the Seven Days' battles in Virginia, Burnside was ordered by McClellan to begin an offensive operation toward Goldsboro. He hoped that such a move would draw troops away from Lee's army east of Richmond. Lincoln, however, had a different idea, and instructed Burnside to move the majority of his force to Fortress Monroe to aid the Army of the Potomac. The commander of the Department of North Carolina departed New Bern with the divisions of Parke and Reno, leaving behind Brigadier General John G. Foster to garrison the city. For the remainder of 1862, Foster improved the defenses of New Bern and continued the policy of raiding towns in eastern North Carolina, including a sizable foray toward Tarboro. Confederate counterstrikes aimed at Federal garrisons in Washington and Plymouth proved annoying but insignificant. Foster closed out the year by conducting a major operation aimed at Goldsboro and the railroad bridge over the Neuse. After engaging Confederate troops around Kinston, advance units of the 11,000-man Federal force arrived at their destination on December 17. Stiff resistance from Brigadier General Thomas L. Clingman prevented Foster from effecting more than minimal damage to the railroad. The Federals retired to New Bern, leaving the Confederates to repair the bridge and track.

Following the battle of Fredericksburg in December, General Robert E. Lee grew concerned about this threat to his supply line in North Carolina and dispatched troops under Major General Daniel Harvey Hill to conduct operations against New Bern and Washington. Neither engagement dislodged the Federals. On April 15, 1863, Hill withdrew his troops to Virginia where they were followed a month later by additional units from North Carolina to participate in Lee's second invasion of the North. Residents of the eastern part of the state were left virtually defenseless in the face of Federal raiding parties and nighttime visits from guerrilla bands composed of native unionists known as "buffaloes."

Northern military gains in eastern North Carolina coincided with the return of political divisions within the state. The secessionist leadership that helped champion the Confederate cause and made the most of the Fort Sumter crisis gave way to a resurgence of individuals who reflected a more conservative point of view. While remaining faithful to the Confederacy, these political and social pundits, many of them former unionists and old Whigs, stressed the primacy of constitutional government and were loathe to surrender individual freedom or state's rights to the Davis Administration or to the Confederate Congress. In 1862 they organized the Conservative Party in the state. Holden's *North Carolina Standard* emerged as the main organ for Conservative Party propaganda and discontent. Ultimately attacked by opponents for his seeming lack of patriotism, Holden increasingly denounced what he considered to be "military despotism" from Richmond while maintaining, for a while at least, a faith in eventual Confederate victory and Southern independence.

One of the first victories for the Conservatives was the gubernatorial election of 1862. Colonel Zebulan B. Vance, a former Whig congressman and unionist, defeated Confederate Party candidate William J. Johnston by a wide margin. Vance, who commanded the Twenty-Sixth North Carolina at the battle of New Bern, chose to stay with his regiment rather than participate in the campaign. His political triumph was due in large measure to an active newspaper crusade that linked Johnston to unpopular wartime policies emanating from Richmond. In addition, supporters of the Confederate Party had a difficult time making the label "unpatriotic" stick to the well-liked colonel. In the end, Vance carried seventy-eight of the state's eighty counties.

Vance championed many causes while governor. One major item on his agenda was to look out for the needs of North Carolina's soldiers without causing undue hardship on the civilian population. He was aided in his task by the work of his predecessors, John W. Ellis and Henry T. Clark, the latter assuming office following Ellis' death on July 7, 1861. Ellis' effort to purchase arms from Northern manufacturers prior to secession had produced an insufficient number of weapons. The April 22, 1861 seizure of 37,000 guns—many outdated flintlocks in need of conversion—in the United States Arsenal in Fayetteville appeared to ease the deficiency somewhat, but the state was allowed to keep only half of them. The transfer of tools, machinery, and ordnance from the arsenal at Harpers Ferry to Fayetteville and from the Norfolk Navy Yard to Charlotte lessened but did not alleviate the problem. With a small manufacturing base to work from, Governor Clark and Adjutant General James G. Martin sought to purchase rifles and shotguns from individuals and to contract with local craftsmen to make the weapons and accoutrements of war. Raleigh, Fayetteville, Charlotte, Wilmington, New Bern, Kenansville, High Point, Asheville, Lincolnton, and Jamestown were involved in military manufacturing. By 1863, few recruits were dispatched to the armies in the field unarmed.

Clothing North Carolina's soldiery was less of a problem. The Old North State was the only member of the Confederacy that, through a special agreement with Richmond, clothed its own troops. Thirty-nine cotton and nine woolen mills provided fabric for shipment to Raleigh where factory workers converted the material into uniforms, blankets, and overcoats. Supplemental shipments of cotton, wool and leather arrived from other states and Europe courtesy of state purchasing agents. Individual donations of clothing also were solicited and became increasingly important as the war progressed. By November 1864, Major General Bushrod Johnson reported to Vance that his soldiers outside Petersburg were "not only comfortably, but genteelly clad."

The business of procurement was one of several that placed Vance on a path of confrontation with the Davis Administration. While espousing loyalty to the Confederacy, the governor's unyielding advocacy for decentralization and his concern for the interests of North Carolina and its citizens inspired him to oppose impressment laws, which he described as "illegal seizures," and the suspension of the writ of *habeas corpus*. Vance likewise challenged the activity of Confederate purchasing agents within the state who were "stripping bare our markets and putting enormous prices upon our [state] agents." Particularly troublesome to the governor was the army's frequent violation of the Conscription Act in assigning North Carolina's conscripts to units from other states. In a letter to Davis, Vance noted that he would have a hard time executing the law if officers "ride roughshod over the people, drag them from their homes, and assign them...to strange regiments and strange commanders, without regard to their wishes or feelings...." Other points of contention between Raleigh and Richmond embraced a wide range of perceived discrimination that included the War Department's neglect of the state's defense needs and the omission of North Carolinians from their share of administrative and military appointments.

As empathic as he appeared to be toward the needs of his people, Governor Vance was unable to shield them from the realities of warfare. Food and salt shortages were felt across the state, while churches and schools suffered for want of financial support and attendance. Inflation and taxation also increased as the war progressed. Many hoped that blockade running would furnish necessities for the military and provisions of all types for civilians that might otherwise be unobtainable. Indeed, North Carolina's irregular coastline provided an ideal haven for these specialized steamships after their journey from Britain, Nassau, or Bermuda. Wilmington alone played host to over 100 different ships. With their gray-painted hulls, collapsible smokestacks, and powerful engines burning (when available) smokeless anthracite coal, blockade runners provided the Confederacy with the sinews of war. In the beginning only one out of every ten ships was captured by the North Atlantic Blockading Squadron.

Burnside's success in eastern North Carolina in 1862 closed much of this shoreline to Confederate navigation, leaving Wilmington on the Cape Fear River as the state's only remaining major port of entry for British goods. Located twenty-eight miles upriver from the Atlantic Ocean, North Carolina's largest town was protected by eleven forts and several batteries as well as the natural defensive features of the Cape Fear. The port was linked by rail to Petersburg and Richmond, thereby serving not only the needs of the state but also those of the Army of Northern Virginia. By 1864, Wilmington emerged as the single most important port in the Confederacy. Yet, as the U. S. Navy increased in size and effectiveness off the coast of North Carolina in 1863, fewer ships made it through the blockade. By mid-1864, only one out of every three attempted runs was successful. Those that did reach Wilmington often unloaded shipments that included profitable consumer goods priced beyond the means of ordinary citizens. Private vessels and those partly owned by the state were required to reserve fifty percent of their cargo for government use, prompting Vance to denounce Richmond for interfering with his effort to provide North Carolinians with essentials—even if many could not afford them.

The growing number of scarcities and unpopular wartime measures, combined with Confederate defeats at Gettysburg and Vicksburg in July 1863, led to widespread state support for a negotiated end to the hostilities. The movement began with the first meeting of peace advocates near Asheboro on March 15, 1862. Following Lee's retirement from Maryland in September 1862, Holden's editorials reflected a diminished hope for Southern victory and suggested that the government sue for an "honorable" peace. During the summer of 1863, his *North Carolina Standard* published selected proceedings from over 100 supposedly impromptu meetings across the state, including one in Wake County that urged citizens to "consult reason and common sense, and to discard prejudice and passion." The similarity of their resolutions and their common dependence upon phrases extracted from Holden's writings called the spontaneity of these assemblies into question. The Conservative editor and his newspaper became the focus of antipathy for those who saw his influence behind what they interpreted to be a movement toward reunification with the North. Soldiers encamped in North Carolina held protest meetings against the paper, and on September 9, 1863, Georgia troops vandalized the offices of the *Standard* and threatened Holden. The next day a mob of citizens destroyed the offices of the pro-Confederate *State Journal* in retaliation. In an effort to establish order and prevent future disturbances, Vance wrote Davis to request that troops passing through the state be prohibited from entering the capital.

In early 1864 Holden actively supported a state convention to pursue separate peace negotiations with the Lincoln Administration. Vance opposed this apparent move toward secession from the Confederacy and told a crowd of 2,000 people in February that, "Instead of getting your sons back to the plow and fireside, they would be drafted...to fight alongside of his [Lincoln's] negro troops in exterminating the white men, women and children of the South." Even though the governor agreed with the essence of Holden's claims of injustice suffered by North Carolina under the Davis Administration, he could not endorse a policy which was to him deleterious and dishonorable. The two men soon became the opposing candidates in the gubernatorial election of 1864—a referendum on the future of the state's relationship to the Confederacy.

In a spirited and bombastic campaign, Governor Vance outlined his complaints against the government and reiterated his determination to safeguard the rights and liberties of the citizens of North Carolina. While avowing his loyalty to the Confederacy, Vance told the electorate that he supported peace talks, but not through independent state action. Holden, meanwhile, struggled to convince voters that he had their best interests in mind more than did his opponent. In the end, Vance won the support of both the moderates and those loyal to the government. Holden and his radical peace supporters were defeated by a vote of 58,065 to 14,471.

With the reelection of Governor Vance, North Carolina reaffirmed its commitment to stay the course chosen by the Confederacy, however long it might last. For some, the end was already in sight. Early in the war, despondency and disaffection caused by military defeats and unpopular wartime measures led citizens living in the western part of the state to ignore state and national laws, including conscription. Vance's efforts to force compliance met with limited success. By 1863, large numbers of army deserters found a haven in the Blue Ridge Mountains as well as sympathy from local citizens. Attempts to apprehend deserters often spawned skirmishes between the state militia (later home-guard units) and armed bands of former soldiers and their supporters. The surrender of most of eastern Tennessee to Federal forces in the fall of 1863 exposed the state's western counties to Federal cavalry raids and rendered the task of controlling the disloyal virtually impossible.

Unable to remedy the situation in the western counties of North Carolina, Confederate strategists placed great hope in an operation against the Federal base at New Bern. A successful push against Foster would eliminate the likelihood of near-future strikes against the Wilmington and Weldon Railroad and return eastern counties and coastal sounds to Southern control. General Lee proposed the plan as early as January 2, 1864, but declined an offer to command the operation personally. Major General George E. Pickett, who had been rebuilding his division after its disaster at Gettysburg, was assigned the task. A small force of sailors and marines under Commander John Taylor Wood were dispatched to attack Federal boats in the Neuse River.

After assembling 13,000 men at Kinston late in January, Pickett divided his force and advanced against New Bern from three directions. On February 1, Brigadier General Robert F. Hoke approached to within one mile of the city. The following day, Brigadier General Seth M. Barton and Colonel James A. Dearing reported that the Federal opposition on their respective fronts was too strong to assail. Pickett had no choice but to withdraw. The operation's only tangible success occurred on water as Wood's naval assault party boarded the U. S. S. *Underwriter* on the evening of February 1 and captured the steamer. Unable to get up enough steam to move his prize out of range of Federal artillery, Wood burned the ship and left the vicinity.

In the wake of his failure at New Bern, Pickett departed for Virginia, leaving Hoke behind to take command of operations in the eastern part of the state. The native North Carolinian focused his attention on the town of Plymouth, located near the mouth of the Roanoke River. Then a Federal supply depot, Plymouth was protected by four gunboats and a garrison of 3,000 men under Brigadier General Henry W. Wessells. Hoke enlisted the aid of the ironclad ram *Albemarle*, even though it was still under construction at Edwards Ferry on the Roanoke River. The battle opened on April 18 as Confederate troops surrounded the town and advanced toward Federal strongholds. Wessells withstood the attack until the *Albemarle* appeared in the river on April 19. It promptly sank one Federal gunboat and forced the others to withdraw. The Federal commander held out for two more days, finally surrendering to Hoke on April 21. The fall of Plymouth forced the evacuation of the nearby town of Washington, which was burned by the withdrawing Federals.

Achieving success unlike his predecessors, Hoke immediately turned his attention back toward New Bern. However, after initiating siege operations against the Federal garrison, the brigadier general was ordered early in May to abandon his position and proceed to Virginia to assist in the defense of the Confederate capital. That same month, the U. S. Navy concentrated its efforts in North Carolina on preventing the *Albemarle* from endangering Federal control of the sounds. After several unsuccessful attempts to destroy the ram, Lieutenant William B. Cushing detonated a spar "torpedo" under the ship's hull while it lay moored at Plymouth on October 27. With the *Albemarle* no longer able to contribute to the defense of the river, Federal troops had little difficulty recapturing Plymouth and Washington.

By late in 1864, the future of the Confederacy did not look bright. General Ulysses S. Grant's relentless campaign against the Army of Northern Virginia drove Lee into the entrenchments of Petersburg and forced him to try, with supplies traveling by rail from North Carolina, to hold his army together under the strain of siege warfare. Major General William Tecumseh Sherman moved south from his base at Chattanooga, captured Atlanta on September 2, and marched toward Savannah and the sea. Lincoln's re-election all but sealed the fate of the Confederacy as it became increasingly obvious that its armies could not withstand four more years of a war of attrition. The year also witnessed the germination of a plan to shut down the port of Wilmington, a goal of Secretary of the Navy Gideon Welles since 1862. To realize their objective, the Federals would have to neutralize Fort Fisher, an "L"-shaped, earthen bastion located at the mouth of the Cape Fear River.

In mid-December, U.S. Navy transports carrying a force of 6,500 veteran troops under Major General Benjamin F. Butler, combined with a fleet of fifty-six warships commanded by Rear Admiral David Dixon Porter, sailed from Chesapeake Bay to a point twenty-five miles off the coast from Fort Fisher. Their plan was to tow the old, shallow-draft U. S. S. *Louisiana*, filled with 200 tons of gunpowder, near the fortress on the night of December 23, ignite the vessel and hope the explosion eliminated many of the Confederate seaward batteries. A naval bombardment from close range the following day would eradicate any remaining resistance. The army then could assault Colonel William Lamb's shocked and defenseless garrison. Nothing went according to plan. The *Louisiana* was anchored too far from shore and its detonation created little more than an interesting pyrotechnical display. Porter's five-hour Christmas Eve bombardment did minimal damage to Fort Fisher's twenty-five-feet thick traverses. Butler, convinced the fort's landface was impregnable, withdrew his troops on December 25 after they had advanced to within seventy-five yards of its walls. The transport ships ferried Butler's frustrated troops back to Virginia while the rest of the fleet remained in North Carolina waters.

General Braxton Bragg, commander of Confederate troops in the Wilmington area, celebrated a victory that could have been much greater had he been less hesitant to reinforce Lamb and attack Butler's troops from the rear. Following the victory, Bragg ignored the advice of Major General W. H. C. Whiting, commander of the Cape Fear District, and made preparations to decrease Fort Fisher's garrison. When the Federals returned in mid-January 1865, 6,000 Confederate troops under Major General Hoke were deployed closer to Wilmington than to the fort.

The Federal plan of attack was similar to the December operation with two exceptions. This time there would be no "floating bomb" and Brigadier General Alfred H. Terry replaced the incompetent Butler as commander of the land assault. An armada of fifty-nine warships, twenty-one transports, and 8,897 troops arrived five miles north of Fort Fisher on January 12. The next morning Porter's ships moved into range and began a bombardment of the fort's traverses, artillery, and surrounding woods. The cannonade continued into the next day as Terry positioned his troops for an assault against the landface. Once again, Bragg, who had over 6,000 troops less than three miles away, made no attempt to challenge the Federals. After bitter hand-to-hand fighting, Fort Fisher fell on the evening of January 15. Soon the other fortifications and batteries protecting Wilmington were abandoned or destroyed. On February 22, the last open port of the Confederacy was in Federal hands as Bragg withdrew his command toward Goldsboro.

As the battle for control of the Cape Fear was winding down, a 60,000-man army under Sherman moved north from Savannah, Georgia, into South Carolina. On March 8, the Federal force entered North Carolina and concentrated on Fayetteville. Confederate cavalry led by Lieutenant General Wade Hampton and Major General Joseph Wheeler struck their Federal counterparts at Monroe's Crossroads on March 10, but were eventually driven back. Blue-clad troops entered Fayetteville the next day and destroyed the arsenal. Leaving Fayetteville on March 15, Sherman's next planned stop was Goldsboro, where he would find fresh troops from Major General John M. Schofield's command and be linked by rail to Wilmington and New Bern.

In an effort to check Sherman's advance, Lee called General Joseph E. Johnston out of his retirement in Lincolnton, North Carolina, and gave him command of what was left of the Army of Tennessee and the Department of South Carolina, Georgia, and Florida. Johnston sent reinforcements under Major General Daniel Harvey Hill to Bragg at Goldsboro, allowing the latter to launch an attack against Federal troops at Kinston on March 8. The division of Major General Jacob D. Cox initially fell back until steadied by reinforcements from New Bern. With 1,000 prisoners and three captured artillery pieces, Bragg disengaged from the battle and withdrew toward Raleigh. Meanwhile, Johnston concentrated all his available forces at Smithfield, located halfway between Raleigh and Goldsboro, and determined to strike at one wing of the advancing Federal army—thus minimizing his numerical disadvantage. After a day-long delaying action at Averasboro on March 16, 21,000 Confederates struck Major General Henry W. Slocum's column on March 19 as it moved near the small town of Bentonvllle. Achieving some initial success, Johnston was unable to rout Slocum before the remainder of Sherman's force converged on the area. Confederate casualties in what was to be the largest battle on North Carolina soil were 2,606; Sherman lost 1,646. Johnston withdrew his army to Smithfield on March 21.

While Sherman seized control in the east, Federal cavalry under Major General George Stoneman raided the western counties of the state. With a force of 6,000 cavalrymen, Stoneman left his base in eastern Tennessee on March 20 and rode through Boone and Wilkesboro before crossing into Virginia to cut the Virginia and Tennessee Railroad. Returning to North Carolina on April 9, Stoneman raided Salem, Mocksville, and Salisbury. The latter town was of special interest to the Federal troopers because it contained a Confederate prison. The would-be liberators were disappointed to discover that the sixteen-acre facility, which toward the end of the war housed over 10,000 captured Federals, was empty, the prisoners having been transferred to other locations. Stoneman burned the abandoned buildings and headed back to Tennessee after stopping in Statesville, Taylorsville, and Lenoir. Concurrent raids aimed at Charlotte, Morganton, and Asheville triggered minor skirmishing with home-guard units as well as junior and senior reserves.

Sherman's occupation of Goldsboro lasted until April 10, when his army began its move toward the state capital and Johnston's Confederate force. On April 11, news arrived in the Federal camp of Lee's surrender to Grant at Appomattox and of the willingness of officials in Raleigh to relinquish their city without a fight. Johnston, having evacuated the capital, rode to Greensboro to confer with Jefferson Davis and suggested that his army no longer could be used effectively against Sherman. With the president's reluctant approval Johnston met with Sherman on April 17 and 18 at the home of James Bennett, approximately halfway between Greensboro and Raleigh. The terms drafted by Sherman, which he claimed were based on a conversation with the now-deceased Lincoln at City Point, Virginia, were extremely generous and consequently drew disapproval from the new president, Andrew Johnson, and Secretary of War Edwin Stanton. The two generals met again on April 26 and Johnston agreed to terms identical to those given to Lee.

With Johnston's surrender, the war came to end in North Carolina and in most of the Confederacy. Those North Carolinians who survived the war inhabited a state that was in economic ruin because of the loss of capital and the devastating impact of warfare. Personal and political acrimony caused by divided wartime loyalties flourished across the state. Former slaves had their freedom but little else. Many whites wondered how long it would be before life returned to normal. It had been a brutal war, one that most people simply wanted to forget.

SUGGESTED READING

John G. Barrett, *The Civil War in North Carolina* (University of North Carolina Press: Chapel Hill, 1963).

North Carolina as a Civil War Battleground (Division of Archives and History, North Carolina Department of Cultural Resources: Raleigh, 1987).

Walter Clark, ed., *Histories of the Several Regiments and Battalions from North Carolina in the Great War, 1861-'65* (Nash Brothers: Goldsboro, 1901).

Daniel Harvey Hill, Jr., *North Carolina, in Confederate Military History: A Library of Confederate States History*, Vol. 4, Confederate Publishing Company: Atlanta, 1899).

Joseph T. Glatthaar, *The March to the Sea and Beyond: Sherman's Troops in the Savannah and Carolinas Campaigns* (New York University Press: New York and London, 1985).

Rod Gragg, *Confederate Goliath: The Battle of Fort Fisher* (Harper Collins: New York, 1991).

William C. Harris, *North Carolina and the Coming of the Civil War* (Division of Archives and History, North Carolina Department of Cultural Resources: Raleigh, 1988).

William C. Harris, *William Woods Holden: Firebrand of North Carolina Politics* (Louisiana State University Press: Baton Rouge, 1987).

Hugh T. Lefler and Albert R. Newsome, *North Carolina. The History of a Southern State* (University of North Carolina Press: Chapel Hill, 1973).

Louis Manarin, compiler, *North Carolina Troops, 1861-1865: A Roster* (North Carolina Department of Archives and History: Raleigh, 1966).

Joseph C. Sitterson, *The Secession Movement in North Carolina* (University of North Carolina Press: Chapel Hill, 1939).

KENTUCKY

by
James Marten

Early in the Civil War, President Abraham Lincoln declared that "to lose Kentucky is nearly the same as to lose the whole game." In this often-quoted passage the native-born Kentuckian noted, "Kentucky gone, we cannot hold Missouri, nor, as I think, Maryland. These all against us, and the job on our hands is too large for us. We would as well consent to separation at once, including the surrender of the capital." This doomsday scenario acknowledged the economic, political, and military significance of Kentucky during the Civil War.

Kentucky ranked ninth in population among the United States in 1860, seventh in the value of her farms, and fifth in the value of the livestock produced on those farms. Her economy depended heavily on tobacco, corn, wheat, hemp, and flax, but her economic well-being reached beyond the farms and plantations of the famed "Bluegrass;" Kentucky ranked fifteenth among the United States in the amount of capital invested in manufacturing and industrial production. Politically, the state had long been a Whig stronghold, and favorite son Henry Clay had raised Kentucky's visibility in national politics. Despite the long-term domination of the Whig Party, Kentucky at times reflected the polarization of the American political system. The "Great Compromiser's" kinsman, Cassius Clay, spoke for a small minority of Kentuckians who disapproved of slavery while at the other end of the spectrum John C. Breckenridge, vice president during the administration of President James Buchanan, accepted the presidential nomination of the Southern Democrats in 1860. Finally, as war-like Southerners and Northerners glared at each other in the spring of 1861, Kentucky loomed as an important factor in their strategic planning. If Kentucky joined the Confederacy, she would provide the fledgling nation's northern frontier with a defensible river boundary, serve as a convenient jumping-off point for offensives into the North's heartland, and effectively block Northern commerce on the great Ohio and Mississippi river systems. Conversely, if the commonwealth remained in the Union, it would rob the Confederacy of those advantages and provide Federal armies with equally important strategic opportunities.

Kentuckians realized their state's value to both belligerents, but were torn over how to respond to the breakdown of the Union. Nothing symbolizes the schizophrenic nature of the attitudes of Kentuckians toward the Federal compact more than the well-known fact that Abraham Lincoln and Jefferson Davis both had been born in Kentucky and had spent significant amounts of time in the state—Lincoln visiting his Lexington in-laws and Davis attending Transylvania University. And other, more substantial paradoxes complicated residents' decisions during the political crisis of 1860-1861. Although slaves comprised nearly twenty percent of the state's population in 1860, and although most Kentuckians supported the right of individuals to own slaves, the percentage of slaves in the total population declined throughout the *antebellum* years and there were relatively few great plantations in the state; out of a total of over 38,000 slaveholders, only seven individuals owned more than 100 slaves, and only seventy owned more than fifty. Aside from the inevitable sales of slaves "down the river"—Cincinatti resident Harriett Beecher Stowe set *Uncle Tom's Cabin* across the Ohio River in Kentucky—the institution of slavery was, in some ways, less harsh than in other slave states. The legislature required jury trials for blacks, permitted the education of African-Americans, and prohibited the importation of slaves purchased out of state. Although Kentucky enjoyed close commercial relations with the Deep South via the Mississippi River and its tributaries, her commerce was drawn increasingly up the Ohio River and, in the 1850s, into the railroad networks developing in the North and Midwest. From an ideological standpoint, Kentucky was famous for her Resolutions of 1798 and 1799, which were important building blocks of state's rights doctrine; yet Henry Clay and his moderate successors spoke for a majority of Kentuckians in seeking to preserve the Union through compromise. There was also a geographic split between Northern and Southern sympathies. Although many Kentuckians traced their origins to Virginia and other Southern states, migrants leaving Kentucky tended to go to nearby border states that, in 1860, remained in the Union. For instance, by 1860, 100,000 former Kentuckians lived in Missouri and a total of 128,000 had migrated to Illinois and Indiana.

The state's fractured but basically moderate personality surfaced in the election of 1860 and the secession crisis of 1861. Although the demise of the Whigs early in the 1850s had led to a brief period of Know Nothing dominance—they elected their gubernatorial candidate in 1855 by a majority of 4000 votes—the state's distaste for the fledgling Republicans left the Democrats the most prominent party in Kentucky in 1860. Yet most voters refused to support Breckenridge and his Southern Democrats in the presidential election that precipitated the Civil War. Although Breckinridge received over 53,000 votes to Abraham Lincoln's 1300, the Northern Democrat, Stephen A. Douglas, garnered over 25,000 votes and the Constitutional Union candidate, John Bell of neighboring Tennessee, won a plurality of 66,000. Rejecting the candidates they perceived to represent the extremes of pro-secession and anti-slavery, Kentuckians gave the moderates a comfortable majority with nearly sixty-three percent of the vote.

Although secession sentiment did exist in the state—Governor Beriah Magoffin, for instance, approved of secession, but did not believe that adequate provocation had occurred—most Kentuckians applauded Kentucky Senator John J. Crittenden's efforts to formulate yet another compromise between the North and South. Public meetings around the state passed resolutions proclaiming their opposition to extremism and to the division of the Union. "Kentuckians!" announced the *Louisville Journal* as Abraham Lincoln took office in mid-March 1861, "You Constitute Today the Forlorn Hope of the Union." Nevertheless, few residents of the state believed that theFederal government had the power to coerce seceded states back into the Union or to intervene in any way with the institution of slavery.

Both Magoffin and the state legislature promoted compromise as the preferable alternative to war, but they disagreed on how it should be accomplished. Magoffin suggested that a convention of the slave states should demand that the fugitive slave law be enforced effectively; that the Missouri Compromise principle be extended to territories farther west; and that the perpetual, uninterrupted use of the Mississippi be guaranteed by the Federal government. He also urged the establishment of a Southern veto of United States Senate legislation regarding slavery. Legislators rejected the slave-state convention idea, preferring a border-state convention. They also sent representatives to the meetings of the ill-fated Washington Peace Conference in February 1861 and resolved in favor of a proposed constitutional amendment protecting slavery in the states where it presently existed.

The fear of military invasion and the destruction of Kentucky's economy and institutions animated both branches of the state government. Kentucky's leaders rightly predicted that if the state seceded, it would be among the first targets of Federal action and quickly become a major battlefield between opposing armies. On the other hand, if Kentucky threw in with the Union, Confederate forces would no doubt enter the state from Tennessee, the institution of slavery would never survive the state's alliance with the Black Republicans, and historic commercial and fraternal ties with the rest of the South would be damaged. When Confederate batteries forced the surrender of Fort Sumter in Charleston Harbor in April 1861, appalled Kentuckians decided that neutrality was the better part of valor. Magoffin refused to cooperate in the call for troops from President Lincoln and, a month later, the legislature formally declared Kentucky's neutrality. This act—quixotic, in hindsight—represented a somewhat naive impression of the nature of warfare. "This state and the citizens thereof," declared the neutrality resolution in the state House of Representatives, "shall take no part in the Civil War now being waged, except as mediators and friends to the belligerent parties."

Despite initial promises by Union General George B McClellan in western Virginia and Governor Isham Harris of Tennessee to respect Kentucky's neutrality, that position soon proved untenable. In June, unionists—aided by an apparent boycott of out-numbered pro-Southern voters—won nine out of ten Congressional seats, while in early August they gained majorities of 76-24 and 27-11 in the state House and Senate, respectively. As authorities attempted to mobilize state military forces to defend Kentucky's borders, relations between the increasingly unionist legislative branch and the governor broke down. Two opposing military forces developed. The State Guards came under the influence of Inspector General Simon B. Buckner and reflected his pro-secession beliefs; a new organization, the Home Guards, found recruits among Union men in the state. Gun-running flourished on both sides. Lexington banker and unionist David Sayre smuggled hundreds of rifles and revolvers from Cincinnati and Louisville and distributed them to "loyal" friends and neighbors. In addition, Confederate and Federal officers established training camps for Kentucky recruits just outside the state's borders and even, in the case of the Union's Camp Dick Robinson, in Garrard County. Blood was nearly spilled in Lexington in August, a month after the first battle of Manassas ended in a Confederate victory, when home guards and Southern militiamen assembled—the unionists dragged out an old brass cannon previously used to celebrate the 4th of July—in response to the arrival of a troop of cavalrymen, in town to pick up a shipment of guns meant for Camp Robinson.

The charade of neutrality ended in September when Confederates seized Columbus, a Mississippi River town in southwestern Kentucky. Nearly simultaneously, a Union force under General Ulysses S. Grant occupied Paducah, upriver from Columbus near the mouth of the Cumberland River. During the next two weeks, the Confederates established a defensive line stretching from Columbus through Bowling Green to Cumberland Gap in the southeastern corner of the state. Easily over-riding Magoffin's veto, the legislature formally demanded that the Confederate forces leave Kentucky soil. The military and political maneuverings shattered Kentucky's neutrality and the state finally entered the War Between the States.

As predicted, Kentucky became a major battlefield in the war between the North and the South, and a number of well-known Civil War generals passed through the Bluegrass State. General Robert Anderson, a native of Kentucky and the Union hero of Fort Sumter, briefly commanded the state volunteers before his retirement; his replacement was General William T. Sherman, whose seemingly unrealistic call for 200,000 reinforcements cost him the job. General Don Carlos Buell took over in November 1861. His subordinates included General George Thomas, in charge of Camp Dick Robinson, and General U. S. Grant, commanding

Union forces in western Kentucky. On the Confederate side, former vice president and presidential candidate Breckinridge slipped out of Kentucky and became a Confederate general; Lexington's John Hunt Morgan and his crack militia unit, the Kentucky Rifles, crossed into Tennessee to join the Confederate forces. Kentuckian Albert Sidney Johnston resigned his colonel's commission in the Federal army to take command of the unwieldy Confederate Department Number Two, which included Kentucky. Simon Buckner commanded the Confederate troops occupying Bowling Green in mid-September 1861.

In addition to a large number of general officers, Kentucky also contributed tens of thousands of enlisted men to the Confederate and Union Armies. Perhaps 90,000 Kentuckians served in the Union army, but probably the most famous and hard-used Kentucky unit campaigned for the Confederacy: the 1st Kentucky Brigade—the 2nd, 4th, 5th, 6th, and 9th Kentucky regiments—which formed in Tennessee and southern Kentucky in the summer and fall of 1861. The "Orphan Brigade" fought in their home state, at the battles of Shiloh, Vicksburg, Murfreesboro, Chickamauga, and Missionary Ridge, and throughout the culminating campaigns in Georgia and the Carolinas.

All of those battles would come later. Although blood was shed in a number of small skirmishes during the fall of 1861, the first major campaigns to affect Kentucky were fought early in 1862. In the eastern portion of the state, at the battle of Mill Springs on January 19, General George Thomas' Union troops forced the small army of Confederate Generals Felix Zollicoffer—who was killed in the battle—and George B. Crittenden back into Tennessee. Grant's successful campaigns against Forts Henry and Donelson in northwest Tennessee exposed the Confederate left flank, and Johnston abandoned Bowling Green. By the early spring of 1862, the Confederate presence in Kentucky practically had disappeared.

This did not, however, eradicate the wishful thinking of Kentucky secessionists. Stung by the actions of the unionist state legislature—which required loyalty oaths from teachers, ministers, jurors, and public officials, and established fines of up to $100 for displaying the Confederate flag—100 delegates from sixty-eight counties, many of them Confederate soldiers or refugees, formed a provisional government, elected George W. Johnson governor, and on December 10, 1861, got themselves unanimously admitted as a state of the Confederacy. The secessionists initially set up their capital in occupied Bowling Green and sent ten representatives to the Confederate Congress. At least one member of the 1st Kentucky Brigade, which elected its own congressmen, thought the proceedings unusual. "As Kentucky has never seceded," he wrote in his diary, "electing Congressmen to represent the state in the Confederate Congress, is all a humbug." Nevertheless, Governor

Johnson attempted to raise troops and collect taxes for the Confederacy, but his inability to enforce his authority limited his effectiveness. The Confederate state government was forced to evacuate their short-lived capital when Confederate troops retreated from the state early in the spring, and suffered another blow in April 1862, when Governor Johnson, serving with a Kentucky regiment in the Confederate army, died at the battle of Shiloh. Richard Hawes took his place and held the largely symbolic post for the duration of the war.

The Southern defeat at Shiloh prevented any major Confederate movement into Kentucky for several months. However, John Hunt Morgan and his 2nd Kentucky Cavalry conducted summer raids into their home state that netted hundreds of Union prisoners and threw the Federals occupying the state into a panic. By mid-August, Confederate Generals Braxton Bragg and E. Kirby Smith decided to follow up on Morgan's success and distract Buell's slow advance into Tennessee with an invasion of their own that would "liberate" Kentucky from the Yankees. Smith darted through the Cumberland Gap and, after a sharp fight at Kingston, managed to occupy both Lexington and the state capital at Frankfort by the first week in September. He then dispersed his troops throughout the bluegrass region and waited for Bragg, who moved into central Kentucky early in September, pursued by Buell. Bypassing the heavily fortified Union defenses at Bowling Green, Bragg fought the Union Army at the battle of Munfordville, which ended when, under a flag of truce, the Federal commander asked Confederate General Buckner whether or not the latter's forces actually outnumbered the former's and for advice about how to proceed. Buckner gave him a tour of some of the Confederate lines and, as a gentleman, recommended that his Union counterpart surrender only if his continued resistance and the resultant casualties could not contribute to the Union cause. He chose capitulation.

Bragg continued toward Louisville, causing panic in Cincinnati, where militia units scrambled to defend the city from attack, but the anticipated junction with Smith failed to occur. Equally distressing was the failure of Kentuckians with Southern sympathies to enlist in Confederate units. Some commanders had hoped for as many as 30,000 volunteers; far fewer actually enrolled. "Their hearts were evidently with us," complained Smith, "but their blue-grass and fat grass [cattle] are against us." The "Confederate" state government formally—and quixotically— installed itself in the state capitol at noon on October 4; aware of approaching Federals, the Confederates evacuated the capital before nightfall. Buell brought Bragg to battle at Perryville on October 8 before the union with Smith could be achieved. Each side suffered over 3000 casualties, and although the Confederates were the tactical victors, they were forced to retire into Tennessee. Confederate armies would never again threaten Kentucky.

Although the repulse of the Confederate invasion of Kentucky helped solidify the unionists' hold on the state government—Southern sympathizer Governor Magoffin resigned in August 1862 and was replaced following a complicated set of maneuvers by James F. Robinson—a division arose among the "loyal" Kentucky Democrats who dominated the state. By the time of the elections in 1863, "Union" and "Peace" Democrats were the primary political parties in Kentucky. The latter accused the former of promoting military excesses and emancipation schemes, while the Union Democrats protested that the Peace Democrats were nothing more than secessionists. Federal troops stationed in Kentucky and General Ambrose Burnside, commanding the Department of the Ohio, aided the Union Party by declaring martial law and requiring voters to take an oath of loyalty. These hard-nosed policies worked and the Union Democratic candidate Thomas Bramlette took over the governorship.

Despite the Union Party's grip on Kentucky government, the war-time policies of the Lincoln Administration, especially regarding slavery, found few adherents among Kentuckians. In 1864, George B. McClellan, the discredited general running for president on the Democratic ticket, carried Kentucky by nearly a three-to-one margin. Although thousands of Kentucky men served the Union cause, nearly 25,000 fought for the Confederacy and the state had chronic problems meeting the quotas set for it by the United States Army, at least partly because the state offered few incentives such as bounties for soldiers who went to war.

The Kentucky Democrats mounted their most stubborn resistance to Republican policies regarding slavery. In March 1863, two months after the Emancipation Proclamation became effective, the state legislature forbade blacks claiming to have been freed by the proclamation from entering the state; authorities treated those who dared to cross the state line as runaway slaves. Kentuckians never wavered in their rigid defiance of Lincoln's urging to end slavery gradually. Governor Robinson denounced the proclamation as an example of Lincoln's having "lent too facile an ear to the schemes of abolition partisan leaders" who had "induced him to publish a manifesto from which nothing but evil" could come. Unaffected by the Emancipation Proclamation and determined to escape the fate of the slave states that had seceded from the Union, Kentucky legislators were still trying to save the institution when the Thirteenth Amendment to the United States Constitution became effective in December 1865.

The 236,000 African-Americans living in Kentucky in 1860 refused to abide by the decisions of politicians regarding their future. As soon as Federal troops entered the state, slaves flooded Yankee encampments. One author has estimated that perhaps ninety percent of the Union regiments stationed in Kentucky ignored fugitive slave laws and official policy and encouraged blacks to desert their masters. Some soldiers did so out of abolitionist principles, but emancipation was also a fitting punishment for arrogant slaveowners and a useful source of cooks, personal servants, and military laborers. Predictably, Kentuckians opposed making soldiers out of African Americans and Governor Bramlette and a number of other opponents of the idea traveled to Washington in the spring of 1864 to express their reservations to Lincoln. Their arguments failed, however, and nearly 20,000 free blacks or fugitive slaves from Kentucky enlisted in Yankee regiments before the end of the war. Several additional thousand signed up after the Confederate surrender. Slave recruits earned liberty for themselves and their families. One officer estimated that perhaps as few as one-fourth of the state's slaves were still bound to their masters by the summer of 1865.

As the debate over slavery and the future role of blacks in Kentucky demonstrated, after the war's second autumn most of the fireworks in Kentucky were political rather than military in nature. Nevertheless, the exploits of Kentucky's own John Hunt Morgan provided hope for desperate secessionists in the state and distractions for perturbed Yankees. Morgan, who eventually commanded two brigades of Confederate cavalry, began a series of raids in October 1862 when he galloped into Lexington, capturing 300 Federals and a wagon train. Morgan launched a much more ambitious raid two months later—the "Christmas Raid"— which surged through central Kentucky as far north as Bardstown. He captured scores of outmaneuvered Union soldiers and interrupted traffic on the Louisville and Nashville Railroad, an important Union supply line.

Morgan's growing fame and confidence led him to disaster in mid-1863, when, against orders, he turned yet another raid—meant to cover General Braxton Bragg's retreat to Chattanooga—into an "invasion" of the North. Morgan's blue-clad pursuers chased the Confederate raiders through Indiana and Ohio for three weeks in July, and the improving Federal cavalry units and the timely intervention of Union gunboats on the Ohio River forced all but a few hundred of Morgan's 2,400 men to surrender. After four months of imprisonment, Morgan and a handful of his officers escaped to the Confederacy. Despite the fiasco in Ohio, residents of Richmond welcomed him as a hero. He was warmly received by the Virginia legislature and thronged by admiring women who granted Morgan something approaching cult status. His military superiors were less admiring; they nearly court-martialed him for disobeying orders. Although Morgan retained command of his decimated brigade, he never regained his effectiveness and his final expedition in June 1864 ended in utter defeat. Union troopers killed Morgan at Greenville, Tennessee, early in September.

Other Confederate cavalry commanders led units out of Tennessee and into Kentucky, most notably General Nathan Bedford Forrest, whose biggest operation—with nearly 3,000 men—entered southwestern Kentucky in mid-March 1864 and engaged a Federal force at Paducah; they retired back into Tennessee after capturing a number of horses and damaging Union supplies. Colonel Adam Rankin Johnson's 10th Kentucky Cavalry, survivors of Morgan's ill-fated Ohio raid, operated throughout central and western Kentucky, attacking supply lines and Federal depots. Other Confederates, such as Colonel George Jessee, detached their partisans from regular Confederate units. Still others worked independently of any authority and often crossed the line into common outlawry. One Kentuckian claimed that the state "swarmed with cutthroats, robbers, thieves, firebugs, and malefactors of every degree and kind, who preyed upon the old, the infirm, the helpless, and committed thousands of brutal and heinous crimes—in the name of the Union or the Southern Confederacy." Guerilla warfare and vigilante activities were, perhaps, inevitable in a state as divided in its pre-war sentiments as Kentucky. Men such as "Sue Mundy"—a former officer under Morgan named Jerome Clarke—and the infamous William Quantrill committed robberies, murders, and other depredations against Federal troops and supporters of the Union, sparking retaliatory actions by Federal authorities. Martial law, the suspension of the writ of habeas corpus, and military tribunals were attempts to quash guerrilla activities; General S. G. Burbridge, commanding the military district of Kentucky, retaliated for guerrilla raids by ordering the execution of four captured raiders for every Union man killed by irregular troops. Confederate sympathizers living in the vicinity of such raids could be arrested and banished from the country.

Although such phenomena left scars that lasted long past the Confederate surrender in May 1865, the war had, at least superficially, a very different impact on the Bluegrass State than it had on the rest of the South. Kentucky did not experience the material devastation suffered by many Confederate states, but, in fact, shared the general prosperity enjoyed by the North throughout the war. Although Union authorities had inhibited Kentucky trade early in the conflict—rightfully fearing that supplies and goods traveling from the North into Kentucky often ended up in Confederate hands—by the time the Mississippi River was opened to Union trade in mid-1863, the Kentucky economy, especially in Louisville, the state's commercial center, was booming.

The Civil War permanently altered the state's political and social dynamics. As E. Merton Coulter wrote in his classic account of this era in Kentucky's history, Kentucky "waited until after the war to secede." During the three years immediately following the war, the Democratic Party unified itself in opposition to the newly organized Republican Party, which was itself split between "Conservatives" and

"Radicals." The Republicans never threatened the Democrats seriously and conservative Republicans soon joined the Democratic fold. The Democratic candidate for governor in 1868, John W. Stevenson, received 115,000 votes to only 26,000 for the Radical candidate, while in the presidential election, Horatio Seymour led the Republican U. S. Grant by nearly a three-to-one margin. Even after African Americans were granted the franchise in time for the congressional elections in 1870, Democrats swept all nine Kentucky seats in the U.S. House of Representatives.

White Kentuckians expressed their late-blooming devotion to the South with racial policies matching those of their recalcitrant fellow former slave states. Politicians resisted all three amendments to the United States constitution ending slavery and granting civil rights to freedmen, and the state managed to put off extending suffrage to blacks until 1870, when pressure from the Republican Party, the Federal government, and black-sponsored state conventions finally accomplished the inevitable. The Ku Klux Klan and "Regulator" groups intimidated African Americans during elections—at least two blacks were killed and a number of others suffered injuries in the "Frankfort Riot" on election day, 1871—and in many instances threatened whites who hired blacks, especially former soldiers. Blacks responded to attacks by drilling as private militia units or by taking steps to defend themselves, and on several occasions, sharp skirmishes broke out between night riders and armed blacks. Early in the 1870s, the state legislature facilitated property ownership for blacks and voted to allow blacks to serve on juries, yet Kentucky suffered from the same violence and racial tension that plagued the rest of the South. While a sort of "polite racism" prevailed in Louisville and other urban areas of the state in the century following the Civil War, mobs lynched over 250 African Americans in Kentucky between 1865 and 1934, with about one-third of those lynchings occurring during the decade after the Civil War. Those numbers account for documented incidents; the actual number of lynchings may have been much higher. Many African Americans fled the state and their population dropped by six percent between 1860 and 1870. Despite increases during the next three decades, they made up only 13.3 percent of the population by the turn of the century.

Less tangibly, the cult of the "Lost Cause" caught on with a vengeance, far out of proportion to Kentuckians' actual war-time loyalty to the Confederacy. Schools used textbooks sympathetic to the Southern cause, survivors decorated the graves of Confederates more religiously than those of their Union counterparts, and memorials and monuments to Confederate heroes sprang up all over the state.

Although Abraham Lincoln and the Union had managed to hold on to Kentucky throughout the Civil War, preventing the fulfillment of the president's dire predictions if Kentucky joined her sister states in a Southern nation, the Bluegrass State figuratively left the Union almost as soon as Confederate and Union guns fell silent. Prior to Fort Sumter, Kentucky had been split deeply by political, economic, and social tensions. Her long history of moderation—the product of those paradoxes—had been a deciding element in the course she followed during the sectional conflict. Unfortunately, the war destroyed the equilibrium enjoyed by Kentuckians, whose Whiggish love for the Union frequently offset a Southern determination to defend slavery. Stripped of the Whig Party and of the "peculiar institution," Kentuckians found unity in the cause of white supremacy and against the party that they believed had upset the comfortable balance of the pre-war years. Most of Kentucky's Civil War soldiers marched behind the "stars and stripes," but, once the Union was preserved, they and their civilian neighbors readily saluted the "stars and bars."

SUGGESTED READING

J. Winston Coleman, Jr., *Lexington During the Civil War* (Henry Clay Press: Lexington, 1968).

E. Merton Coulter, *The Civil War and Readjustment in Kentucky*   (University of North Carolina Press: Chapel Hill, 1926).

William C. Davis, *The Orphan Brigade* (Doubleday: New York, 1980).

Lowell H. Harrison, *The Civil War in Kentucky* (University of Kentucky Press: Lexington, 1975).

Victor B. Howard, *Black Liberation in Kentucky: Emancipation and Freedom, 1862-1884* (University Press of Kentucky: Lexington, 1983).

J. Stoddard Johnston, *Kentucky*, in *Confederate Military History Series*(Confederate Publishing Company: Atlanta, 1899), .

James A. Ramage, *Rebel Raider: The Life of General John Hunt Morgan* (University Press of Kentucky: Lexington, 1986).

William H. Townsend, *Lincoln and the Bluegrass: Slavery and Civil War in Kentucky* (University of Kentucky Press: Lexington, 1955).

George C. Wright, *Racial Violence in Kentucky, 1865-1940: Lynchings, Mob Rule, and "Legal Lynchings"* (Louisiana State University P r e s s : B a t o n Rouge, 1990).

James B. Martin, "Black Flag over the Bluegrass: Guerrilla Warfare in Kentucky, 1863-1865" *Register of the Kentucky Historical Society* , 86 (Frankfurt, Autumn 1988), pp. 352-375.

MISSOURI

by
Phillip Thomas Tucker

No state caught amid the vortex of the Civil War's storm experienced more divisiveness or suffered more than Missouri. The fratricidal struggle in the western slave state on the frontier was as much of a social and ethnic conflict as a sectional confrontation. And by any measure, the war in Missouri was waged on as destructive a scale as anywhere else in the nation. Indeed, the modern concept of total war was given free reign in Missouri and became more merciless and savage there than even in the invaded Southern states. As one historian stated, "Missouri was plunged into the most widespread, prolonged, and destructive guerrilla fighting in American history." The four-year holocaust in Missouri was the epitome of the "brothers' war," with more families divided and more family members fighting on opposite sides than in any other state. More neighbors sighted muskets on their neighbors and kinsmen in the western-most border state than anywhere else.

Missouri contributed almost 110,000 soldiers to Union ranks, and approximately 40,000 men fought for the South. Missouri's tragic paradox was exemplified by the fact that the state "gave liberally of our blood and treasure to the side of the Confederacy [but] still we were the sixth state in furnishing troops for the preservation of the Union although we were seventh in population" in the nation. Missouri supplied more than sixty percent of its total population of military age to the great national epic. Missouri's internal turmoil was anguished because of an unique mixture of geographic, social, and demographic factors which were not found on such a scale elsewhere.

Missouri was militarily vulnerable. On the state's western border stood Kansas, the scene of the "first" civil war in the 1850s before Southern cannon roared their defiance upon Fort Sumter in Charleston Harbor, South Carolina. For Missourians, the war began in the mid-1850s and for them the specter of American killing American early became a reality. Like her people who were deeply torn by sectional ambiguities, divisions, and complexities, Missouri was in a complicated position in 1861, a frontier border state with slaves hemmed in on three sides by potential adversaries: Iowa in the north, Nebraska to the northwest, Kansas on the west, and Illinois to the east.

After earning statehood in 1821, prosperous Missouri continued to be dominated by a strong Southern influence almost four decades later in 1860. From the beginning, Missouri had reflected a distinctive Southern heritage. It was settled by hardy frontiersmen and farmers from the Upper South, mostly Kentuckians, Tennesseans, Virginians, and North Carolinians. By 1860, three-fourths of all Missourians either had been born in the South or their parents were from Dixie, fulfilling the promise of a Jeffersonian Democracy and an agrarian utopia in the west. These Southern immigrants had settled in Missouri primarily during the pre-statehood period and up until the 1840s.

Later, another group of culturally distinct migrants—the German people—came to Missouri and were equally motivated in fulfilling the dream of a better life and possessing an idealistic vision of opportunity in the new world. During the 1850s, tens of thousands of Germans poured into the state. Existing ethnic feuds carried over from Europe and were further fueled by the sectional tension and polarization in St. Louis, Missouri's largest and wealthiest city.

Pro-centralized government and pro-Republican, the Germans were pitted against the native Americans of pro-Southern sentiment because of deep social tensions, ethnic hostilities, economic competitions, and cultural differences. The social upheaval that emerged during the last decade before the war polarized many Missourians, especially those in St. Louis. By 1860, the Southern-born populace had become a minority in Missouri for the first time in the state's history.

The German population of Missouri played a decisive role not only in helping to heighten sectional tensions before the war, but also in eventually winning the state for the Union. Pro-Southern Missourians felt that this "foreign" tide would destroy not only a unique Southern culture on the western frontier but also the great Jeffersonian dream: a yeomen society of middle-class farmers. Hence, pro-Southerners viewed the Germans as a political, economic, and cultural threat, and these fears in part caused them to side with the South. In addition, the Irish community of St. Louis was divided by sectional antagonism, with many Irish strongly anti-German and pro-Southern, while other sons of Erin were pro-Union. Clearly, the confused social situation in Missouri not only spawned divisions but also gave rise to ethnic feud within ethnic feud.

By 1860, deep currents beneath the Southern fabric of the state brought change and altered the destiny of Missouri. A tightly interwoven economic infrastructure, which historically had linked Missouri with the South, had unraveled. The rich farm lands along the Missouri and Mississippi river valleys had long supplied the foodstuffs, such as corn and pork, that helped feed the people of the Deep South and their slaves. In part, Missouri had been built and made rich not only from slave labor, but also from the heavy volume of commerce and lucrative trade flowing south to the great mercantile center of New Orleans.

By 1860 the traditional network of a largely rural and subsistence agricultural economy had been altered dramatically by the new economic realities of an industrial age. Now a strange new world of eastern and northern bankers, centers of investment and capital, more profitable markets, and free labor far from the state's borders had transformed the old economic balance that had existed for generations into something new and unrecognizable: a modern economy.

Unknown to the average yeoman farmer in the field, now the economic destiny of Missouri was bound tightly to the railroads that linked the state with the new markets of the manufacturing, trade, and industrial centers of the North, shattering the traditional dependence on Southern markets and a frontier economy. Now the exports went east and north by rail and brought back imports as well, bypassing the backward and staple-crop dominated South. The secure world of Missourians already had been torn apart by subtle realities far beyond their control by 1860.

Elected governor of Missouri in 1860 with the help of a moderate disguise, Claiborne Fox Jackson continued to look toward the past and Dixie. Feeling that the state's destiny still lay solidly with the South, he failed to grasp the implications of the dawning of an industrial age. Ironically, a conservative populace that only wanted peace and nothing to do with radicals, North and South, had elected a secret secessionist as governor of their state.

According to the beliefs of pro-Southerners, the political, social, and economic bonds with the South could not be severed by the progressive transformations occurring in the state. So when the Southern states departed the troubled Union during the winter of 1860-1861 as secessionist fever spread, Governor Jackson was eager to take Missouri out of the Union by any means possible. He felt that Missouri's "honor, her interests and her sympathies alike point in one direction"— to the South.

Despite being out of step with the march of the industrial age and modernization, Governor Jackson correctly ascertained the intimate feeling that many Missourians felt toward Dixie. Contrary to popular mythology, pro-Southerners of Missouri were not bound to the South by a blind support for slavery. Indeed, the number of African Americans in bondage was less than ten percent of the state's population in 1860 and only a small percentage of Missourians owned slaves. Instead, a vibrant Southern heritage, social and cultural factors, and the conflict in "Bleeding Kansas," rather than a direct economic stake in the "peculiar institution," better explain the motivations of pro-Southern Missourians. When slavery served as a factor in personal motivation, it was the fear of slave insurrection sparked by abolitionists from nearby Kansas, Illinois, and Iowa.

Despite pro-Southern sentiment among many Missourians, they were an independent-thinking frontier people not to be swayed easily by events in the East or South, and they were anything but radical extremists. Like most Americans in 1861, the people of Missouri wanted to avoid the nightmare of civil war at all costs, so they embraced a strict neutrality. On February 18, 1861, Missourians demonstrated their conservatism when 110,000 out of 140,000 voted for moderate candidates during the state convention election called by Governor Jackson to determine Missouri's relationship with the Union. Overwhelmingly, Missourians rejected the radicals of both sides. In an interesting paradox, the common people of Southern antecedents and of a slave state refused to sever ties with the Union at a time when secession fever swept across much of the South.

Jackson was shocked by the election results, and his designs to bring revolution to Missouri were thwarted. Not even the subsequent firing on Fort Sumter or the governor's refusal to provide the United States government with troops was enough to spread secession sentiment on the Western frontier. For the majority of pro-Union and pro-Southern Missourians, neutrality seemed to be the rational solution to avoid the national holocaust.

While Missourians remained calm, the actions of radicals of both sides soon altered the fate of their state. As throughout the nation, a handful of extremists intensified the sectional antagonisms in Missouri, deepening the divisions earlier brought about by the social and economic revolution of the *antebellum* period. Pro-Southerners in Missouri faced the greatest threat in Captain Nathaniel Lyon, who was the perfect foil to Governor Jackson and the Southern cause in Missouri. Lyon arrived in St. Louis to take charge of the Federal arsenal there in February 1861.

The destiny of Missouri, in large part, would be determined by the contest for St. Louis, especially for control of the United States Arsenal. The arsenal would prove a decisive asset to the side which secured permanent possession of the largest military storehouse in the entire South. It contained 60,000 rifles and muskets, dozens of artillery pieces, and 90,000 pounds of black power, the means to make the Southern dream of revolution successful in Missouri.

Assisting Lyon and the Union cause was a new demographic reality fatal to Missouri's relationship to the Confederacy: by doubling in size during the last decade, St. Louis now consisted of approximately sixty percent foreign-born, making it one of the most cosmopolitan cities in the nation. This vital manpower pool would swell the Union ranks, tipping the scales in the North's favor. Not only had St. Louis been integrated into the Northern economy, but also the balance of demographic power likewise swung to the unionists' advantage. In many ways, the

Civil War in Missouri already had been decided by the many changes brought about during the 1850s.

Much was at stake during the spring of 1861 because the side that controlled St. Louis would win Missouri and have the upper hand in the Trans-Mississippi. And the strategic United States Arsenal was the key to St. Louis. The Union eventually won the war by successfully turning the Confederacy's left flank and winning control of the Mississippi River and the Mississippi Valley. Of all the border states, Missouri was the most strategic, and the struggle for its possession would be more decisive than even Kentucky—the border state previously considered to be the most vital by many historians. The launching of the strategic turning movement began with Union victory in St. Louis.

In 1860, Missouri was the richest and most populous of the border states and of the Trans-Mississippi states. The fact that Missouri was the second most populated state in the South, besides Virginia, was a critical factor for a manpower-short Southern nation caught in a long war of attrition. Despite Missouri's obvious significance, historians have long underestimated the strategic importance of both Missouri and the Trans-Mississippi area.

Missouri's strategic importance was enhanced by the Mississippi and Missouri rivers located within or along its borders, and with its position out-flanking Illinois on the west. This posed a threat to Union advances east of the Mississippi and south along the Tennessee and Cumberland river systems in Tennessee. To the west, a Confederate Missouri would isolate Kansas and the Indian Territory. If the Mississippi River was the key to the west, then Missouri was the key to the Mississippi. A Confederate Missouri might well result in a Confederate southern Illinois and, more important, a Confederate Kentucky. Resource-rich Missouri also could serve as the bread basket of the South, as during the *antebellum* period.

While the common people of Missouri naively wished for neutrality, the radical leaders of both sides enthusiastically geared for war during the fateful spring of 1861. In St. Louis, the energetic Lyon, Francis P. Blair, and the German leader Franz Sigel, mobilized Union forces, primarily among the Germans, and began drilling their soldiers for action. Pro-Southern leaders of St. Louis likewise began training volunteers.

To help launch his revolution after being thwarted at the ballot box, Governor Jackson called out the Missouri Volunteer Militia of St. Louis, and General Danial Marsh Frost's brigade established their annual encampment at Camp Jackson on the western outskirts of St. Louis early in May. Here, the majority of St. Louis' most militant pro-Southerners, including Frost, were concentrated. Under the guise of a legal encampment, Frost planned to attack the United States Arsenal when the governor reconvened the state convention to pass an ordinance of secession.

To assist in reducing the arsenal, Confederate President Jefferson Davis sent a small amount of artillery at Governor Jackson's request which had been captured at the United States Arsenal at Baton Rouge, Louisiana, to Frost at Camp Jackson. When Lyon learned that Confederate aid had been sent to Frost's militiamen of Camp Jackson, he struck immediately. On May 10, approximately 6,000 Unionists, mostly Germans, surrounded and captured almost 700 defenders of Camp Jackson. In one stroke, Lyon eliminated the best organized and most thoroughly trained pro-Southern force in Missouri.

After the surrender of Camp Jackson, Frost's militiamen marched to the St. Louis arsenal as prisoners-of-war. Hardly had the column of captives departed Camp Jackson when a pro-Southern mob of engaged citizens attacked the Federal troops. The unionists fired into the crowd, killing or wounding approximately 100 civilians. Both the capture of Camp Jackson and the "Camp Jackson Massacre" lit the powder keg of revolution in Missouri; the difficult task of choosing sides and the horror of civil war had been forced upon the people of Missouri. Indignant over acts committed by the Federal government in St. Louis, the General Assembly of Missouri passed a law for the organizing and arming of the Missouri State Guard to defend the state from Union invasion. Now convinced of the despotic nature of the newly elected Republican administration of Abraham Lincoln, thousands of citizens rose up in arms across rural Missouri, fearing that the unionists would bring the same high-handedness beyond St. Louis and attempt to occupy the entire state. Lyon had turned thousands of conservatives into revolutionaries.

St. Louis was secured by the unionists with the capture of Camp Jackson, and they would never lose their grip on this most important city. In addition, the strategic United States Arsenal in St. Louis would remain in Union hands for the remainder of the war. The arsenal could have armed Confederates across the state, providing the artillery and munitions needed if the South was yet to win Missouri. Indeed, one of the Confederacy's most pressing difficulties during the war was the acquisition of artillery and small arms, especially in the Trans-Mississippi. Possession of the St. Louis arsenal might have turned the tide in the South's favor in Missouri, and perhaps in the Trans-Mississippi as well. Also western Confederate armies fighting on the eastern side of the Mississippi would have benefited from the arsenal's capture. Rebellion in Missouri had been dealt a severe blow because Lyon's actions had kept much of the state's populace unarmed.

After depriving the South of hundreds of the best-trained soldiers in the state, a gold mine of arms and munitions at the arsenal, and the great mercantile center of St. Louis, Lyon struck another lightning-quick blow to end Confederate aspirations in Missouri. By mid-June, 1,500 of Lyon's troops steamed up the Missouri River and easily captured the state capital, Jefferson City. The governor and the pro-Southern administration lost legitimacy and credibility after being chased from the seat of state government and forced into exile.

Governor Jackson's Missouri State Guard, under the command of General Sterling Price, could not stop Lyon, who scattered Price's men in the small fight at Boonville, Missouri. Besides ending the attempt of Confederate forces trying to rally to Price's standard, Lyon also deprived pro-Southern Missourians of sizable manpower reserves north of the Missouri River. Southern control of the key waterway that cut the state in half and led to Kansas and the far west was vital. In a classic example of the concept of divide-and-conquer, Lyon effectively divided the state by gaining control of wealthy northern and central Missouri, making conquest of the state almost inevitable.

A state convention at Jefferson City to vote for secession was now impossible after the state's political apparatus was driven out of the capital. For the war's duration, the Confederacy would never tap the abundant resources and manpower reserves of the richest portion of Missouri located north of the Missouri River. After gaining control of the key rivers of the state, the Federals next seized the vital railroad lines across northern Missouri, and these thrusts into Missouri's interior further scattered the already isolated and disorganized local forces in the occupied areas. And, most important, Lyon's aggressive actions put out the fire on a simmering revolt in both St. Louis and the rural counties.

Thanks to the timely initiatives of Lyon, the unionists gained the upper hand in the struggle for Missouri. Now Price's Missouri State Guard and the exiled governor and other officials fled to southern Missouri to escape Lyon's wrath. Price hoped that Missouri might yet be won with Confederate assistance from Arkansas, and Price moved southward to link with forces there.

Next to Lyon, ironically, the man who most doomed Missouri in 1861 was President Davis. In contrast, President Lincoln and Union military strategists did not fail to grasp the strategic importance of Missouri. Because the state government had been forced from the capital and because the state was invaded by Union troops from Kansas, Illinois, and Iowa, an ordinance of secession could not be passed at an early date. But an act of secession was President Davis' requirement before he would extend substantial Confederate aid and dispatch Southern troops to Missouri.

Davis already had erred in not trusting Missouri's pro-Southern leaders and underestimating the strategic importance of the state by not sending sufficient aid to save them. By so doing, he practically guaranteed that Missouri would be lost to the Confederacy.

Without substantial Confederate assistance, the Missouri State Guard had little chance. To keep Price's forces from linking with the Confederates under General Ben McCulloch in Arkansas, Lyon's troops pursued the fleeing Missouri troops into southwestern Missouri. Sigel and Jackson forces clashed at Carthage, Missouri, early in July, and the Southern forces won a minor victory during the race southward. In another example of Southern mismanagement and lack of cooperation, Price encountered as much difficulty with McCulloch as with Sigel. Providing a classic case of Confederate efforts doomed by provincialism and the doctrine of state's rights, McCulloch refused to unite with Price to meet Lyon and Sigel in part because Missouri had not seceded officially.

By early August, McCulloch finally agreed to limited coordination of action after President Davis eased his hard-line attitude and instructed him to assist Price. To reclaim Missouri and upset the state convention about to install a provisional Union government, Price and McCulloch advanced northward from southwest Missouri to meet Lyon at Springfield. Again, Lyon seized the initiative. His Federal troops marched out to catch Price and McCulloch by surprise, striking first as he had done at Camp Jackson three months earlier.

Lyon attacked the Confederates in their camps along Wilson's Creek, hitting the Confederates hard at dawn on August 10. Despite the surprise, superior Southern numbers prevailed after the Union battle plan that divided the forces of Lyon and Sigel back-fired. Price and McCulloch won a victory and killed the pesky Lyon, but took heavy losses so that pursuit was impossible to exploit their success.

After Wilson's Creek, Price's troops advanced northward to "liberate" western and central Missouri in mid-August. McCulloch, however, refused to join him, and again lack of cooperation largely doomed the effort to reclaim Missouri. Nevertheless, Price's Missourians pushed on to the Missouri River, and captured Lexington, Missouri, and several thousand unionists on September 20. But military victory did not bring political success, for pro-Southern Missourians failed to rise up to disrupt the establishment of the Union provisional government.

Responding to political pressure, Union forces were galvanized by Price's invasion. General John C. Fremont gathered a strong army and forced Price to withdraw southward by the end of September. Without Confederate assistance and with desertions among his army increasing, Price could not hold central Missouri. He had to retire and forfeit gains. Price's withdrawal ended at the small village of Neosho in southwestern Missouri during the third week of October. Here, the remnants of the exiled state legislature passed an ordinance of secession and elected delegates to the Confederate Congress. Missouri officially became the twelfth member of the Confederate States of America on November 28, 1861. But it was too little, too late. The exiled governor eventually would be forced to take refuge in Arkansas and then Texas.

Early in November, Price again withdrew further south to link with McCulloch. Lincoln replaced Fremont with General David Hunter, and then replaced Hunter with General Samuel R. Curtis early in 1862. With new determination and 10,000 troops, Curtis advanced from Rolla, Missouri, to drive Price out of Springfield, where the Missouri State Guard had established winter quarters.

In February 1862, the outnumbered Missouri Confederates were chased into northwestern Arkansas, where they united with McCulloch. Once the confident Curtis had pursued too far south into Arkansas and distanced himself from his supply base and support, the combined Confederate force under Price and McCulloch turned north to attack Curtis, after Major General Earl Van Dorn arrived early in March to take overall command. But Van Dorn only brought defeat, losing a decisive battle on March 7 and 8 at Pea Ridge, Arkansas.

Sometimes called the "Gettysburg of the West," the bloody, two-day battle of Pea Ridge sealed the fate of Missouri. The South had lost much, and perhaps the Confederacy even lost the war by letting Missouri slip away. A Missouri won for the Union was the beginning of the end of Confederate hopes in the west, eventually leading to the fall of Vicksburg and the isolation of the Trans-Mississippi. The extreme left flank of the Confederacy had been turned, hastening the dismemberment of the South and leading to Union control of the Mississippi.

Military operations in Missouri by regular opposing field armies ended after Pea Ridge. Both sides now funneled troops east and across the Mississippi, including Price's Missouri Army. But the North drew many more reserves from Missouri than did the South. Union garrison troops from Missouri became key players in adding muscle to General U. S. Grant's efforts in winning the Mississippi Valley.

While east of the Mississippi young Missouri soldiers in blue and gray fought in the Southern states, the war was only beginning for the people of Missouri. The most savage guerrilla war in American history consumed Missouri for the remainder of the war. Thousands of citizens of four western Missouri counties—one of the state's richest sections—were forced to abandon their homes by Order Number Eleven in an effort by Federal authorities to deprive the guerrillas of their sanctuary. Nevertheless, important military results came from guerrilla activities. Guerrillas in Missouri effectively tied down tens of thousands of Union troops, negating the North's superiority in manpower and resources and lengthening the war.

Battles and skirmishes continued for years without decisive results, with only Virginia and Tennessee witnessing more clashes than Missouri. The total number of engagements in Missouri has been tabulated at 244(sixty-five in 1861; ninety-five in 1862; forty-three in 1863; and forty-one in 1864), while skirmishes were countless. In comparison, Virginia witnessed 519, and Tennessee 298 engagements. More battles were fought in Missouri than in any other state west of the Mississippi.

In a futile bid to turn back the tide, General Price launched an ill-fated raid in Missouri during the autumn of 1864, but no permanent gains resulted. He briefly threatened St. Louis and Jefferson City but was too weak to attack. Defeat at Westport, near Kansas City, drove Price's raiders south and back to Arkansas.

Missouri's fate was decided by events in the war's beginning. Guerrilla warfare continued not only throughout the war, but also after the conflict ended. As nowhere else in the nation, the plight of the common people of Missouri best illustrated the axiom that the most suffering in war is experienced by the general population. As no other people in the nation, the citizens of Missouri were victims to both the forces of blue and gray from 1861 to 1865.

SUGGESTED READING

Galusha Anderson, *A Border City During the Civil War* (Little, Brown and Company: Boston, 1908).

Richard S. Brownlee, *Gray Ghosts of the Confederacy: Guerrilla Warfare in the West. 1861-1865* (Louisiana State University Press: Baton Rouge, 1958).

Albert Castel, *General Sterling Price and the Civil War in the West* (Louisiana State University Press: Baton Rouge, 1968).

Michael Fellman, *Inside War: The Guerrilla Conflict in Missouri During the American Civil War* (Oxford University Press: Oxford, 1989).

Duane G. Meyer, *The Heritage of Missouri* (River City Publishers: St. Louis, 1963).

William E. Parrish, *Turbulent Partnership: Missouri and the Union, 1861- 1865* (University of Missouri Press: Columbia, 1963).

Christopher Phillips, *Damned Yankee: The Life of General Nathaniel Lyon* (University of Missouri Press: Columbia, 1990).

Hans Christian Adamson, *Rebellion in Missouri, 1861: Nathaniel Lyon and His Army of the West* (Chilton Company: New York, 1961).

James Neal Primm, *Lion of the Valley: St. Louis, Missouri* (Pruett Publishing Company: Boulder, 1981).

Walter H. Ruyle, *Missouri: Union or Secession* (George Peabody College for Teachers: Nashville, 1931).

The Civil War News

For people with an active interest in the Civil War today

Monthly current events newspaper produced by a national staff of reporters and photographers covering what's happening on the Civil War scene today:

Preservation, Southern Heritage Issues, Living History, Coming Events, Book Reviews, Internet, Collecting, Letters, Research, Firearms, plus News, Photos, Features, Columns. Display and Classified Ads for a wide variety of Civil War-related products.

See what our readers say in unsolicited comments:

• "I truly applaud your fine efforts to offer a balanced view of the oftentimes difficult and still controversial subject matter... the Civil War."   *Virginia*

• "For news, reviews and intelligent balanced articles, nothing can beat your publication."   *Idaho*

• "Your publication surpasses everything on the market for keeping abreast of what's happening in this exciting field. I only wish that *The Civil War News* was a weekly newspaper."   *Pennsylvania*

Free sample issue
(800) 777-1862

mail@civilwarnews.com

www.civilwarnews.com

The Confederate Shoppe

William G. Mori, Proprietor

"One Has An Obligation To Seek The Truth"

Books, Tapes, Flags
Confederate Memorabilia

Visit Our Table At Most
Major Shows and
SCV, U.D.C. Conventions

or

Contact Us For Your
Confederate Needs

928 Delcris Drive
Birmingham, Alabama 35226
Tel.: (205) 942-8978 / Fax: (205) 942-7881
E-Mail: Conferedate@wwisp.com
Internet: www.pointsouth.com/c-shoppe.htm

Join The Civil War Society Today

The magazine.

Civil War magazine is the cornerstone of the Society. Published bi-monthly, *Civil War* features original scholarly articles covering all facets of the war. Our writers are opinionated, often conflicting in their interpretations, but that is the essence of scholarship. We work to ensure that each issue is balanced in its representation of the subject matter, and covers as large a geographical area as possible. *Civil War* does not shrink from controversial or unconventional subjects, and we present the traditional topics in a fresh light to broaden understanding.

Our seminars. We believe

in action. Our Society seminars, held year-round, are hosted by the leading academic experts and regularly attract participants from as far as the west coast, Canada and Europe. Come to one and you'll see why. Some of our recent seminars have included an intense focus on the Seven Days Battles in Richmond, and a novel perspective of Antietam by canoe. Our seminars are excellent for deepening your appreciation of the mastery of a successful strategy, the strengths and limitations of field command, and the personalities of the commanders themselves. They are also relaxing social events that allow members to become acquainted. Anyone can visit a battlefield — we bring it alive!

The **Civil War Society** is a unique organization: personal, yet far-reaching, impartial yet provocative, informed, yet entertaining. Our publications have won awards, our seminars have drawn praise, and our funds have helped save battlefields. We have a vibrant, active, and growing membership — we invite you to become a part of it!

Membership Includes:

• *Civil War* bi-monthly magazine

• Our historical **calendar,** thoroughly researched and really stunning

• The **Society newsletter,** where members keep abreast of preservation activities and society events.

• A personalized parchment **membership certificate**

• Our **guide** to tracing your Civil War ancestors

• The opportunity to obtain a **Civil War Society MasterCard,** with a portion of every purchase going towards preservation.

Call 1-800-247-6253

or use the order form below

☐ For a Gift ☐ For Myself / ☐ 1 yr. $39.00 ☐ 2 yrs. $68.00 (save $10) ☐ 3 yrs. $89.00 (save $28)

Name _____

Address _____

City _____ State _____

Zip _____

gift card to read _____

☐ Check ☐ 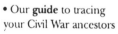 ☐ ☐ ☐

Card Number _____

Exp. Date _____

Signature _____

The Civil War Society • P.O. Box 770-CW • Berryville, Virginia 22611

Please allow 4 to 6 weeks for delivery. For foreign shipping please add $10, $8 for Canada

Are you a Southern Conservative?

Then you should be reading *Southern Partisan*, the Southern Conservative Quarterly.

Call (800) 23-DIXIE

Student Subscription only $10!

DIXIE DEPOT

Over 600 Southern Items

VIDEO TAPES: as "The South Speaks Out!," "Camp Sumter," "Above the Wind," & Many More!

AUDIO TAPES & C. D.s: as "In Defense of Dixie & Our Flag," "Confederate Manhood" + artists as Bobby Horton, Wayne Erbsen, 12th Louisiana String Band, 11th N. C. Troops, Southern Lace, Stone Grey Day, The Rebelaires & many others with over 65 from which to choose!

BOOKS: Hundreds, old & new, from which to choose!

Bumper Stickers; Cookbooks; Relic/Collectors' Books; Poetry Books; License Plates; Anecdotes, Humor & Misc. Booklets; Gifts & Special Items; Children's Section; Metal Signs & Goodies; Clothing & Wearables & Decorator Pieces; Flags; Belt Buckles; Coins; Key Rings; Out-of-Print Books; Patches; Lapel/Hat Pins & Tie Tacs; Warning Stickers, etc.

A RARE GIFT!!! As you probably know, Southern symbols of the Old South were not welcomed at the 1996 Olympics in Atlanta. But, one Olympic pin was made *with the Georgia State Flag on it!* The Republic of Georgia sold one with their flag AND the host flag. The ONLY pin with the flag + the 5 Olympic rings. Many pins now sell for big bucks, but this is truly a rare one! DIXIE DEPOT has **ALL** the remaining pins. There are NO others! The pin reads: "Two Georgias, United in Friendship, Atlanta '96." The Republic of Georgia sold them to help pay expenses BUT they were *NOT* sold in commercial outlets. The pin is beautiful, well made & will certainly get attention worn as a lapel, vest or hat pin or tie tac. It was approved by the IOC (International committee, not acog).

ORDER #001 now for $20.00 + $4.00 S&H

to order or obtain a catalog, write

DIXIE DEPOT

P. O. Box 1448 or 72 Keith Evans Road
Dawsonville, Georgia 30534---or---
Call: 706-265-7533(RLEE) or Orders Call, 1-800-942-2447 ---or---
FAX: 706-265-3952 --- or--- E-Mail: DIXIE_DEPOT@STC.Net
---or---visit our Website at: http://www.ilinks.net/~dixiegeneral

Visa, MasterCard & Discover accepted
(dealers welcomed)

EDUCATE! To preserve, promote & protect our Southern Culture, Heritage & History!